A Constructively Critical Conversation between Nonviolent and Substitutionary Perspectives on Atonement

A Constructively Critical Conversation between Nonviolent and Substitutionary Perspectives on Atonement

Theological Motifs and Christological Implications

Hojin Ahn

Foreword by Joseph L. Mangina

PICKWICK *Publications* · Eugene, Oregon

A CONSTRUCTIVELY CRITICAL CONVERSATION BETWEEN NONVIOLENT AND SUBSTITUTIONARY PERSPECTIVES ON ATONEMENT
Theological Motifs and Christological Implications

Copyright © 2021 Hojin Ahn. All rights reserved. Except for brief quotations in critical publications or reviews, no part of this book may be reproduced in any manner without prior written permission from the publisher. Write: Permissions, Wipf and Stock Publishers, 199 W. 8th Ave., Suite 3, Eugene, OR 97401.

Pickwick Publications
An Imprint of Wipf and Stock Publishers
199 W. 8th Ave., Suite 3
Eugene, OR 97401

www.wipfandstock.com

PAPERBACK ISBN: 978-1-6667-3141-5
HARDCOVER ISBN: 978-1-6667-2388-5
EBOOK ISBN: 978-1-6667-2389-2

Cataloguing-in-Publication data:

Names: Ahn, Hojin, author. | Mangina, Joseph L., foreword.

Title: A constructively critical conversation between nonviolent and substitutionary perspectives on atonement : theological motifs and christological implications / by Hojin Ahn.

Description: Eugene, OR: Pickwick Publications, 2021 | Includes bibliographical references and index.

Identifiers: ISBN 978-1-6667-3141-5 (paperback) | ISBN 978-1-6667-2388-5 (hardcover) | ISBN 978-1-6667-2389-2 (ebook)

Subjects: LCSH: Christian ethics. | Atonement—Biblical teaching. | Violence—Religious aspects—Christianity.

Classification: BT265.3 A36 2021 (print) | BT265.3 (ebook)

12/03/21

Scripture quotations marked (NIV) are taken from the Holy Bible, New International Version®, NIV®. Copyright © 1973, 1978, 1984, 2011 by Biblica, Inc.™ Used by permission of Zondervan. All rights reserved worldwide. www.zondervan.com The "NIV" and "New International Version" are trademarks registered in the United States Patent and Trademark Office by Biblica, Inc.™

Contents

Foreword by Joseph L. Mangina | vii
Acknowledgements | ix

Introduction | 1
    Research Questions | 2
    Methodology | 6
    Overview | 6
    The Language of Atonement: A Brief Glossary of Terms | 9

1. The Nonviolent God's Nonviolent Atonement: Theologically Justified? | 13
    1.1 The Theological Issue of Violence | 14
    1.2 Brock's Feminist Critique of God's Judgment as Divine Violence | 16
    1.3 Schwager's Girardian Application of Scapegoat Theory | 25
    1.4 Weaver's Anthropological View on God's Nonviolent Atonement | 36
    1.5 Systematic Theological Review | 49
    1.6 Constructively Critical Suggestion | 52

2. The Nonviolent Jesus: A Functional Christology
    for the Sake of God's Kingdom | 55
    2.1 Brock's Erotic Power-Oriented Christology | 56
    2.2 Schwager's Dramatically Christological Discussion | 68
    2.3 Weaver's Ethically Oriented Christology | 82
    2.4 Systematic Theological Review | 100
    2.5 Constructively Critical Suggestion | 103

3. God's Sovereign Purpose in Christ's Crucifixion:
    Violence or Restoration? | 106
    3.1 Anselm: God's Honor and his Restorative Satisfaction | 107
    3.2. Calvin's Paradoxical View on the Simultaneity
        of Judgment and Salvation | 116
    3.3 Barth's Unifying Perspective on God's Being
        and His Work of Atonement | 128
    3.4 Systematic Theological Review | 141
    3.5 Constructively Critical Reflection | 144

4. Christ the Mediator's Self-Sacrificial Atonement *Pro Nobis* | 149
    4.1 Anselm's Cultic-Feudal Perspective on
        Christ's Atoning Death | 150
    4.2 Calvin's Biblical Reflection on Christ's
        Sacrifice and Victory for Us | 158
    4.3 Barth's Penal-Cultic Substitutionary Doctrine of
        Atonement and the Socio-Political Implications
        of Christ's Apocalyptic Victory | 170
    4.4 Systematic Theological Review | 195
    4.5 Constructively Critical Reflection | 197

Conclusion: Towards a Holistic Perspective
    on Atonement Theology | 201

Bibliography | 209

Foreword

DO WE REALLY NEED one more book about the atonement? In recent decades the doctrine of Christ's atoning work has been the subject of fierce disagreement among Christians. These arguments have pitted evangelicals against liberals, Anabaptists against Calvinists, defenders of penal substitution against feminists and others who worry about the "violent" God of the Old Testament. Meanwhile, theological textbooks encourage the idea that there is no one "right" view of the atonement and that we can cheerfully mix and match among different models: sacrifice, substitution, *Christus victor*, Abelardian, and so on. This eclectic approach is appealing, but also seems too easy. It can leave us wondering whether any of it is actually *true*.

Into this morass of controversy steps Hojin Ahn, a Reformed theologian-pastor with a strong commitment to a substitionary view of the cross. Among his theological heroes are Anselm of Canterbury, John Calvin, and Karl Barth. But Ahn is not *so* enamored of substitution that he is unwilling to listen to its critics. Among the many virtues of this book is its thoughtful dialogue with scholars who bring revisionist perspectives to bear on the *theologia crucis*. These include Rita Nakashima Brock, a well-regarded Christian feminist; J. Denny Weaver, a Mennonite and author of *The Nonviolent God*; and Raymund Schwager, a Roman Catholic indebted to the thought of social philosopher René Girard. Ahn skillfully brings these critics into fruitful dialogue with the mainstream of Western Christian thinking on the work of Christ. He reads their work with charity, takes seriously their concerns over God and violence, but is also not afraid to push back when he believes they have misconstrued Scripture and classical Christian teaching. Not unlike Barth, he is able to take his opponents' best arguments and incorporate them into his own. The upshot is a creative and nuanced re-reading of the Anselmic tradition, one that will have widespread ecumenical appeal.

Do we really need one more book on the atonement? Yes, when the book is as thoughtful and generative of fresh insight as this one is. Thank you, Hojin Ahn.

Joseph L. Mangina
Professor of Theology
Wycliffe College, Toronto

Acknowledgements

THIS BOOK IS A minor revision of my doctoral thesis, and I am sincerely indebted to my doctoral supervisor, Professor Joseph L. Mangina, who directed the original project. He graciously allows me to write on the evangelical doctrine of substitutionary atonement and guides me with his academic excellence and theological openness. Also, I have to express my heartfelt gratitude to my lovely wife, Sooyeon Han, and my adorable son and daughter, Hwiseong and Hwimin, for their joyful companionship during my long theological journey in North America. Finally, I dedicate my monograph to our Savior Jesus Christ, who loved sinners just like me and gave himself at the cross for their salvation (Gal 2:20). The whole of my book is nothing but a humble pointer to glorify the eternal truth and life in his person and atoning work *pro nobis*.

Introduction

IN RECENT YEARS, TRADITIONAL substitutionary accounts of Christ's atoning work have increasingly come under criticism for what is said to be their propensity for encouraging violence.[1] Theologians from a variety of viewpoints—feminists, pacifists, and Girardians, among others—have contributed to a large literature on this subject.[2] In this book, I will take these critics seriously, but then try to show how a modified substitutionary account actually addresses these concerns—perhaps better than the nonviolent theories themselves. Through a conversation with theologians such as St. Anselm, John Calvin, Karl Barth, Rita Nakashima Brock, Raymund Schwager, and J. Denny Weaver, I will sketch the outlines of a "holistic" character of atonement that both stands in line with Scripture and tradition and addresses contemporary ethical concerns.

In particular, nonviolent perspectives attempt to dismantle any objective concept of God sovereignly accomplishing the atonement in Christ's person. The modern reinterpretation of atonement argues that

---

1. At the heart of Christian theology lies the doctrine of atonement—how God reconciles the world to himself by Jesus Christ's person and work. The culmination of the atonement is generally understood to be the death of Jesus in place of sinners. Christ's sacrificial death, satisfying God's judgment against human iniquities, accomplishes the reconciliation between God and humanity and liberates humans from the power of evil. Nevertheless, a few modern theologians cast doubt on the hermeneutical viability of the idea of the substitutionary atonement.

2. Weaver, *The Nonviolent Atonement*; Schwager, *Jesus in the Drama of Salvation*; Brock, *Journeys by Heart*.

if God punishes Christ instead of sinners in order to satisfy God's justice, God must justify divine violence against the innocent. In order to avoid these consequences, the nonviolent interpretation suggests that Christ's victimized death reveals the dualistic conflict between evil and God. The most representative case will suffice to illustrate the point. *Cur deus homo?*, the question about God's sovereign purpose in Christ's atoning work, is radically transposed into "Who killed Jesus?," a provocative inquiry into the ethical issues surrounding divine violence. The transposition is especially apparent in J. Denny Weaver's *The Nonviolent Atonement*, which criticizes both classical and modern versions of Anselmian satisfaction theories of atonement, characterizing them as justifications of God's intrinsic violence for the sake of his retributive justice. Weaver justifies his own nonviolence-centered biblical interpretation in a theological dialogue with the nonviolent approaches of Rita Nakashima Brock's feminist perspective, Raymund Schwager's biblical application of Girardian theory, as well as Gustaf Aulén's *Christus Victor*. It is no exaggeration to say that, due to the dualistic background of God and evil, Weaver's ethically-reoriented narrative model of *Christus Victor* denies the doctrinal content of God's sovereignty in the atoning work of Christ. The radical re-interpretation of the saving death of Christ necessitates a vindication of a biblical doctrine of substitution from the standpoint of Reformed and evangelical theology. As regards the theological motifs and Christological implications of the atonement, I comprehensively critique the nonviolent atonement theologies of Brock, Schwager, and Weaver, with an in-depth analysis of the substitutionary doctrines of St. Anselm, John Calvin, and Karl Barth. Moreover, in contrast to Weaver's bias against the classical view of Christ's atoning death in the place of sinners, this monograph explores both an integrative and critical conversation between nonviolent and substitutionary interpretations, in order to move towards a holistic view of atonement.

Research Questions

Previous scholarly enquiries on this topic have not been without hope of finding a theologically mediating position between traditional substitutionary doctrines and modern nonviolent atonement theories.[3] Yet I will

---

3. Due to the fundamental division between classical-substitutionary and modern-nonviolent groups of scholars, only a few theological dialogues have mediated

present a more biblical, revelation-centered, systematic-theological, and comprehensive study of the controversial concerns regarding the question of whether Jesus' nonviolent death happens solely by evil, without God's sovereignty in Christ. My own theological questions in this study are as follows. First of all, what are the essential issues in Brock's feminist interpretation, Schwager's Girardian scapegoat theory, and Weaver's narrative *Christus victor* model? Concerning a biblical concept of the three offices of Christ—prophet, priest, and king—as well as Jesus' vicarious humanity *pro nobis*, are there any theological common grounds on which nonviolent and substitutionary atonement theologies can intersect? Is it possible to find a justification for the dualistic confrontation between God and evil as the sole objective cause of Christ's inevitable death? Instead of the classical formulation of God's sovereign necessity and intervention—his forgiveness of sinners and the removal of sin, and the restoration of the fallen world—in Christ's substitutionary death, can the new nonviolent interpretation of the crucifixion of Christ offer an ethical and soteriological solution to the issue of violence and evil in our world?

To get to the heart of controversial issues of divine violence or God's righteous judgment against sin and evil through Christ's atoning death, I employ four systematic categories that seek to clarify the relation between the epistemological and ontological dimensions of Christ's death.[4]

---

between these opposing views. Hans Boersma contributes to harmonizing the two opposing views by introducing the postmodern philosophical concept of "hospitality" in his book *Violence, Hospitality, and the Cross*. Similarly, Robert W. Jenson reaches a more holistic position on the atonement by following the scriptural testimonies in *Systematic Theology I*. Jenson not only argues for God's sovereign intervention in Christ's atoning death, as in the case of substitutionary doctrine, but also criticizes Anselm's satisfaction theory by noting (along with nonviolent atonement scholars) that it separates Christ's atoning death from the entire biblical narrative of Christ's life and ministry. Additionally, in terms of representation and substitution, Jeannine M. Graham provides us with a penetrating analysis of three influential theologians. Graham, *Representation and Substitution in the Atonement Theologies of Dorothee Sölle, John Macquarrie, and Karl Barth*.

4. According to Rosalene Bradbury, there is a "negative epistemology of the cross" and a "positive epistemology of the cross" in the discussion of atonement theology. The former can be summarized as follows: "the self-glorifying human attempt to reach up the knowledge of God and know as God knows, but the inability to do so, and therefore the crucicentric rejection of that attempt." By contrast, the latter can be defined as "the summons of the cross to vicarious death in and with the crucified Christ, in whom the creaturely presumption to know as God is overcome. In exchange union with Christ's mind, consolidated through an ongoing sanctifying process of death to the natural attempt to know as God." Bradbury, *Cross Theology*, 3–4. Following Bradbury's

Here I define "epistemology" as referring to *how* humankind perceives the crucifixion phenomenologically, while "ontology" indicates *what* God has in fact done in Christ's person and his atoning work. The core ideas of both nonviolent and substitutionary atonement theologies will be examined with respect to: 1) negative epistemology, or the revelation of human sinfulness (both as harm done to victims and as personal guilt) as that which God condemns; 2) negative ontology, the annihilation (or transformation) of evil by the divine act of judgment in Christ; 3) positive epistemology, the revelation of God's restorative nonviolence and his saving righteousness in Christ; and 4) positive ontology, the liberation of suffering victims from the powers of evil and God's reconciliation with sinners; more broadly, the restoration of the world. With this classification, I will review how both the nonviolent and substitutionary atonement models maintain hermeneutical integrity in their theological logic and biblical interpretations.

Moreover, concerning the inseparable relation of atonement theology and Christological implications, I adopt the hermeneutical assumption that Christ's person is in his work and the work is in the person.[5] Here I assume that while the nonviolent atonement theories functionally imply Christ's humanity for God's kingdom, the substitutionary models have the ontic basis of the Mediator, the incarnate Son of God for us. What I mean by "functional" and "ontic" perspectives on the person of Christ is critically summarized by Richard Bauckham, as follows.

> The distinction commonly made between "functional" and "ontic" Christology has been broadly between early Christology in a Jewish context and patristic Christology which applied Greek philosophical categories of divine nature to Christ. Even when ontic Christology is seen to begin well within the confines of the New Testament, it is seen as the beginnings of the patristic attribution of divine nature to Christ . . . The whole category of divine identity and Jesus' inclusion in it has been fundamentally obscured by the alternative of "functional" and "ontic,"

---

theological distinction, I accept Barth's unifying view of Christological soteriology in which there is both an epistemological dimension of revelation and an ontological view of reconciliation in the person and work of Christ. Barth, *Church Dogmatics* IV/1, 637. Barth states that "he (Christ) is both the ontic and the noetic principle, the reality."

5. Torrance, *Atonement*, 94. Thomas F. Torrance claims that "atonement in act is identical with Christ himself, and the fact that Christ is God and human means that once the act of atonement is made, it is made once for all, and it lives on for ever in the person of the mediator."

Introduction

understood to mean that either Christology speaks simply of what Jesus does or else it speaks of his divine nature.⁶

As Bauckham rightly puts it, the New Testament proclaims the historical Jesus' "unique divine identity," not just a human one.⁷ However, what is lacking in Bauckham's view is the holistic identity of Christ, because he has both the ontological dimension of the Son of God and the functional one of the human Jesus for God's kingdom. From the Christological standpoint, I will ask more specific questions. What is the identity of the victimized Jesus, as it is tragically described in the nonviolent models of atonement? Is he the savior of humans oppressed by evil, or is he nothing but the representative of innocent victims? Correspondingly, what are the distinctive themes in the substitutionary perspectives of Anselm, Calvin, and Barth? Who has the closest theological affinity with the assumption in the nonviolent atonement models that God's negative judgment is incompatible with his positive restoration? As Colin E. Gunton asks in *The Actuality of Atonement*, how are the three principal scriptural themes of sacrifice, judgment, and victory holistically harmonized into their atonement theologies?⁸ Or are there other crucial theological dimensions such as the "apocalyptic"⁹ that need to be re-illuminated?

Moreover, how do substitutionary understandings of Christ's objective reconciliation between God and sinners overcome the dualism between God and the hostile powers in the nonviolent atonement theories? Unlike the radical dichotomy envisioned by Aulén between God's satisfaction by the death of Christ's humanity and Christ's victory solely by his deity, do these three scholars have a balanced view of the relationship between Christ's person in two natures and his atoning work? How can their theological motifs of atonement be objectively substantiated by the dynamic unifying principle between the person and work of Christ? On the other hand, should anything be reconsidered in Anselmian satisfaction theory regarding God's honor, or the Calvinistic notion of Christ's penal substitutionary death, or Barth's integrative approach of restoration and judgment in his own Christologically modified satisfaction model? In

6. Bauckham, *God Crucified*, 41–42.
7. Bauckham, *God Crucified*, 41–42.
8. Gunton, *The Actuality of Atonement*.
9. Beker, *Paul the Apostle: The Triumph of God in Life and Thought*. According to Johan Christiaan Beker, the Apostle Paul's "apocalyptic" soteriology confirms that Christ's crucifixion and resurrection reveals God's negation of the evil world and his recreation of a new world in Christ.

addition, how could Anselm, Calvin, and Barth respond to the modern criticism that Christ's substitutionary death in fact brings about the disintegration of eternal oneness between God the Father and the Son? Finally, could there be *critically constructive* engagement between the substitutionary doctrines and the nonviolent approaches to atonement, without compromising the crux of evangelical doctrine in Christ's saving death?

Methodology

This study will be a systematic-theological examination of the nonviolent and substitutionary perspectives on atonement. However, I do not intend to survey the theological development of these topics throughout the entire history of Christian doctrine. Due to the limited scope of the book, I will concentrate on the selected works of the representative theologians from both the classical and modern camps. For the classical view, I will present Anselm's *Cur Deus Homo*, Calvin's *Institutes of Christian Religion* II (1559) and his *Commentary on Hebrews*, and Barth's *Church Dogmatics* II/1 and IV/1. Among the modern or nonviolent views, I have selected Brock's *Journeys by Heart*, Schwager's *Jesus in the Drama of Salvation*, and Weaver's *The Nonviolent Atonement*. I will use concept analysis to verify and develop these theologians' hermeneutical presuppositions regarding the theological motifs and Christological implications of the atonement. I will give much more considerable attention to the assessment of Weaver's and Barth's thoughts on the atonement, since as later theologians they possess a more wide-ranging theological repertoire than the earlier ones.

Overview

As a whole, I will demonstrate that the theological differences between nonviolent atonement theories and substitutionary perspectives are attributable to their contrasting Christological implications and theological understandings of the relationship between God's sovereignty and evil.[10] Nonviolent atonement theories replace the theological motifs and Christological presuppositions of the God-centered doctrine of substitution—sin

---

10. Weaver himself confesses that the theological difference between nonviolent and substitutionary atonement theology "goes to the heart of discussion of the nature of Christian faith and practice, our understanding of God, and how we live out our calling as disciples of Jesus." Weaver, *The Nonviolent Atonement*, 271.

to be atoned for by God's sovereign righteousness and the atoning work of Christ as God and human—with their own anthropological and ethical issues of victimization, exemplified by Jesus' innocent but inevitable death at the hands of cosmic-structural evil. The nonviolent models give a functional meaning to Jesus' human solidarity with victimized people in the dualistic conflict between evil and God. By contrast, from the substitutionary perspectives, the uniqueness of Christ's person as God-human corresponds to his own substitutionary atoning work in the objective sense. Christ's saving death never justifies human victimization by evil in the yet-suffering world. Rather, it reveals the divine judgment against sin and evil, which violently resist God's kingdom of justice and peace. We can realize that the crucified and risen Christ not only actualizes God's ethical justice of nonviolence for the sake of his peaceful reign in the world, but also demonstrates God's alien righteousness for the sake of the objective reconciliation between God and humans.

My monograph will consist of two major sections: (1) a theological critique of nonviolent atonement models with suggestions for pursuing the common denominator towards substitutionary atonement theories; and (2) a doctrinal vindication of substitutionary perspectives, followed by a critical re-assessment, and a conclusive analysis with a holistic perspective on the two conflicting types of atonement. Chapter 1 will open with the controversial issue of divine violence in Jesus' saving death for sinners. In terms of the biblical interpretation of nonviolence, I will engage Brock's feminist healing-oriented critique of the penal satisfaction model as God's "cosmic child abuse," Schwager's theological understanding of the nonviolent God through the lens of the Girardian atonement theory of the scapegoat, and Weaver's narrative *Christus victor* theory of a God who never intended to execute his Son. I will not only criticize the justification for the absence of the nonviolent God in the violent death of Jesus, but also show how the human-ethical ideology of nonviolence is projected onto God in these nonviolent atonement theories.

Chapter 2 shifts the Christological focus of the monograph to both the negative motif of Jesus' human victimization, and the positive one of his resurrection by God. This section starts with a Christology in which God's kingdom of nonviolence is historically actualized in a violent world through the vulnerable humanity of the nonviolent Jesus. I will examine Brock's human approach to Jesus as a prophet of feminism, insofar as his death reveals the structural evil of patriarchy. I will also discuss Schwager's dramatic description of the crucified Christ's identification with victims and his transforming power over evil, as well as Weaver's human-ethical interpretation of Jesus' person and work insofar as they nonviolently resist the violent evil in the world. Consequently, I will clarify their phenomenological understandings of the tragic event of Jesus' prophetic-cultic death, which inevitably reaches back to a dualism between a nonviolent God and violent evil.

Correspondingly, in terms of Jesus' resurrection as restoration, Brock places a heavy emphasis on the healing motif of feminist communities by focusing on the visualizing and spiritualizing dimension of Jesus' resurrection by "erotic power." Likewise, Schwager only concentrates on elaborating a Girardian re-interpretation of Christ's resurrection as God's nonviolent forgiveness. By contrast, Weaver pursues the apocalyptic reorientation of Christ's resurrection in both cosmic and historical milieus. We can observe the discontinuity between crucifixion and resurrection by contrasting the nonviolent perspectives.

In the second part, Chapter 3 will turn to a crucial motif in the substitutionary atonement perspective: God's sovereign intervention in the problems of sin and evil in the crucifixion of Christ. In order to re-vindicate God's sovereignty and the divine necessity of atonement in Christ, I will review how God's mercy and justice are mutually related to each other in the three substitutionary atonement types. I will seek theological similarities between the nonviolent atonement theories and Anselm's view of the restoration of the fallen world and the doctrinal denial of God's punishment. I will demonstrate that Calvin's seemingly violent understanding of God's satisfaction in his righteous judgment against sin and evil is related to God's positive and restorative will toward fallen creation. More substantially, I will deal with Barth's integrative perspective on God's restorative judgment in both the doctrine of God's being (*CD* II/1) and of reconciliation as God's work (IV/1). Yet I will critique the absolutizing tendency of Calvin's and Barth's forensic metaphor of atonement.

Chapter 4 will develop a reflection on Christ's person and work as the Mediator in relation to three great representatives of the substitutionary perspective: Anselm, Calvin, and Barth. My goal here is to show that a retrieval of cultic imagery, along with aspects of the forensic judgment and *Christus victor* motif, can help us move toward a genuinely holistic view of atonement. Anselm's understanding of Christ's voluntary sacrifice furnishes an important resource, despite his regrettable tendency to separate Christ's death from his own person. Next, I will address Calvin's dynamic understanding of Christ's priestly-sacrificial atonement in the

Commentary on Hebrews, offering a systematic-theological evaluation of Calvin's biblical and revelation-centered Christology. Lastly, by re-illuminating Barth's theological exegesis of Christ's eternal priesthood, I will evaluate Barth's own Christocentric perspective on atonement thorough the lens of God's being and act in Christ as the divine humiliation for us.

Correspondingly, regarding Christ's resurrection, I will start with a theological question regarding Anselm's failure to mention the *Christus Victor* motif in the atonement event and his disregard of the relationship between Christ's crucifixion and his resurrection. Next, I will lay out how Calvin's doctrine of Christ's substitutionary death for sinners can be holistically harmonized with his triumph over the hostile authorities, in light of the divine continuity between crucifixion and resurrection. More importantly, I will not only emphasize Barth's divine-apocalyptic characterization of Christ's resurrection, but also reflect on the socio-political implications of atonement. Yet I will also review whether the evangelical doctrine of substitutionary atonement can apply Christ's liberating power to current issues regarding structural evils, as modern critics point them out.

At the conclusion of this study, I will offer a self-critical reflection that seeks harmony among the modern and classical scholars' views on atonement. I will reflect on the intersection of the two conflicting types of atonement—the cultic dimension of the prophet Jesus' inevitable sacrificial death, which discloses structural evil, and the necessity of God's sovereignty and Christ's person in accomplishing the atonement. Therefore, at the heart of Christ's saving death lies the simultaneity of Jesus' victimization by evil, and Christ's reconciliation between God and humankind.

The Language of Atonement: A Brief Glossary of Terms

In the glossary below, I offer a preliminary clarification of some of the major terms and concepts I will use to describe the doctrine of atonement.

Substitutionary Atonement: This view confirms that Christ died instead of fallen sinners, in order to achieve their reconciliation with God.[11] Sinners must but cannot do this by themselves. Christologically speaking, in his own person as truly God and human for us, not only does Christ's incarnation take our fallen humanity, but his crucifixion also makes a

---

11. There is no doubt that Christ's substitutionary death for us [ὑπὲρ ἡμῶν] is at the heart of Pauline soteriology. "When we were still powerless, Christ died for the ungodly . . . But God demonstrates his own love for us in this: While we were still sinners, Christ died for us" (Rom 5:6, 8).

substitutionary atonement for all our sins and sinful nature itself.[12] In other words, according to Balthasar, "He [Christ] gives himself 'for us' to the extent of *exchanging places with us*. Given up for us, he becomes 'sin' (2 Cor 5:21) and a 'curse' (Gal 3:13) so that we may 'become—that is, share in—God's [covenant] righteousness.'"[13] As Luther rightly observes, without the radical substitution that is the "admirable exchange" between sinful humankind and Christ *pro nobis*, there cannot be the salvation of sinners.[14]

Satisfaction: A theological concept of God's satisfaction by Christ's atonement is originally attributed to St. Anselm.[15] In fact, Anselm is the first theologian who systematically deals with the necessity of atonement as the objective satisfaction of God. He believes that God's honor should be objectively restored by the incarnate Son of God, who compensates for the disorder of the entire creation caused by human sin.[16] There is an objective necessity for God's satisfaction by the restoration of the fallen world. The problem of sin cannot be solved simply by God's benevolent forgiveness of sinners or their subjective repentance.

Penal/Forensic Substitution: When Anselmian satisfaction theory is developed under the pressure of legal categories, it becomes a forensic theory, with penal substitution as an important subtype. The penal substitutionary doctrine is inclined to emphasize that God's justice is satisfied with Christ's substitutionary death. The theory highlights that Christ's vicarious suffering and death are due to God's retributive punishment, a punishment that sinners deserve as if in a legal context at a human court of justice.[17] Biblical support for the penal view may be found in Pauline texts, e.g., "In his [crucified] body, our sin and hostility are condemned" (Rom 8:3; cf. Eph 2:14).[18] Yet it is of particular importance to note that there are forensic models that do *not* emphasize punishment. The forensic approach may, for example, underscore God's restorative or apocalyptic judgment of fallen creation by his saving righteousness in

---

12. Torrance, *Atonement*, 126.
13. Hans Urs von Balthasar, *Theo-Drama IV*, 241.
14. Balthasar, *Theo-Drama IV*, 284.
15. Balthasar, *Theo-Drama IV*, 255.
16. Anselm, "*Cur Deus Homo*," *Basic Writings*, 191–302.
17. Berkhof, *Systematic Theology*, 414–15. The Reformed orthodoxy scholar Louis Berkhof attempts to prove the hermeneutical validity of penal substitution through the lens of purely juridical reasoning.
18. Berkhof, *Systematic Theology*, 241. This theory may also suggest "the suffering Servant who bears sins" (Isa 53:4).

Christ's vicarious death, without appealing to any sort of penal logic or mechanism.[19] At this point, Barth's apocalyptically forensic perspective on substitutionary atonement can strengthen the hermeneutical weaknesses of modern penal substitutionary theories.

Christus Victor: Gustaf Aulén revives the classical idea of *Christus Victor*, which has been overshadowed by the Anselmian satisfaction theory.[20] Aulén re-interprets the fathers and Luther as understanding sin and death as the evil powers that are conquered by the Son of God in a dualistic struggle between God and Satan. Aulén's patristic concept of *Christus Victor* is "a cosmic drama" involving Christ's conquest over evil in the dualistic perspective. The "dramatic" view of Aulén's can be summarized as follows: "Christ—*Christus Victor*—fights against and triumphs over the evil powers of the world, the 'tyrants' under which mankind is in bondage and suffering . . . the triumph over the opposing powers is regarded as a reconciling of God himself."[21] Nonetheless, it is to be noted that Aulén's over-emphasis on Christ's deity impairs the theological integrity of Christ's person and his atoning work.

Cultic/Priestly-Sacrificial Atonement: The cultic perspective is directly based on the liturgical sacrifices and ordinances in Leviticus. They enable the forgiveness of sin with the atoning blood of animal sacrifices that are dedicated by a priest to the holy God. Yet the cultic dimension of atonement should not be misunderstood as "a pagan notion of placating God," because the biblical perspective confirms that the subject of reconciliation is God: "God reconciles himself to man and reconciles man to himself in Jesus Christ."[22] According to Hebrews, Christ's ministry of reconciliation is essentially done by the eternal priesthood in Christ's self-sacrificial work of atonement.[23] Christ's priestly-sacrificial atonement reveals the double identity of the crucified Christ in that the offerer,

---

19. For thoughtful research on the issue, see Smythe, "The Place of Atonement in Barth's Forensic Apocalyptic Doctrine of Justification," in *Forensic Apocalyptic Theology: Karl Barth and the Doctrine of Justification*, 113–44.

20. Aulén, *Christus Victor*.

21. Aulén, *Christus Victor*, 5.

22. Torrance, *Atonement*, 53.

23. "Such a high priest truly meets our need—one who is holy, blameless, pure, set apart from sinners, exalted above the heavens. Unlike the other high priests, he does not need to offer sacrifices day after day, first for his own sins, and then for the sins of the people. He sacrificed for their sins once for all when he offered himself. For the law appoints as high priests men in all their weakness; but the oath, which came after the law, appointed the Son, who has been made perfect forever" (Heb 7:26–28).

the eternal priest, becomes one with the offering, the lamb of God.²⁴ Because of its uniqueness, the incarnate Son of God's self-giving sacrifice perfectly accomplished the essence of all the cultic rituals in Leviticus. In this sense, the crucifixion of Christ is cultically understood to be the "shedding of blood," the atonement itself.²⁵

Propitiation/Expiation: "Propitiation" means that God's righteous wrath against sin and evil is satisfied or appeased by his own "holy love" in the self-giving sacrifice of the crucified Son of God.²⁶ Accordingly, "expiation" is the removal of sinners' guilt by the atoning blood of Christ. Thus, without expiation of sin, there cannot be propitiation of God's wrath. In this way, the two cultic terms are not mutually exclusive.²⁷

---

24. Torrance, *Theology in Reconciliation*, 133–35.
25. Balthasar, *Theo-Drama IV*, 241.
26. Torrance, *Atonement*, 68–69.
27. Stott, *The Cross of Christ*, 122–25. C. H. Dodd argues that the English translation of the Greek word *hilasterion* (Rom 3:25) must be "expiation," not "propitiation," because the Apostle Paul never argues for God's intentional wrath itself against sinners, Dodd, *Bible and the Greeks*, 82–95. However, Leon Morris rightly observes that there is substantial evidence in Paul's writings for propitiation as the appeasement of God's "personal divine revulsion to evil," Morris, *Cross in the New Testament*, 190–91.

1

The Nonviolent God's Nonviolent Atonement

Theologically Justified?

A God without wrath brought men without sin into a kingdom without judgment through the ministrations of a Christ without a cross.[1]

Religion is human nature reflected, mirrored in itself. That which exists has necessarily a pleasure, a joy in itself, loves itself, and loves itself justly; to blame it because it loves itself is to reproach it because it exists. To exist is to assert oneself, to affirm oneself, to love oneself . . . There also is it already exalted to that state in which it can mirror and reflect itself, in which it can project its own image as God. God is the mirror of man.[2]

WHY DO WE NEED to research the nonviolent atonement theologies of Brock, Schwager, and Weaver? What is the point? Above all, I will begin with my own theological reasons, which especially focus on Weaver's discussion of violence and atonement. Next, I will outline the core ideas of how the nonviolent God accomplishes the nonviolent work of atonement through the lens of Brock's feminist-relational view, Schwager's biblical

1. Niebuhr, *The Kingdom of God in America*, 193.
2. Feuerbach, *The Essence of Christianity*, 63.

application of Girard's scapegoat mechanism, and Weaver's nonviolent atonement theology in his *Christus victor* theory. I will demonstrate that a purely nonviolent concept of God who never violently judges sin and evil is none other than the hermeneutical projection of human nonviolence. I will also suggest that God's nonviolence in the salvation of victims and restoration of the suffering world must be preceded by divine judgment as intervention, or by the annihilation of evil in a violent world.

1.1 The Theological Issue of Violence

Given his commitment to a nonviolent account of atonement, Weaver assumes that since violence is an all-inclusive and universal issue in our modern world, nonviolence is the practical solution to an urgent problem. Following Glen Stassen and Michael Westmoreland-White, Weaver defines two aspects of violence: "(1) destruction to a victim and (2) by overpowering means. *Violence is destruction to a victim by means that overpower the victim's consent.*"[3] He specifies concrete cases of violence from his own theological standpoint.

> Violence as harm or damage includes physical harm or injury to bodily integrity. It incorporates a range of acts and conditions that include damage to a person's dignity or self-esteem. Abuse comes in psychological and sociological as well as physical forms: parents who belittle a child and thus nurture a person without self-worth . . . Such forms as racism, sexism, and poverty are frequently referred to as systemic violence. It is necessary to keep all these forms of violence in mind, from direct violence of bodily injury and killing through psychological abuse and the multiple forms of systemic violence.[4]

Weaver's claim that there are multidimensions of violence in the world is surely plausible. He examines the three major areas of contemporary violence: "domestic," "social," and "criminal." Moreover, Weaver engages Brock's and Schwager's critiques of divine violence in the satisfaction theory of atonement in order to reconstruct his own alternative atonement theology of nonviolence. Firstly, Weaver comprehensively surveys feminist and womanist theologians' accusations that penal

---

3. Weaver, *The Nonviolent Atonement*, 8. Cited from Strassen and Westmoreland-White, "Defining Violence and Nonviolence," 18.

4. Weaver, *The Nonviolent Atonement*, 8.

substitutionary theory is "divine child abuse or divine surrogacy" and that it forces victimized womankind "to submit passively to abuse" in the domestic milieu of violence.[5] Secondly, Weaver not only reflects on the anthropological ideas of René Girard's scapegoat theory, but also accepts Schwager's biblically dramatic application of the Girardian perspective.[6] Following Girard and Schwager, Weaver observes that as the innocent victim of evil, Jesus nonviolently "unmasks the violence of the scapegoat mechanism" at the social-communal dimension.[7] Lastly, Weaver assumes that the modern American judicial system indeed reflects retributive justice in the form of violence against criminals, as found in the penal substitutionary theory of atonement, because the common goal is to inflict punishment upon sinners.[8] By doing so, Weaver reaches the conclusion that domestic, communal, and criminal violence—the three primary dimensions of modern violence—have the negative effect of justifying the violent motifs of God's satisfaction in Anselmian atonement theory. Weaver concludes that divine violence in the doctrine of satisfaction is the projection of a human ideology of violence that can maintain the *status quo* of social order.

Correspondingly, concerning nonviolence, Weaver illustrates a wide-ranging "spectrum of stances and actions ranging from passive nonresistance at one end to active nonviolent resistance at the other."[9] The passive application of nonviolence is "persuasion" that influences "the action of others without denying their freedom or harming their person."[10] It is noteworthy that for Weaver, the active practice of nonviolence can encompass "some forms of punishment for children, physically restraining children from running into the street, knocking a person out of the path of a vehicle, and physically restraining a person attempting suicide."[11] Yet since Weaver himself practically concedes "coercion used positively,"[12] it must be possible for power's compulsory role to ultimately

---

5. Weaver, *The Nonviolent Atonement*, Chapter 5, "Feminist Theology on Atonement," and Chapter 6 "[African American] Womanist Theology on Atonement."

6. Weaver, *The Nonviolent Atonement*, 48–51, 57–61, 294–300.

7. Weaver, *The Nonviolent Atonement*, 51.

8. Weaver, *The Nonviolent Atonement*, 2–3. Weaver's claims are indebted to Timothy Gorrinage, *God's Just Vengeance*, 1–29.

9. Weaver, *The Nonviolent Atonement*, 9.

10. Weaver, *The Nonviolent Atonement*, 9.

11. Weaver, *The Nonviolent Atonement*, 9.

12. Weaver, *The Nonviolent Atonement*, 9.

bring about good to persons and the community. Weaver neglects to consider that nonviolence itself cannot exist in a pure and absolute sense, because it is involved in real contexts that necessitate the coercive force of control and judgment.

1.2 Brock's Feminist Critique of God's Judgment as Divine Violence

The Feminist Healing of Broken-Heartedness by Erotic Power

Writing from a feminist perspective, Brock takes a much more radically critical position on the penal-substitutionary perspective than other nonviolent atonement theologians such as Schwager and Weaver.[13] Before discussing why Brock censures the idea of God's judgment through Christ's substitutionary death, I will lay out the hermeneutical foundations of her own feminist healing-oriented soteriology.

Brock appeals to a personal-practical dimension of feminist theology that is different from previous socio-political theories of "liberation" from patriarchalism.[14] Instead of "the overturning of patriarchal power hierarchies"—that is to say, "the turning of oppressed and oppressor upside down as essential to liberation"—Brock emphasizes "turning patriarchy inside out" in order to "illuminate the power that heals" the "broken heart."[15] Brock's intrapersonal analysis reveals broken-heartedness as the destructive result of patriarchal evil. Her paradigm shift provides a positive and constructive framework for the healing of abused women's "broken-heartedness," caused by a male dominance that functions as a negative and destructive power. For Brock, since the "ontological relational existence, the heart of our being" has been seriously damaged by patriarchal evil, there is a necessity for the ontological-relational healing

---

13. A group of feminist theologians have fundamentally deconstructed a traditional understanding of the sovereign God and his atoning work in Christ. They have a common premise that a substitutionary doctrine of atonement is based on the violence and evil that are inherent in patriarchy as a social-political and economic power structure of masculine dominance. Migliore, *Faith Seeking Understanding*, 211. For representative scholars, see Fiorenza, *Jesus: Miriam's Child, Sophia's Prophet*; Johnson, *She Who Is: The Mystery of God in Feminist Theological Discourse*; Sölle, *Christ the Representative*; Radford Ruether, *Sexism and God-Talk: Toward a Feminist Theology*.

14. Brock, *Journeys by Heart*, xv.

15. Brock, *Journeys by Heart*, xv.

of the broken-heartedness.[16] It is correct to say that healing is one of the most crucial aspects of Christ's salvation for suffering sinners. Jesus himself declares that he is the spiritual healer by saying that "it is not the healthy who need a doctor, but the sick. I have not come to call the righteous, but sinners" (Mark 2:17). Given that sin is the most fatal disease that destroys the whole of a human being, Brock employs the biblical metaphor of healing in the appropriate sense. Thus Brock asserts that "sin is a sign of our broken-heartedness, of how damaged we are, not of how evil, willfully disobedient, and culpable we are. Sin is not something to be punished, but something to be healed."[17] Brock's theological assumption is that without healing, wounded people cannot break out of a vicious circle of hurting each other.[18] Accordingly, the problem of sin is "a symptom of a wound" in an interpersonal dimension, not "a state of being" in the objective sense.[19] Moreover, in Brock's feminist thought, a traditional view of sin in which objective guilt is to be forgiven in a penal sense is replaced by the modern-contextual image of a subjective wound to be restored in the therapeutic sense. Instead of an abstract and ahistorical explanation of original sin, Brock argues for "a phenomenology of the brokenness" as "a historical, concrete wounding" that happens through "abusive relationships" at home.[20] Brock effectively employs the "micro-examination of interpersonal family relationships" in order to disclose the communal-relational effect of real sins' destructive force, which corresponds to the "female experience" of domestic violence and abuse.[21] For Brock, what matters is not a textual discussion on the logical cause of original sin, vertically related to God in the Bible, but its destructive consequence among suffering humans in the contextual and horizontal sense. This is her own contribution to overcoming the abstracting tendency of Western hamartiology, in which there are not sufficient human-relational solutions to the destructive phenomenon brought about by fallen humans themselves. In this regard, Brock's feminist theology not only reveals the relational dimension of patriarchal evil, but also offers a nonviolent

---

16. Brock, *Journeys by Heart*, 7.
17. Brock, *Journeys by Heart*, 7.
18. Downie, "Discerning Redeeming Communities," 73–74.
19. Downie, "Discerning Redeeming Communities," 73.
20. Downie, "Discerning Redeeming Communities," 75.
21. Downie, "Discerning Redeeming Communities," 74–75.

curative approach to the broken-heartedness of abused women, instead of their violent vengeance against social and interpersonal evil.

Next, in order to address the problem of broken-heartedness, Brock proposes her creative formulation of "erotic power" grounded upon "relationship and community as the whole-making, healing center of Christianity."[22] Brock defines erotic power in a relationship-centered perspective by contrasting the feminist nonviolent power of creation and cooperation with the violent masculine power of possession and dominance.[23] It is noteworthy that she suggests an ontological dimension of the femininity-oriented power.

> Erotic power as an *ontic* category, that is, as a fundamental ultimate reality in human experience, is a more inclusive and accurate understanding of the dynamics of power within which dominance and willful assertion can be explained. Power as a causal concept is better understood when set into the *ontic* framework of erotic power as the most inclusive principle of human existence. Hence all other forms of power emerge from the reality of erotic power.[24]

Erotic power is the feminist ontological-relational resolution to the universal problem of broken-heartedness, insofar as it is caused by patriarchal violence and deeply entrenched in our contemporary society.

Finally, Brock uses process theology, in which "relationship and change are ultimate principles of reality," to confirm that the structure of feminist erotic power corresponds to "a nondualistic relational understanding."[25] She vividly describes erotic power through the lens of process theology. The power that "emerges from creative synthesis" is "the fluid product of a highly interactive process that begins with birth and buoys us throughout life."[26] She goes further to argue that "erotic power is the fundamental power of existence-as-a-relational-process," because "all existence comes to be by virtue of connectedness" through "the erotic power" of "being/becoming."[27] Likewise, according to Brock, since sin is broken-heartedness in a personal dimension, the ultimate solution

22. Brock, *Journeys by Heart*, 52.
23. Brock, *Journeys by Heart*, 26.
24. Brock, *Journeys by Heart*, 26.
25. Brock, *Journeys by Heart*, 34.
26. Brock, *Journeys by Heart*, 39.
27. Brock, *Journeys by Heart*, 41.

should come from the relationships between humans. Thus, healing cannot be brought about by an almighty savior in lieu of powerless and fallen sinners, because any salvation coming from a divine work destroys the human's "irreplaceable" identity and freedom in an intrinsic sense.[28] Rather, a "self-healing" power lies in victims' own connection with their true selves and intimate solidarity with their fellow human beings.[29] For Brock, erotic power is immanently present in every human being. Due to the brokenness of the heart, we are disconnected from the divine power and love. Yet when erotic power realizes itself in us, we not only begin to receive life-giving power, but also connect with each other heart to heart. A human being "only exists in relationships as it focuses and structures those relationships."

> Such a view of power may seem new, but it, in fact, is a more primal awareness of life that taps the energy sources of our earliest beginnings when, as children, we were most vulnerable and needed to connect to others. The childhood birth of play and the rebirth of heart lead us into the many realms of erotic power.[30]

Here I observe that Brock's feminist formulation of erotic power shares a common denominator with the classical-biblical understanding of creation and salvation. Brock's rhetoric on childhood echoes our perfect humanity before the fall. The erotic power in us not only recognizes the broken-heartedness in the present but also remembers the original image in the past. This self-awareness sets up our new identity so we can start to heal our wounded heart until we reach a future of perfect restoration. In fact, Brock seems to keep in mind the doctrines of justification, sanctification, and the glorification of our fallen nature by God's grace in Christ, though all the procedures are understood and described by her own feminist-process theology in the human-immanent sense. Regarding a personal-relational understanding of humanity, Brock's feminist theology not only illuminates the analogy of humankind as *imago Dei* but also re-affirms Calvin's insight that truly knowing who we are is inextricable from obtaining the true knowledge of God.[31]

---

28. Sölle, *Christ the Representative*, 43. Brock agrees with Sölle's feminist critique of the substitutionary view of salvation.

29. Brock, *Journeys by Heart*, 16.

30. Brock, *Journeys by Heart*, 39.

31. Calvin, *Institutes* I.1.3.

However, I realize that for Brock, "all power emerges from erotic power." There are two contrasting responses: the "life-giving form" of humans' reception or the "destructive form" of their rejection ("broken-heartedness").[32] In this sense, erotic power has ultimate sovereignty over healing broken relationships. Brock's feminist definition of erotic power is almost the same as God's sovereign justice, love, and power. At this point, I wonder how Brock would respond to the role of erotic power in the case of disconnected beings who violently reject personal persuasion. In this case, if healing takes place, the positive and constructive event must be preceded by a negative and deconstructive confrontation with the aggressor's force. There must be violent intervention by the nonviolent erotic power. Such might be a case of sovereign judgment by erotic power that Brock would reject. I surmise Brock would choose the nonviolent option: As healing by erotic power depends on the process itself, erotic power becomes too powerless to heal any violent resistance. Ultimately, it comes to lose the life-giving power of connection.

The fundamental reason why Brock encounters the same deadlock as process theology is that there is a gap in the logic of her healing-oriented soteriology. She only tells us *what* healing is occurring, without describing *how* the healing happens through the relational dimension between God and women wounded by men's violence. Consequently, Brock's own subjective discussion of broken-heartedness and healing fails to deal with the issues of abused women's "shame" and "despair," which patriarchal sin itself causes.[33] Abused women's right recognition of their own selves and other fellows cannot automatically guarantee their actual restoration from sin and evil. Brock's idealizing tendency never considers that, although broken-heartedness as the destructive effect of sin needs to be healed, the destructive sin itself cannot be annihilated by the self-healing of wounded women themselves.

Penal Substitution as Cosmic Child Abuse?

Within the feminist process-theological framework, Brock hastily concludes that traditional concepts in Christianity that are described by

---

32. Brock, *Journeys by Heart*, 41.

33. Downie, "Discerning Redeeming Communities," 197–98. Downie's critique goes to the root of the matter. Wounded women should not only face "the injustice of what has been done to them," but also overcome "the pain of being deeply wounded by others." Yet the wounded women have no self-recovering power by themselves.

androcentric language, such as God the Father and the Son, are nothing but the socio-religious ideology of masculine domination.

> Christian theology has done so, both through almost exclusively masculine symbols such as father, king, Lord, and savior and through theological doctrines of omnipotence and divine *apatheia*, judgment, and reason . . . The doctrine of omnipotence, by connection to such images, has tended to reinforce their hierarchal, controlling aspects.[34]

For Brock, women cannot participate in the masculinizing history of salvation. She contends that "through androcentrism, the experiences and reality of women are made invisible."[35] It is understandable that Brock explores a feminist redemption of Christian theology from the prison of patriarchalism by re-illuminating women's experience of immanent life in this world. However, regarding the feminist experience of victimization-oriented salvation, Brock makes the provocative claim that masculinity-centered soteriology causes a theological problem, as there is "cosmic child abuse" in the penal substitutionary doctrine.[36] She claims,

> The shadow of omnipotence haunts atonement. The ghost of the punitive father lurks in the corners. He never disappears even as he is transformed into an image of forgiving grace. Hence the experience of grace is lodged, I believe, not so much in a clear sense of personal work gained from an awareness of interdependence and the unconditional nature of love, but in a sense of relief from escaping punishment for one's failings. Paternalistic grace functions by allowing a select group to be in a favored relationship with the powerful father, but the overall destructiveness of the oppressive systems of the patriarchal family is not challenged by such benevolence. Hence judgment on the unsaved is a necessary component of atonement. Such doctrines of salvation reflect by analogy, I believe, images of the neglect of children or, even worse, child abuse, making it acceptable as divine behavior—*cosmic child abuse*, as it were. The father allows, or even inflicts, the death of his only perfect son. The emphasis is on the good goodness of power of the father and the unworthiness and powerlessness of his children, so that the father's punishment is just, and children are to blame. While atonement doctrines emphasize the father's grace and forgiveness, making

34. Brock, *Journeys by Heart*, 49.
35. Brock, *Journeys by Heart*, xiii.
36. Brock, *Journeys by Heart*, 56.

it seem as if he accepts all persons whole without the demand that they be good and free of sin, such acceptance is contingent upon the suffering of the one perfect child.[37]

For Brock, all the masculinizing concepts of God's almighty power that unilaterally determine salvation are nothing but the projection of a violent patriarchalism that must be dismantled in the current society and world. According to Brock, the penal substitutionary atonement theory is the glorification of Christ's redemptive suffering of God's divine violence, because God's arbitrary wrath is appeased by the Son's obedient death. Brock also censures the Trinitarian concept of atonement, in which God the Father takes the divine judgment of sin and evil in the Son Christ, because the "fusion" of the two masculine persons has nothing to do with the "intimacy" that is based upon interdependence.[38]

Similar to Brock, other feminist theologians also point out serious problems in the traditional theological perspective. They associate Jesus' crucifixion with suffering that is mostly attributed to violence and evil in the present world.[39] Brock's feminist analysis of child abuse within patriarchalism is convincing in that domestic violence happens again and again in the fallen world, including here and now. Therefore, we need to critically accept Brock's interpersonal analysis of women's victimization by persisting evils in the patriarchal family and society. Against the false ideologies of oppression and subjugation, we must proclaim Christ's gospel of liberation to suffering victims.

Nonetheless, regarding Brock's nonviolent interpretation of God's therapeutic work for victimized women, Kathryn Tanner argues that "God in the moral example or influence model might seem a sentimental patsy, without righteous anger or horrified concern for the destructive and wayward effects of sin on human life."[40] Although Brock's restorative motif of healing by erotic power is justifiable and necessary in the reconciliation process of salvation, God's nonviolent healing of wounded women cannot supersede the divine judgment against the sin and evil that actually causes the victimization. Tanner rightfully argues for the righteousness of God's sovereign act on the cross:

---

37. Brock, *Journeys by Heart*, 56.
38. Brock, *Journeys by Heart*, 57.
39. Duff, "Atonement and the Christian Life," 21–33.
40. Tanner, "Incarnation, Cross, and Sacrifice," 37.

The cross is the final expression of God's wrathful condemnation of sin, the place where sin, and the suffering and death it entails, are borne by Christ and put to death, destroyed. The cross is the ultimate expression of God's loving choice to be with sinners, in all the sufferings of a spiritual and physical sort that burden human life in its sinful condition.[41]

This is the revelation of God's own righteous solidarity with victimized sinners and his annihilation of sin in the personal and socio-political context of suffering and evil. However, Brock unfairly overlooks the divine judgment—how God tackles and solves the problem of evil—and she radically narrows down the universal and historical drama of God's salvation into the particular and spiritual aspect of abused women's healing. Correspondingly, Serene Jones affirms that the destructive "oppression" of patriarchalism is not merely "a social phenomenon," but one "which defies the will of God" and needs to be re-illuminated through Luther's and Calvin's biblical understanding of sin, justification, and sanctification.[42] From Jones's Reformed-feminist perspective, "God's judgment" is no longer the divine violence to oppress women, but the justifying force to "dismantle" all the patriarchal ideologies of "gender categories and the binarism of sexual difference."[43] God's justification of victimized women in a divine judgment on structural evil guarantees the new identity of forgiven and restored women in Christ.[44] Receiving divine grace—i.e., reconciliation, restoration, and forgiveness—from a loving God, they are empowered to forgive offenders and embrace themselves. Thus, they can be actually liberated from the bondage of self-deprecation and torment.

Jones concludes that Brock's subjective analysis of the concrete and historical issue of domestic violence relies on "universalizing and/or ahistorical frames of reference to structure their [women's] accounts of human experience."[45] Likewise, the nonviolent atonement scholar Weaver criticizes Brock's feminist process theology insofar as "her discussion of the healing of broken relationships on the basis of erotic power is a kind of one-size-fits-all solution."[46] Brock, while rejecting any ahistorical understanding of God's saving power in Anselmian satisfaction theory, still

41. Tanner, "Incarnation, Cross, and Sacrifice," 36.
42. Jones, *Feminist Theory and Christian Theology*, 109.
43. Jones, *Feminist theory and Christian Theology*, 66.
44. Jones, *Feminist theory and Christian Theology*, 108.
45. Jones, "Women's Experience Between a Rock and a Hard Place," 34.
46. Weaver, *The Nonviolent Atonement*, 177.

uncritically universalizes and eternalizes the phenomenon of women's suffering. In regard to substitutionary atonement, Brock unjustly projects the evil of abusive families onto the objective and unique act of God's salvation in Christ. The hermeneutical integrity between universality and particularity collapses in feministic process theology, which unconditionally reads all theological propositions in light of its foundational assumption that the broken hearts of women can be healed within female communities. If there is a universal phenomenon of patriarchal and androcentric structural evil, why does Brock never concede the necessity of God's universal justice against that evil in the objective sense? Without divine judgment, feminist liberation movements ironically justify the dualistic relationship between oppressed women and dominant men in the socio-political, cultural, and economic framework in our human society. Horizontal reconciliation in broken societies and families will never take place without the vertical saving work of God in Christ.

Despite Brock's denial of God's judgment through Christ's death, I suggest that Brock's insights about salvation as healing can be critically harmonized with the substitutionary model of atonement. Brock's nonviolent motif of healing is fundamentally analogous to the human body's recovery during medical treatment. However, unlike Brock's nonviolent understanding, the practical healing of a human body goes hand in hand with the violent extermination of a virus or removal of a tumor by a doctor. The seemingly nonviolent recovery of a wounded body is based on a violent intervention to remove the harmful things in the body. In terms of atonement, if we rely on the analogy of healing, there must be a synthetic procedure: the removal of sin and evil is followed by the recovery of a broken-hearted victim. If we holistically re-interpret Brock's life-giving healing motif through the lens of substitution, Christ's substitutionary death would be God's spiritual transplant surgery for sinners through the self-sacrificial love of his Son, who voluntarily becomes the substitutionary transplanter. At first glance, God's divine operation, removing evil from humankind and transplanting eternal life into them, seems to be merely a human killing—the crucifixion of Jesus—and is misunderstood as divine violence. Nonetheless, the divine event ultimately turns out to be the life-giving procedure by which God sovereignly heals spiritual patients through Christ's substitutionary death. If God's judgment were divine violence against his Son, Christ would have been annihilated in the process. Instead, the Son of God was raised because of God's divine operation.

Given that, as Brock says, broken-heartedness is a symptom of sin like a "sickness unto death," the feminist healing by erotic power should not remain at the level of alleviation. The sin itself that causes the broken-heartedness must be annihilated. Unfortunately, Brock's erotic power-oriented healing never pursues a biblical solution for divine judgment on patriarchal sin and evil. It is self-contradictory that although Brock insists that erotic power has an ontological dimension, she only focuses on an inter-relational healing of the broken-heartedness. Yet, as Brock acknowledges with regret, the powerless Goddess who is the projection of a vulnerable humanity is ultimately unable to save victims from the repetition of evil and violence. Thus, God and the victimized women are to be imprisoned in the cage of a suffering and healing process. That is the inevitable cruelty of a feminist goddess that Brock never wants, but implies.

1.3 Schwager's Girardian Application of Scapegoat Theory

The Dramatic Perspective on the Nonviolent God

Schwager attempts to engage René Girard's anthropocentric theory of the scapegoat and violence with Jesus' dramatic salvation in the Bible.[47] For Girard, the scapegoat mechanism is the universal manifestation of human communities' inherent violence throughout ancient myths, cultures, and religions into modern society. Girard's understanding of the crucifixion emphasizes the subjective realization of humankind, in line with the Abelardian theory of atonement. The Girardian perspective decisively reveals the concealed nature of "mimetic violence" in the scapegoat mechanism, in contrast with myths that never tell the truth about the victimization, because Jesus' narratives of life, death, and resurrection unveil human "ignorance" and "a persecutory unconscious."[48] It is important to see that, as with Girard, Schwager's emphasis on the universality of evil accords with a classical doctrine of human depravity. Such depravity leads to a cognitive distortion of God's truth and to human

---

47. Schwager, *Jesus in the Drama of Salvation*, 127–30. For the Girardian theory on violence and atonement, see Girard, *The Scapegoat*, and Girard, *Violence and the Sacred*.

48. Boersma, *Violence, Hospitality, and the Cross*, 142, cited from Girard, *I See Satan Fall Like Lightning*, 126. Girard does not acknowledge any objective or ontological reality in Christ's atoning death, only highlighting the cognitive and epistemological aspect of human evil and violence in the event.

self-destruction. Thus, Schwager is alert to the ways in which depraved humans uncritically project violence upon a God who has nothing to do with "the world of sin":[49]

> Since God does not will sin, we may not treat as revelation of the Father anything which *immediately* and *directly* arises from sin, otherwise God and sinners would merge into one another. The unjust condemnation and violent death of Jesus were unambiguous fruits of sin, and therefore nothing of God—in direct fashion—was disclosed in them.[50]

It is noteworthy that within the Girardian perspective, Schwager creatively develops his own dramatically reoriented atonement theology. Instead of a dogmatic concept of a transcendental and sovereign God who acts so unilaterally as to accomplish his own salvation of the entire world, Schwager proposes a dynamic understanding of God's being and work that is "dramatically" influenced by the human world.

> *Does not all unilinear thinking fall short, and should not the action of God be seen more dramatically*—not in the sense of cosmic catastrophes, but in the sense of events which have their particular moment in time and which involve the interplay of free agents? The nearest available horizon of understanding, the Old Testament, shows how God made promises, met the resistance of his people, "repented" of his actions, acted in anger and overcame his own anger by his mercy, and made possible new beginnings of his people.[51]

The compassionate God struggles with disobedient humans to the point that he manages to solve the dilemma between retribution and forgiveness, as if God himself were the principal character of his own drama of redemption in Christ. Thus, according to Schwager, the entire drama of Jesus' salvation consists of five principal stages in the Triune God's dramatic acts, which dynamically respond to human agents' free decisions toward his kingdom.[52] Above all, Schwager argues for his own hermeneutical principle of harmony in the Bible, in order to set forth

---

49. Schwager, *Jesus in the Drama of Salvation*, 168.
50. Schwager, *Jesus in the Drama of Salvation*, 194.
51. Schwager, *Jesus in the Drama of Salvation*, 35.
52. These are "the dawning of the kingdom of God," "the rejection of the kingdom of God and judgment," "the bringer of salvation brought to judgment," "resurrection of the Son as judgment of the heavenly Father," and "the Holy Spirit and the new gathering."

The Nonviolent God's Nonviolent Atonement

the divine-human drama of salvation. He believes that "no contradictory opposition is introduced into God's will in accordance with Scripture."[53] Schwager concedes that, in contrast to Jesus' nonviolence as the complete revelation of God, there are a number of problematic events of divine violence in the Old Testament. In order to solve the dilemma of how the violent God of justice and retribution can be identical with the nonviolent God of love and forgiveness, Schwager not only confirms a theological unity between the two Testaments, but also relies on an anthropological perspective on violence and religion.[54] For Schwager, the Old Testament's metaphors of "retribution" are deeply interrelated with "the primitive sense of vengeance."[55] The two concepts of violence had affected the ancient Jews' consciousness and even their belief in who God is.[56] Thus Schwager demythologizes the human concept of the retributive God in the Old Testament. For Schwager, given that God is nonviolent, he cannot be involved with any violent will or act that contradicts his being of nonviolence.

Schwager attempts to dismantle all the violent interpretations of atonement in the entire Scripture. Regarding the suffering servant of God in Isaiah 53, Schwager gives a nonviolent interpretation of God's being:

> There remains a certain ambiguity in the songs of the stricken servant. Does their central message consist in the new and surprising way retribution was carried out? Or is it decisive here that God inspired the servant to nonviolence? In the first case, there would be no breakthrough from the old idea of vengeance; they would simply have found a new and surprising variant. In the second place, however, God, as proclaimed in these songs, would have to have been understood as a *nonviolent God*. On this assumption, the "retribution" which fell on the suffering servant would have to be understood in a new way. It would be the result, no longer of a direct act of will from God, but only the consequence of a (bad) human and social way of behavior.[57]

The key point of this new nonviolent perspective is to identify the human misunderstanding of divine violence, in which "yet we considered

---

53. Schwager, *Jesus in the Drama of Salvation*, 166.
54. Schwager, *Jesus in the Drama of Salvation*, 17.
55. Schwager, *Jesus in the Drama of Salvation*, 17.
56. Schwager, *Jesus in the Drama of Salvation*, 17.
57. Schwager, *Jesus in the Drama of Salvation*, 24. Emphasis mine.

him punished by God, stricken by him, and afflicted" (Isaiah 53:4).[58] Rather, the suffering and death of the righteous servant are totally attributed to "our transgression and iniquities" (Isa 53:5). Thus, God does not directly punish the innocent servant instead of sinners.[59]

Yet, in contrast to Schwager's nonviolent perspective, God's judgment on the Israelites is inseparable from his restoration of the kingdom of God, because the faithfulness of God confirms his sovereign actualization of both judgment and restoration as a whole.[60] Thus Schwager's nonviolent interpretation of God's judgment is misconstrued, in that the Old Testament prophets essentially agree with the claim that God's righteous judgment goes hand in hand with his gracious restoration. The Bible itself testifies that there is no hermeneutical contradiction between the judgment of God and his work of salvation, for God as a holy judge of the disobedient Israelites is the same Lord as the Father who embraces the repentant sinners as his loving children. Moreover, Schwager unfairly assumes that the Old Testament is the imperfect revelation of a wrathful God who is appeased by the innocent blood of animal and human sacrifice. I suspect that this is a modern version of Marcionism, in which the whole of the Bible is judged by the absolute standard of human nonviolence, as if all the violent concepts and narratives were an interpolation by humankind.

Correspondingly, regarding the nonviolent exegesis of Paul's doctrine of atonement in the New Testament, Schwager claims that God's wrath is his revelation of sinners' self-deceptive desires and their self-judgment by evil deeds (Rom 1:18–32).[61] Schwager contends that Paul never argues for God's "direct punishment" against sinful humankind.[62] It is interesting to see that although Schwager gets rid of God's direct punishment, he acknowledges God's indirect judgment, in which God hands over the fallen humans to their own sinful desires and evil deeds. Schwager argues that Jesus' proclamation of God's judgment brings about

58. Belousek, *Atonement, Justice, and Peace*, 236.

59. Belousek, *Atonement, Justice, and Peace*, 240.

60. Gowan, *Theology of the Prophetic Books*, 169. Gowan insists that God is both the Judge and Savior. Eichrodt, *Theology of the Old Testament*, 467. Eichrodt claims that the return of the repentant Israelites demonstrates the fulfillment of the "prophetic message of judgment and new creation" and the realization of their "hope" to solve the problem of sin as "obstacle" to the righteous reign of God.

61. Schwager, *Jesus in the Drama of Salvation*, 165.

62. Schwager, *Jesus in the Drama of Salvation*, 165.

"the self-judgment of people hardening their hearts."[63] Schwager's nonviolent interpretation of the "self-judgment" of sinners confirms his own application of the Girardian perspective on human misunderstanding and collective violence against innocent victims. Above all, the infinite chasm between God and sinful humans in a vertical dimension is replaced by the cognitive gap in the horizontal sense between humans' right understanding of themselves and the miscomprehension of their evil deeds. As an innocent victim, Jesus reveals the collective violence of the scapegoat mechanism. Thus, for Schwager, God never wills the death of Christ because the punishment of Christ is carried out by self-deceiving sinners.[64]

> It cannot be said that the Father handed over the Son because he wanted to judge him and punish him in place of sinners. *The judgment did not start from God but from humankind*, and the will of the Father was only that the Son should follow sinners to the very end and share abandonment, in order thus to make possible for them again a conversion from the world of hardened hearts and distance from God.[65]

In this regard, for Schwager, there is no link between God's wrath and the divine judgment, because the former implies God's nonviolent response, whereas the latter shows his violent retribution. Concerning God's work of reconciliation in Christ (2 Cor 5:19), Schwager argues that there is neither "an anger of God toward his son" nor "a destruction of sin through him."[66] Likewise, Schwager asserts that God the Father never makes Christ into sin, but the evil force of sin is so strong as to convert him into sin. What follows is Schwager's nonviolent theological interpretation of the substitution of Christ.

> The power of sin is so cunning that it can get completely within its grasp the good and holy law and can so distort it that it works against God and his envoy . . . The power of evil rather turned back the command which came from God against the Son. Working from this insight, we are finally led to the interpretation of 2 Corinthians 5:21, that God did not himself destroy Christ in judgment. Certainly, he sent him into the world of sin, but entirely with the aim of saving humankind. However, the

63. Schwager, *Jesus in the Drama of Salvation*, 116.
64. Schwager, *Jesus in the Drama of Salvation*, 117–18.
65. Schwager, *Jesus in the Drama of Salvation*, 118. Emphasis mine.
66. Schwager, *Jesus in the Drama of Salvation*, 118.

power of sin was so great that it was able by means of its own mechanism and dynamic to draw him into its world and thus to make him into sin.[67]

What enables Jesus to achieve substitution is not God himself, but the scapegoat mechanism. For Schwager, it is an unquestioned assumption that judgment is nothing but violence and evil, because to judge an innocent victim is the violent process of the scapegoat mechanism. Here Schwager fails to distinguish God's righteous judgment on evil from evildoers' unrighteous punishment of an innocent victim. Thus, Schwager firmly believes that the nonviolent God of love cannot and should not perform any kind of violent judgment. Moreover, according to Schwager, even if Paul seems to literally declare God's violent judgment on the crucified Jesus, i.e. God's condemnation of the sinful nature (Rom 8:3), the act has nothing to do with God himself. Paul's divine expressions concerning God's work in the crucifixion are not about God's intervention but the manifestation of "a reality" of violence and evil in the human world.[68] God's "eternal mission" in Christ's incarnation comes to take "a concrete form in the history of salvation" of the violent world.[69] By contrast, if anyone advances the violent interpretation that the God of nonviolence revealed in Christ violently judges the innocent Jesus, the case will cause a serious theological "contradiction" between God's nonviolent being and his violent work.[70] Therefore, all the violent judgments in the Bible are totally attributable to self-deceived sinners, because they are enslaved by the evil powers to the extent that "they did not know what they were doing."[71] In this regard, Schwager's anthropocentric perspective on God's saving work sheds light on the nonviolent character of God's love and the historical actuality of Christ's crucifixion as a violent judgment by sinners.

According to Schwager, there is no biblical evidence that God the Father is the direct agent of his Son's execution, because Jesus was crucified by an evil force, not by God. Rather, God "remained the 'Abba' to whom Jesus entrusted himself absolutely," to the moment of crucifixion.[72] Thus Schwager employs the notion of divine permission, in which God

67. Schwager, *Jesus in the Drama of Salvation*, 168.
68. Schwager, *Jesus in the Drama of Salvation*, 162.
69. Schwager, *Jesus in the Drama of Salvation*, 162.
70. Schwager, *Jesus in the Drama of Salvation*, 162.
71. Schwager, *Jesus in the Drama of Salvation*, 169.
72. Schwager, *Jesus in the Drama of Salvation*, 116.

allows the forsakenness of Jesus as the authorities on earth execute him. Thus Schwager insists that Jesus' desperate prayer at Gethsemane has nothing to do with his voluntary submission to God's violent will. Jesus' spiritual agony signifies "the absence of the heavenly Father" who never wills his Son's crucifixion.

> The subsequent anguish shows how Jesus had to undergo a drama into which he was drawn with his innermost soul, and in which, therefore, something experientially new was able to come about, something which had already been made clear at the objective level. The scene at the Mount of Olives reveals how existential the drama was and that even his inner most space of belief and trust did not remain unaffected. The darkness which attacked his soul was an expression of how deeply he was struck by those forces over which he himself had pronounced judgment. He was the one taking action, and yet he became the victim of what he had released. Certainly, the dark night was possible only because the Father permitted it, but it should not be concluded from this that he was struck directly by his God, who had suddenly transformed himself from a kindly Father into a despotic master.[73]

Schwager concludes that the loving Father had no responsibility for his Son's death, for there was no divine violence in the crucifixion. It was solely evil that existentially overwhelmed and crucified Jesus. In this way Schwager seems to solve the hermeneutical and ethical dilemma as to how a loving God brings about the crucifixion of Christ for humans. Instead, by describing the dramatic absence of God the Father and his permissiveness toward the hostile powers, Schwager safeguards the integrity of the relationship between the Father and the Son. The nonviolent and powerless God is the complete manifestation of Christ on the cross, because "the concept of power in its application to God needs to be criticized by means of the crucified one's nonviolence and powerlessness"[74] Subsequently, the dramatic process of atonement, according to Schwager, reveals God's persuasive will for the nonviolent salvation of self-judging sinners. What takes place in the death of Jesus is not God's retribution against sin and evil, but his salvation of sinners as "victims of evil" and

---

73. Schwager, *Jesus in the Drama of Salvation*, 116.
74. Schwager, *Jesus in the Drama of Salvation*, 205.

the "transformation" of evil itself.[75] Here, Schwager paradoxically argues for God's saving power in the crucifixion.

> The event of the cross became a sign that God allowed himself to be thoroughly touched and affected in his Son. But in its turn this process again had the bitter limit that it was won by means of the greatest imaginable human misdeed and lived out as suffering and torment. But in the Easter response to this misdeed there was finally revealed an eternal goodness, which cancelled out even this evil and yet did not overwhelm people with divine power, but continued to court their freedom by means of the Spirit. Unlimited goodness is shown to be truly endless goodness and is clearly separated from any vague kindness and weakness.[76]

God's suffering and self-openness toward violence in the world not only reveal his solidarity with victimized humans in his Son's crucifixion, but also make possible the divine declaration of the dismantling of evil through Christ's resurrection. The paradoxical power of God's nonviolence and love, which finally conquer violence and hostility, lies at the heart of Schwager's dramatic atonement model. Therefore, I sense that Schwager's atonement theory corresponds to a substitutionary emphasis on God's atoning work in Christ once-and-for-all, because the transforming power of God's nonviolent love annihilates evil as the obstacle that alienates sinners from God.

Nonetheless, we cannot but wonder whether Schwager's God of nonviolence has the sovereign power of forgiveness regarding the death of his own Son or not. The outcome of Schwager's task of de-mythologizing the righteous God and his judgment revealed in Scripture is that there never exists "a violent and wrathful God" and that he only remains as "a powerless God who does not engage in retribution."[77] If the powerless God only passively waits for Christ's inevitable death at the hands of the violent powers of spiritual darkness, it would not be unfair to say that this is also the hidden divine violence of abandonment. Here, we must take notice of Schwager's moral exemplar view of atonement. The nonviolent God abandons Jesus in order that sinners' inner hearts might be transformed by God's persuading love via the cruel crucifixion. The bottom line is that God neither judges sin nor saves sinners in the active

---

75. Schwager, *Jesus in the Drama of Salvation*, 194.
76. Schwager, *Jesus in the Drama of Salvation*, 201.
77. Balthasar, *Theo-Drama IV*, 312.

The Nonviolent God's Nonviolent Atonement

sense. Even after the death of Jesus, God merely waits for the response of sinners. In contrast to God's pure passivity in Schwager's dramatically reoriented Girardian view, Balthasar argues for God's sovereign intervention in the death of Christ. Unlike Schwager, Balthasar claims that in order to fully reveal the dramatic dynamics of God's salvation in the Bible, "there must be an interplay" between God's "initiative" act of grace and the sinner's "freedom."[78] God's plan of salvation is not passively achieved by the merciful decision of divine forgiveness regarding the crucifixion of Jesus. Rather, the loving and forgiving God actively sent his own Son into the violent world, in order to make Christ the self-sacrificial atonement that judges sin and evil in his own person as God-human. Schwager should have reflected on the simultaneity of God, who is both an actor in and the writer of his own drama of salvation. Therefore, I constructively suggest that for Schwager, in order to move beyond the limitation of a dramatically oriented atonement model, God as the divine author can and must play both a transcendental and immanent role in all the plots throughout the entire drama of redemption.

In addition, it is through the lens of his own nonviolent perspective that Schwager dynamically re-illuminates the reconciliation between God and humans in the Anselmian doctrine of atonement.[79] Schwager fully accepts the Anselmian perspective on God, whose "goodness is greater than any that can be thought."[80] At this point, Schwager's subjective perspective on God accords with an objective understanding of substitutionary atonement, in that the latter also focuses on the dramatic change from the human recognition of God's wrath to a recognition of his grace—which the former highlights. To illustrate, Calvin emphasizes that due to human incapacity, it is not until sinners are terrified by God's wrath that they start to realize God's eternal love toward them in the crucifixion of Christ.[81] Correspondingly, Schwager underlines the human cognitive turn:

> As long as people are trapped in sin, they can perceive everything only from the perspective of their own closed worlds, and God must necessarily appear to them as an alien and hostile power. Only after a genuine conversion does their capacity to

---

78. Balthasar, *Theo-Drama IV*, 318.
79. Schwager, *Jesus in the Drama of Salvation*, 165.
80. Schwager, *Jesus in the Drama of Salvation*, 197.
81. Peterson, *Calvin and the Atonement*, 20–23. Cited from Calvin, *Institutes* II.16.2.

see things alter, and thus also their picture of God. Now he no longer has to appear as the angry one, but can show himself as he is, the one who is kind above all others.[82]

Yet although Schwager dramatically describes the fact that the nonviolent God has revealed both himself and the evil of humankind, he fails to explain *how* the relational-cognitive dimension of God's being can be the same as his objective reconciliation of the entire fallen world here and now. Like Girard, Schwager exposes his tendency to focus exclusively on the nonviolent God who permits the evil that the scapegoat mechanism causes. Thus the Giradian perspective reaches the non-biblical conclusion that God decisively reveals divine nonviolence through the human violence of the crucifixion. God intends to enlighten human ignorance regarding his true self in the Old Testament, which highlights God's violent retribution against the disobedient Israelites. Due to human failure and rebellion, God plans to give up his own Son to the cruel hands of evildoers, in order to reveal the violence of the scapegoat mechanism and his own unconditional forgiveness towards those who are unaware of their violence. However, if God allows human violence in the historical-immanent sense, in order to reveal his nonviolence to the human consciousness, it paradoxically points to the inherent violence of the nonviolent God. While God's nonviolence only functions in a verbal sense, the phenomenon of violence is unremittingly connected with God's permission. God purposes to maximize the dramatic contrast between human violence and divine nonviolence. Yet why cannot God take the initiative to demonstrate his transforming power of nonviolence before the violent event happens? It is thus more problematic that God passively reveals his nonviolence only after the dramatic maximization of human violence. The hidden truth is that the nonviolent God willfully leaves the violent situation as it is, in order to finally reveal his nonviolent salvation. It is dubious that Schwager's nonviolent God is nonviolent in a real sense.

Likewise, according to Schwager, God's "turn" toward those who violently crucified Christ does not have any objective implication of reconciliation. It merely shows the cognitive "process" as God's revelation. Correspondingly, the divine response to the violence is not God's active decision but his passive one. Thus Schwager fails to guarantee the simultaneity of God's revelation and reconciliation in Christ. God's

---

82. Schwager, *Jesus in the Drama of Salvation*, 196.

revelation of his unconditional love towards sinful humankind remains as the condition of their self-awakening to their violent crime and God's forgiveness of evil. God's radical conversion towards sinners is not the accomplishment of atonement in Christ, but the condition for their salvation. If God's revelation never confirms his objective reconciliation in Christ, but only prepares the process for sinners' subjective realization, the content of the divine revelation is indeed empty. In this way, God's justice, God's judgment by his own righteousness, and his reconciliation are totally replaced by his love and the dramatic acts of his revelation and forgiveness through Christ's violent death. In other words, without human self-awareness of God's revelation, there is no way to confirm God's objective reconciliation. In this regard, God absolutely necessitates his own drama of redemption, in which God reveals his eternal goodness stage by stage, in order to enlighten the ignorant. The bottom line is that figuring out how to know God is the be-all and end-all of the biblical drama of salvation. Human awakening to the true knowledge of God's infinite love is the point on which God's atonement stands or falls. Schwager naively believes that sinners' cognitive conversion not only has a decisive effect on interpersonal reconciliation between persons, but also brings about the restoration of the entire creation.[83]

Moreover, a number of self-contradictory arguments impair Schwager's hermeneutical principle of God's consistency in his being and work in atonement. To begin with, while Schwager believes in God's "absence" at the moment of Christ's crucifixion,[84] in order to prevent misunderstandings about divine judgment, it is self-contradictory for him to argue for God's self-openness as his solidarity with the crucified Son.[85] Schwager never offers any clue on how the absent Father can be so suddenly present with the dying Jesus on the cross. How can the powerless God in his nonviolent act unexpectedly turn into the almighty God in his violent intervention against evil? Schwager cannot help acknowledging that his own nonviolent concept of God and the sovereign one from the substitutionary perspective are not mutually exclusive. Rather, I believe that by harmonizing the two contrasting approaches, we will have a holistic perspective on a multifaceted dimension of God's being and work beyond the human scope of reason and experience.

---

83. Peter Stork, "The Drama of Jesus and the Non-Violent Image of God," 202.
84. Schwager, *Jesus in the Drama of Salvation*, 116.
85. Schwager, *Jesus in the Drama of Salvation*, 201.

1.4 Weaver's Anthropological View on God's Nonviolent Atonement

Narrative Christus Victor

In contrast to Brock and Schwager, it is noteworthy that from the outset Weaver not only critically engages with the three doctrinal types of atonement—i.e., Anselmian satisfaction, *Christus victor*, and moral influence—but also constructively proposes his own atonement model, the narrative *Christus victor*. Before directly demonstrating the logic of nonviolent atonement, Weaver firstly offers a theological interpretation of Revelation, in order to "take an indirect route to narrative *Christus Victor*."[86] Unlike Brock and Schwager's use of anthropological ideas such as feminist healing and the scapegoat mechanism, Weaver's nonviolent atonement theology is solidly based on the biblical testimonies as a whole.[87] By placing an essential emphasis on the biblical and historical actuality of atonement in the Revelation of John, Weaver positively reconstructs Aulén's *Christus Victor* model. This model focuses on the mythological and transcendental dimension of the dualistic conflict between God and the hostile powers. Unlike Aulén, and in lieu of a violent image of Christ as the cosmic warrior who conquers evil, Weaver describes the crucified and resurrected Christ as the nonviolent victor, because he is the slain lamb of God in heaven in Revelation.

> The elements of cosmic confrontation and victory appear throughout Revelation, making the book virtually an extended, multifaceted statement of the *Christus Victor* image—a confrontation between good and evil, between the forces of God and the forces of Satan, between Christ and anti-Christ . . . The lion and lamb of symbols of ch. 5, which both refer to Jesus, portray one instance of a conqueror motif—the lion as a symbol of victory and the slaughtered lamb signifying the (nonviolent) manner of the victory . . . In chs. 6 and 7, it is the nonviolent conqueror—the slain lamb—who has earned the right to open the seals, and it is the lamb's victory over the forces that oppose the reign of God that is celebrated by the two great multitudes of the second scene of seal six . . . The juxtaposition of this celebration in seal six with the utter chaos and destruction in the scene of 5:12–17

---

86. Weaver, *The Nonviolent Atonement*, 20.

87. Weaver, *The Nonviolent Atonement*, See Chapter 2, "Narrative *Christus Victor*: The Revisioning of Atonement," 13–86.

suggests the greatness of the victory. This celebration matches that of ch. 5, which acclaimed the victory of the slaughtered lamb, the resurrected Christ.[88]

It is of great importance to see that for Weaver, God's salvation comes from the resurrection of the nonviolent Christ. Moreover, in order to overcome the mythologizing tendency of Aulén's *Christus Victor*, Weaver qualifies his own exegesis by confirming "the correlation between the historical church of the first century and *Christus Victor* in the book of Revelation."[89] According to Weaver, Revelation's "cosmic imagery" plays a hermeneutical role in demonstrating "the universal and cosmic significance of events in our historical world."[90] Weaver specifically proposes that "the sequence of seven seals corresponds to the reign of Roman emperors" from Tiberius to Domitian. "Seals one through four and six progress through various kinds of oppression and destruction, culminating with the highest level of evil—utter chaos—in the first scene of the sixth seal."[91]

> The message to be learned from the image of the cheering throngs is that the rule of God has already triumphed for those who live in the reality of the resurrection. Even when confronted with the devastation wreaked by the rule of Rome, culminating with the destruction of the temple and the sacred city of Jerusalem, they do not face ultimate despair. Though earthly rule appears to culminate in destruction, the rule of God has already begun on earth with a victory, the resurrection of Jesus. With the scenes of cheering throngs in seal six, the writer of Revelation makes a statement about a historical event, namely, the fall of Jerusalem. These celebratory scenes convey the message that in the grand scheme of things as defined by the reign of God, even the fall of Jerusalem pales in significance to the resurrection of Jesus. Here in a different form is the confrontation of reign of God and reign of evil, with God's reign victorious in the resurrection of Jesus. This is *Christus Victor* depicted in the realm of history.[92]

In this way, Weaver's narrative *Christus Victor* comes to declare God's nonviolent victory "in both human historical and cosmic realms," and to

---

88. Weaver, *The Nonviolent Atonement*, 20–22.
89. Weaver, *The Nonviolent Atonement*, 23.
90. Weaver, *The Nonviolent Atonement*, 23.
91. Weaver, *The Nonviolent Atonement*, 21.
92. Weaver, *The Nonviolent Atonement*, 26.

highlight Jesus' nonviolent life and work in the world.[93] We need to pay attention to Weaver's emphasis on his own biblical positivism regarding nonviolent atonement and reconciliation. His revelation-centered interpretation agrees with that of Robert Jenson. Like Weaver, according to Jenson, there can be neither a hidden story—like Anselm's speculation about God's broken honor "behind" Scripture—nor a mythological one like Aulén's idea of Christ's victory in the cosmic battle between God and the evil powers "beyond" the Bible.[94] Rather, it is solely through the biblical narratives that we can access God's historical revelation of his concrete work of nonviolent atonement for humankind. In this light, it seems impossible to deny that Weaver' narrative *Christus Victor* has much more hermeneutical validity than the other nonviolent atonement theories.

However, regarding all the literal meanings of divine violence, Weaver himself directly contravenes the fundamental principle of mutual correspondence between God's revelation and historical events. It is noteworthy that Weaver's interpretation of nonviolence neutralizes every violent concept of God's judgment or cosmic war in Revelation in a sort of spiritualizing and demythologizing process. According to Weaver, no historical event actually corresponds to the divine symbols of violence.[95] Weaver fails to distinguish God's nonviolent victory from a number of passages on God's violent judgment of evil. If the reign of God is purely nonviolent, why does he not only prohibit of the evildoers' entrance to his Kingdom but also throw them into the fiery lake of burning sulfur (Rev 21:8)? Since Weaver intends to ground nonviolent atonement upon the military image of God's victory in Revelation, not on a doctrine of reconciliation through crucifixion or a Eucharistic understanding of forgiveness, the nonviolent perspective ironically amplifies the theological issue of divine violence. Weaver never answers the important hermeneutical questions. How is God's nonviolent victory achieved? How can evil be annihilated in a purely nonviolent way? Does Weaver naively assume that evil is on a path to self-destruction? Revelation uses the violent image of God's fiery wrath destroying the hostile powers on the earth. Why does Weaver not apply the principles of nonviolent atonement literally and directly onto the issue of God's divine retribution against evil? Weaver is not unaware of the biblical testimony. He writes,

---

93. Weaver, *The Nonviolent Atonement*, 23.
94. Jenson, *Systematic Theology I*, 189.
95. Weaver, *The Nonviolent Atonement*, 34.

> Seal five shifts the viewpoint from an earthly scene to the heavenly realm, where the souls of the martyrs under the altar somewhat petulantly bemoan the slowness of God in avenging their deaths—deaths that resulted from the oppression and death depicted in seals one to four.[96]

Furthermore, Weaver reluctantly acknowledges that "God's judgment occurs" in order to save God's people from Satan in Revelation.[97] If Weaver believes in Revelation's divine and transcendental "symbolism," which universally and actually corresponds to all the human and historical events in the world, it would not be correct to say that there remains only a nonviolent interpretation of themes such as judgment, war, and victory.[98] More seriously, even after the resurrection of the nonviolent Christ there have been wars, famines, and catastrophes all over the world, as Revelation's universal and actual symbolism predicts. In this regard, Weaver's narrative *Christus Victor* provides a theological reductionism of nonviolence that exclusively confines biblical events to the lens of the absolute standard. For Weaver, there is no essential difference between God's divine judgment and human violence, because he assumes that every violent event is evil itself, without discerning what purposes underlie the violent phenomenon and who initiates the event.

The Nonviolent God's Human Inevitability in the Death of Christ

The definitive goal of Weaver's theological task is to reconstruct God's atoning work through the lens of nonviolence. Weaver censures the traditional theological discussion of atonement for justifying God's execution of the innocent Jesus on the ground that his violent death paradoxically brings about eternal life and salvation for humankind.

> Atonement theology starts with violence, namely, the killing of Jesus. The commonplace assumption is that something good happened, namely, the salvation of sinners, when or because Jesus was killed. It follows that the doctrine of atonement then explains how and why Christians believe that the death of Jesus—the killing of Jesus—resulted in the salvation of sinful humankind.[99]

---

96. Weaver, *The Nonviolent Atonement*, 21.
97. Weaver, *The Nonviolent Atonement*, 21.
98. Weaver, *The Nonviolent Atonement*, 32–33.
99. Weaver, *The Nonviolent Atonement*, 2.

For Weaver, all the atonement theologies that actively or passively imply God's violent intervention and the necessity of Jesus' atoning death are nothing but a distortion of God's saving truth of nonviolent salvation through Jesus. Weaver criticizes the commercial or penal aspects of God's satisfaction in "Anselmian" or "substitutionary theory" more than any other traditional types. The hermeneutical deconstruction of God's intrinsic violence is the principal purpose of Weaver's nonviolent atonement model.[100] Concerning divine violence, Weaver appreciates that Brock's feminist critique of God's judgment as cosmic child abuse discloses "the abstract formula of satisfaction" that not only justifies patriarchal violence but also the unethical implication of Jesus' substitutionary death.[101] In contrast to the traditional atonement theologies, Weaver pursues the obliteration of God's divine intentionality. By doing so, Weaver strives to guarantee the nonviolent being and work of God in the crucifixion of Jesus. According to Weaver, regardless of whether God crucifies Jesus directly or indirectly in the Anselmian satisfaction theory, the theory manifests "intrinsic violence."[102]

> Who was responsible for the death? or most provocatively, "Who killed Jesus?" These questions focus on the agency behind the death of Jesus. In an Anselmian approach to atonement, God obviously did not directly kill Jesus. In some lights, however, God seems implicated in Jesus' death . . . It is God's honor or God's law that was violated and had to be satisfied. Most obviously, sinful humankind cannot arrange its own satisfaction of God's offended honor . . . For satisfaction atonement, it appears that the only remaining option is that God is the agent behind Jesus' death. It would appear that God is ultimately the one who arranged for the death of Jesus as the payment that would satisfy divine honor or as the compensatory punishment required by the divine law. Although the traditional language has focused on Jesus' death for sinners, asking about the agent behind the death points to God as both the author of the process or the agent behind the transaction that requires the death of Jesus as innocent victim, as well as the recipient of the death as payment to God's honor.[103]

---

100. Weaver, *The Nonviolent Atonement*, 18.
101. Weaver, *The Nonviolent Atonement*, 174.
102. Weaver, *The Nonviolent Atonement*, 96.
103. Weaver, *The Nonviolent Atonement*, 89–90.

Weaver contends that there should not be any aspects of divine intentionality, necessity, or satisfaction in Jesus' death, in order to absolve God from any violence. Next, Weaver also criticizes the Abelardian moral influence tradition, because God has the divine purpose of awakening subjective responses from saved sinners towards God's ultimate love, as manifested in the crucifixion of Jesus.

> For the moral theory, God appears quite specifically as the agent of Jesus' death. In this motif, God the Father sent his most precious possession to die in order to display an ultimately loving act. Apparently the death of Jesus has no salvific purpose in this motif if it is not God-intended.[104]

Even the moral influence theory does not reject the absolute necessity of Jesus' death and the objective work of God's reconciliation, according to Weaver: "God the Father needed the death as the way to demonstrate the Father's love for sinful humankind."[105] If there remains the issue of God's sovereignty over Jesus' execution, Weaver thinks that Abelard's new perspective on atonement can hardly be free from the theological influence of Anselm.

Likewise, from the perspective of his narrative *Christus Victor*, Weaver also critically summarizes the non-biblical assumptions in Aulén's *Christus Victor* motif.

> Paying a ransom assumes that even Satan has certain rights that must be respected. Another variation denies such rights and pictures the defeat of the devil via deception. Failing to perceive the presence of God or the deity of Christ hidden under the flesh of Christ, analogous to the way bait covers a fishhook or cheese baits a mouse trap, the devil assumes an easy prey, swallows the bait of humanity of Jesus, and is caught by the deity hidden under the human nature.[106]

Even though Weaver includes the biblical motif of Christ's resurrection and conquest in his narrative *Christus Victor*, he points out that in the classical type, there still remains a demonic necessity for Christ's sacrificial death. The necessity indicates "an obligation in a contract to which God agrees."[107] For Weaver, the logic of atonement is "offensive

---

104. Weaver, *The Nonviolent Atonement*, 90.
105. Weaver, *The Nonviolent Atonement*, 89.
106. Weaver, *The Nonviolent Atonement*, 16.
107. Weaver, *The Nonviolent Atonement*, 88.

in its acceptance of rights for the devil," because "without the death to meet the agreement, souls of sinners remain in bondage."[108] The classical *Christus Victor* theory reasons inductively that God intends to satisfy the evil powers by sacrificing Christ, though an ultimate purpose of the deception is to defeat the devil through the resurrection.

Furthermore, Weaver argues that even the Girardian perspectives of Anthony Heim and S. Mark Barlett, the nonviolent atonement theologians, cannot escape from the hermeneutical problem of "divine intentionality" in the execution of Jesus.

> Girardian analysis, which pictures Jesus dying in abyssal compassion or stepping into the scapegoat mechanism in order to stop it, successfully invalidates all of these exchangist or transactionist images, in which the death affects God or humankind. However, the Girardian perspectives walk right up to the line of divine intent (to suggest an image) without quite stepping over it. When the intent is to show compassion and halt the scapegoat mechanism, that comes painfully close to the divine intention that Jesus should die, which allows the idea of a God who uses or sanctions violence to creep past the line via a back way.[109]

At this point, Weaver distances himself from Schwager's Girardian application of the scapegoat mechanism. Rather, Weaver's purely nonviolent atonement theory is "fully in accord with Brock in identifying forces of evil as the ultimate agency behind the death of Jesus."[110] Weaver refutes all the theological interpretations that God intervened in Christ's death. It is evident that Weaver's nonviolence-oriented atonement theory indeed deconstructs all the classical and modern hermeneutical models of God's sovereignty in the atoning death of Christ. Accordingly, it is through the denial of God's intentionality in Jesus' death that Weaver successfully absolves God of all responsibility for the crucifixion. Weaver's objection to satisfaction theory is persuasively grounded upon his contextualizing assumption that social, cultural, and historical backgrounds have a deep impact on the hermeneutics of atonement. Just as penal substitution appeals to modern Protestants because of its legal logic of retributive justice, Anselmian satisfaction theory reflects the cultural image of God as a Lord who has to restore his honor for the purpose of maintaining the

---

108. Weaver, *The Nonviolent Atonement*, 88.
109. Weaver, *The Nonviolent Atonement*, 299.
110. Weaver, *The Nonviolent Atonement*, 175.

The Nonviolent God's Nonviolent Atonement

social hierarchy of feudalism.[111] Exposing the hidden errors in the cultural interpretations of atonement, Weaver concludes that the underlying motif of retribution in both penal substitution and Anselmian satisfaction theory vindicates God's violent punishment of Jesus.[112]

Nevertheless, Fleming Rutledge forcefully criticizes Weaver's nonviolence-centered atonement theory, because violence itself has never been considered as an essential motif of Christ's substitutionary death that accomplishes God's plan of salvation.[113] Thus the dualistic premise between violence as evil and nonviolence as good cannot be the solid hermeneutical grounding to discuss the doctrine of atonement. Rather, it is ironic that although Weaver supports *Christus Victor* model as the theological-ethical base of nonviolence, the theory is misused to justify violence in the historical sense. According to Hans Boersma, we need to take a notice of Weaver's historical and theological miscomprehension in which *Christus Victor* theory is based on early church's nonviolent confrontation against the Roman Empire.

> In the case of Constantine, it is evident that he retained a powerful link with the traditional *Christus Victor* theme of the atonement. Constantine, or at least the historian Eusebius, did not see a discrepancy between the *Christus Victor* theme of the atonement and an imperial embrace of the Christian faith. Weaver's claim that the *Christus Victor* theme depended on a situation of confrontation between church and state is simply not borne out by the facts. Constantine drew on the *Christus Victor* tradition to underwrite his imperial power. The *Christus Victor* theme does not lend itself to easy domestication in the service of a stance of nonviolent opposition to the existing structures of society.[114]

Weaver cannot naively justify his own narrative *Christus Victor* model of nonviolence by disregarding Anselm's theory of satisfaction as violence. In order to criticize Weaver's radical theological bias, Telford Work rightly observes that throughout church history of doctrine, the apostolic and holy catholic tradition have confirmed Christ's substitutionary death by God's will.[115] To illustrate, Thomas Aquinas is never

---

111. Weaver, *The Nonviolent Atonement*, 8.
112. Weaver, *The Nonviolent Atonement*, 9.
113. Rutledge, *The Crucifixion*, 498.
114. Boersma, *Violence, Hospitality, and the Cross*, 158.
115. Work, "Review of *The Nonviolent Atonement*," 510–513. Work asserts that "Weaver blames the continuing theological power of retributive justice on

hesitant to declare the biblical actuality of the atonement event by God's sovereignty, emphasizing that there should be the "necessity of the end proposed" in which God accomplishes all the prophecies of the Scripture on sinners' salvation through the passion and death of Christ himself.[116] For Aquinas, we cannot realize the reconciling work of God in Christ without the revelation of God, because the Bible itself declares and interprets the whole of what God intends to accomplish in the atoning death of Christ. The church's history of doctrine clearly proves that God revealed in Christ decides the crucifixion of the incarnate Son of God and fulfills the salvation of sinners for all of us. The biblical and theological theme of God's necessity of Christ's substitutionary death has nothing to do with divine violence. Rather, as Weaver acknowledges, violence and evil that crucify Christ are those of fallen humankind and the hostile powers that must be judged by God's righteousness and power in Christ's self-sacrificial death for sinners on the cross.

Therefore, in contrast to Weaver's unjustified theological assumption, a specific model of atonement such as *Christus Victor* has never been sanctioned as the sole and absolute standard that judges the other theories as ethical or not. If Weaver believes his narrative *Christus Victor* model of nonviolent atonement to be the timeless and objective truth that can and must censure the Anselmian satisfaction theory as violence, it would not be unfair to argue that his nonviolent perspective would be nothing but the theological violence to indiscriminately eradicate all the other biblical, classical, and catholic reflections on atonement.

Yet it is striking that Weaver goes on to argue that God the Father nonviolently sacrificed his Son for the sake of God's kingdom. According to Weaver, Christ's "mission" to the point of death is to "make present and live for the reign of God."[117] What is at stake here is whether Weaver's nonviolent atonement can avoid the issue of Jesus' victimization in a sacrificial death or not. It seems plausible that the obliteration of God's divine intentionality makes it possible to rescue the miserable Son as the innocent victim from the cruel Father as the revenging punisher. However, Weaver cannot help but encounter the theological issue

---

Constantinianism and punitive Western and American structures of justice, but contrary biblical evidence is a more significant explanation for it, and for the appeal of something like satisfaction theory from as early as Athanasius (not just Anselm!) through today." Work, "Review of *The Nonviolent Atonement*," 512.

116. Aquinas, *Summa Theologica* III.46.1.
117. Weaver, *The Nonviolent Atonement*, 94.

of victimization in Jesus' death. Instead of the direct question of *who* the agent of Jesus' death is in the classic Anselmian satisfaction theory, the indirect question of *what* eventually causes his death emerges in the new nonviolent atonement model. For the Anselmian satisfaction theory, including the doctrine of penal substitution, God is the essential agent of Jesus' death for the sake of sinners, whereas according to Weaver, the "confrontation of ultimates" between God and the power of evil brings about the "inevitable" death of Jesus.[118] While Anselm's God autonomously willed that Jesus die for the sake of God's retributive justice, Weaver's nonviolent God unavoidably intended Jesus' death for the purpose of realizing God's reign. In order to confirm that the nonviolent God has no divine intentionality in the death of Christ, Weaver deploys the human logic of inevitability. This is his own exegetical way to erase God's intended violence and to explain the relationship between Jesus and God in the crucifixion. Weaver says,

> "No, God did not will the death of Jesus." There is a sense, however, in which narrative *Christus Victor* can respond, "Yes, God did will the death of Jesus." Jesus' mission was to witness to the reign of God. It was God's will that Jesus carry out that mission faithfully, even when it meant death. In fact . . . his mission made his death *inevitable*. The reign of God in Jesus made an ultimate claim, which was confronted by the ultimate claim of the powers of evil. This confrontation of ultimates *inevitably* resulted in death, but the death was a function of Jesus' mission and not the purpose or the goal of the mission. Jesus could have escaped death at the hands of Rome, but that escape would have meant failing his mission. God willed that Jesus face this death rather than abandon his mission. A similar question of intentionality concerns Jesus' attitude to death. If Jesus' mission was to give living witness to the reign of God breaking into the world, then his mission was not to die . . . However, the ultimate character of his mission produced an ultimate response, namely, killing him. In fact, the ultimate character of the confrontation made death *inevitable*. It appears that Jesus faced this *inevitability*.[119]

According to Weaver, the crucifixion is an event of Jesus' human inevitability, in which God nonetheless willed that his Son die, whereas resurrection is God's sovereign plan of forgiveness to the evil world. This

---

118. Weaver, *The Nonviolent Atonement*, 92.
119. Weaver, *The Nonviolent Atonement*, 91–92. Italics mine.

view is manifestly non-biblical because Weaver contrasts Jesus' human death in the crucifixion with God's divine plan in the resurrection of the crucified Jesus. For Weaver, God's sovereignty only starts to emerge in the resurrection. Did God the Father and Son disappear or die in the crucifixion? Where were they in the event? In fact, Weaver's nonviolent God is too incompetent to save his Son from the execution on the cross. More problematic is Weaver's anthropological perspective on the relationship between the Father and the death of the Son. The Almighty God the Father and the Son are nothing but a miserable human "daddy and son" in a story of missionary martyrdom. Weaver fails to reckon with the fact that to abandon God's divine intentionality in Christ's death is to delete God himself from the history of biblical salvation. It is obvious that Weaver justifies the anthropocentric view of the nonviolent atonement theory at the expense of a Triune God-centered biblical soteriology.

> An analogy from human experience can perhaps add clarity to how death can be willed without seeing it as the goal or purpose of a life-bringing mission. Most of us know stories of people who risked death for the sake of a cause to which they were committed—Christian martyrs who died rather than recant, parents risking death to rescue a child, environmental activists trying to save trees, peace activists working to prevent or halt a war, and more. Examples abound. In some cases, people died from these efforts rather than abandon their mission or pursuit. In such instances, the death occurred not because they chose it or undertook a suicide mission, nor was dying their purpose or goal in acting, nor did the organizers of the activity send them out for the purpose of being killed. Rather death came as a result of pursuing another agenda; and without making death the goal, it was willed in the pursuit of the life-bringing mission.[120]

Does Weaver actually want to say that if God had predicted the death, he would not have sent the Son into the world? Otherwise, is the crucifixion an unexpected horrible event beyond God's sovereign knowledge and power? Who is God at the moment of the death of his Son? Jettisoning God's sovereignty and satisfaction theory, Weaver is left with a very vague, indeterminate picture of God. It is theologically unconvincing that Weaver indiscriminately identifies God's will and act with a human intention and deed. The judgment of God against evil cannot be reduced

---

120. Weaver, *The Nonviolent Atonement*, 92–93.

to cosmic child abuse, in that God the Father's only and eternal judging act has no correlation to the repetitive sins of violent human beings.

In order to get to the heart of the matter, let me illustrate the historical human agents in the death of Jesus. While the Jewish high priests had to execute Jesus in order to maintain their religious hierarchy, the Roman governor Pontius Pilate inevitably handed over the innocent Jesus for the sake of the Roman Empire's political stability in Jerusalem.[121] A key question for Weaver is whether Pilate's inevitable act is guilty or not. Obviously, he is a sinner, just as we confess that Jesus "suffered under Pontius Pilate" in the Apostles' Creed. There might be sufficient excuse for his serious iniquity. Pilate not only strove to protect the socio-political status quo of Israel as a colony of the Roman Empire, but also attempted to rescue Jesus from the violent crowd. Nevertheless, the judge who should have been righteous inevitably surrendered himself to the unrighteous judgment of Christ's crucifixion, because he was desperate to avoid an uncontrollable riot at Jerusalem and political accusations against himself, all of which would unavoidably follow from the acquittal of Jesus. As Barth rightfully claims, the evil deed of Pilate, though it seems inevitable, is nothing but a "contradiction" to his official position, in which he must enforce Roman law with fairness and impartiality.[122] Yet, due to his own human dignity and survival instinct, he abandoned both a human-legal justice based on Jesus' innocence and God's righteousness in Christ's person and work. Therefore, inevitability cannot justify the crime of killing, no matter what the consequence is.

Why does Weaver overlook the dark side of Jesus' inevitable death, which was willed by a God who decided to perpetuate his reign in the world? Although Weaver criticizes the intrinsic violence of God's intentionality as child abuse in the Anselmian satisfaction theory, Weaver forces God to be involved with child abandonment because of human inevitability in the nonviolent atonement model. More seriously, the concept of God's human powerlessness during the death of his Son raises the theological question of who this God is. For the sake of the everlasting dominion of his kingdom, Weaver's nonviolent God allows his Son to be viciously murdered on the cross. In this case, God is no longer omnipotent and merciful, but becomes a powerless and selfish human god.

---

121. For a theological discussion on Pontius Pilate, see Barth, Chapter 16, "Suffered under Pontius Pilate," in *Dogmatics in Outline*, 108–13; and Stott, *The Cross of Christ*, 48–52.

122. Barth, *Dogmatics in Outline*, 111.

Although it appears that Weaver justly removes the image of God as a vengeful king who executed his innocent son on the cross, he unjustly proposes that God is fundamentally analogous to Pilate, who avoided any violent intervention in the crucifixion. Pilate was at pains to justify his innocence by attributing the killing of Jesus to both the Jewish religious ruling class and the violent crowd at Jerusalem. In the same manner, the nonviolent God himself demonstrates that there is no divine violence in the crucifixion, because the death of Jesus is solely due to the evil powers and self-deceived sinners in the world. It is more problematic that, just as Pilate succeeded in preserving the Roman Empire's dominion over Judea by allowing the inevitable crucifixion of Jesus, God also achieves the realization of his kingdom through the inevitability of his own son being killed by evil powers. There is no doubt that this is the nonviolent justification of Christ's violent death by Pontius Pilate and by God in Weaver's atonement theory. Although Weaver may also believe that Pilate is a hypocrite, according to the biblical testimony and the Apostles' Creed, I suspect that Weaver is yet unaware of his projection of Pontius Pilate's human inevitability onto the nonviolent God. Weaver badly distorts God's divine sovereignty in the crucifixion of Christ, turning it into human inevitability through his own projection of human nonviolence onto God's being and work. Regarding God's sovereignty, if Weaver at least wants to be in line with the omniscient God, he needs to say that God already foresaw Jesus' death under his plan. This inevitably means that Weaver has to acknowledge the hermeneutical logic of divine intentionality in Anselmian satisfaction theory. Weaver cannot but realize that the nonviolent God in heaven permits the crucifixion of Christ by evil powers so that he will not have Jesus' innocent blood on his hands. The nonviolent God not only watches over the evil powers' killing of his own Son, but also justifies the crime of abetting the murder. The cruel facts prove that the nonviolent God has nonviolent intentionality regarding the atoning death of Jesus. In this light, Weaver's theological argument for God's human inevitability not only causes a collapse of the inner logic of God's non-intervention, but also exacerbates the problems of violence and evil rather than solving them. The nonviolent God has no saving power, justice, and love during the death of Christ—just like Pilate.

1.5 Systematic Theological Review

Here I will constructively recapitulate who the nonviolent God is from what we have critically observed in the nonviolent atonement theories of Brock, Schwager, and Weaver. The theological common denominators are as follows.

1. There is a hermeneutical causality in which positive life and restorative nonviolence can and must originate from the life-giving God and his restorative work of salvation.[123]

2. The negative and destructive phenomenon of God's retributive judgment in Christ's death, especially in the penal substitutionary model, cannot result in the positive and constructive work of life-giving salvation.

3. In nonviolent soteriology, the nonviolent God reveals the problem of violence and evil in the crucifixion of Jesus, who is a representative innocent victim. Jesus' death has nothing to do with the direct intention of God, even if the tragic event occurs in the world that God creates. Rather, the victimization by evil *inevitably* happens beyond the scope of God's reign of peace and nonviolence. God's nonviolent intervention solely heals innocent victims and restores the suffering world from violence and evil. Thus God nonviolently saves the human world from violence and evil, by conforming himself to the human-ethical standard of nonviolence.

4. A strong dualism is posited between the negativity of violence and the positivity of God's being and work.[124] By removing all the

123. Love, *Love, Violence, and the Cross*, 70. Love rightly observes that "in the generative [nonviolent] model of salvation, redemption is *biophilic*; life flows out of life. The metaphor is organic rather than militaristic. We come to life as we are held in being by a nurturing, creative center, a living and life-giving 'other.' The organic paradigm of life-generating-life is reflected in the model's saving images: God is like a strong woman beside a sheltering tree protecting all life. God is like a mother who births, breastfeeds, befriends, teaches to walk, guides. God's power is like the saving power of love between lovers, or friends."

124. Aulén, *Christus Victor*, 149. To illustrate a precursor of modern nonviolent atonement theory, according to Aulén: "Salvation is therefore regarded *positively*, not *negatively*. It is always *positive*, wherever the classic idea is dominant, whether the actual terms used be the forgiveness of sins, union with God, the deifying of human nature, or some other. On the other hand, with the Latin doctrine the natural tendency is for forgiveness to be regarded *negatively*; for it is the fruit of the satisfaction made by Christ that the punishment deserved by man is remitted . . . The fundamental mistake

negative and destructive themes of God's vindicatory judgment and Christ's satisfaction of divine justice, we can restore the positive and constructive dimension of God's continuous work of salvation toward victimized humans.

5. This approach affirms the divine attributes of nonviolence and healing love aimed at unconditional forgiveness and restoration. Thus, the nonviolent atonement theologian assumes that God is not a pair of scales balancing his violent justice and arbitrary omnipotence and begrudging mercy, which require satisfaction by Jesus' sacrificial death.

6. From a human-relational perspective, how to properly conceive of the nonviolent God is the main point on which nonviolent soteriology stands or falls, because the God of nonviolence already saves us in a nonviolent way, beyond our human misunderstanding of divine violence.

7. There is a paradox in God's nonviolent salvation, because the vulnerable and suffering God who inevitably abandons his Son ultimately overcomes evil powers in a divine-restorative way, not a human-retributive one.

The most meaningful contribution of nonviolent atonement models is in the area of the epistemological dimension of the crucifixion of Christ. The ethical perspective proves that the loving God is never meant to be a violent deity that must be arbitrarily placated by the human sacrifice of an innocent victim, as ancient myths tells about the violent satisfaction of gods. In a consequent sense, the nonviolent atonement theories fairly defend God's self-sacrificial love and his nonviolence for humanity. Atonement has nothing to do with any external exchange between God and sinful humans. Therefore, substitutionary atonement theologies agree with the nonviolent perspective on atonement, in that an arbitrary God's satisfaction by Jesus' atoning death is nothing but a theological myth. Reformed and evangelical theology never justifies a doctrine of a violent God who arbitrarily executed his Son.[125] Concerning the historical death

---

is that the critic has a conception of forgiveness as *negative*." Italics mine.

125. Williams, "Penal Substitution: A Response to Recent Criticism," 77–78. Penal substitutionary atonement is not based on the divine violence by God the Father against his Son, but on the eternal harmony within the Triune God that Augustine, John Own, and Calvin confirm. Thus, the evangelical doctrine has nothing to do with "the ludicrous railroad illustration where the father switches the points to rescue his

of Jesus, it seems fair for the nonviolent atonement theologians to make a distinction between the nonviolent God and violent evil, because the historical agents of the crucifixion are sinners and evil powers, not God himself. The nonviolent God never justifies the crucifixion of Christ.

As I mentioned above, while the ontological dimension of atonement is God's being and act at the crucifixion, the epistemological one consists in the human perception of Christ's saving death. Regarding the noetic and ontic understandings of the nonviolent atonement theories, three dimensions are lacking in the nonviolent perspective. First is a positive epistemology in which God's saving power and righteousness, hidden to human reason and experience, are revealed to us by faith in the crucifixion of Christ. Second is a negative ontology in which God must annihilate sin and evil in order to rescue the suffering world from hostile powers. And third is the vertical aspect of positive ontology, in which God reconciles with violent perpetrators who conspire at the crucifixion of Jesus, the representative of victimized humankind. The bottom line is that the negative epistemology that fallen humankind violently collaborates with is radically moved to a positive ontology involving the nonviolent God's restoration in an unexpected way. However, Brock, Schwager, and Weaver paradoxically argue for a positive ontology that is immediately followed by a negative epistemology, because, despite God's absence from the violent phenomenon of Christ's death, the nonviolent God never abandons Jesus or humankind to the extent that God finally accomplishes the nonviolent salvation of victims and even the restoration of the violent world. At this point, what I criticize is the dualistic approach to the nonviolent God's nonviolent salvation. Nonviolent atonement theologians struggle to affirm the saving truth that God can and must engage the negative phenomenon of Jesus' violent death, as a

---

passengers and in so doing kills his wandering son. The son has no idea of what is going on, and presumably should not have been standing around on a railway track in the first place . . . this illustration is a total travesty of penal substitution." Likewise, John Stott deals with the anthropocentric misunderstanding of the relationship between God and the crucified Christ: "We must not then speak of God punishing Jesus or of Jesus persuading God, for to do is to set them over against each other as if they acted independently of each other or were even in conflict with each other. We must never make Christ the object of God's punishment or God the object of Christ's persuasion, for both God and Christ were subjects not objects, taking the initiative together to save sinners . . . The Father did not lay on the Son an ordeal he was reluctant to bear, nor did the Son extract from the Father a salvation he was reluctant to bestow. There is no suspicion anywhere in the New Testament of discord between the Father and the Son." Stott, *The Cross of Christ*, 151.

necessary step in his restorative salvation. Due to the radical separation they posit between the nonviolent God's positivity and evil's negativity, there remains a reign of evil where God cannot but allow the death of Jesus. The tragic fact inevitably makes God himself the passive and vulnerable victim facing the urgent issue of violence and evil in the crucifixion of Jesus. Therefore, according to nonviolent atonement theories, the negative epistemology of the innocent Jesus' crucifixion tragically results in what Weaver illustrates above: like the human father of a martyr, even God himself inevitably becomes victimized by the overwhelming power of evil. Since nonviolent atonement theories consider God's judgment against sin to be divine violence, the evil powers are absolved from God's righteous verdict. Socio-political evils justify themselves, because, at the moment of Jesus' death, there is no God who condemns and annihilates them. If God remains as the passive victim of the overwhelming power of evil, who can reveal the evil itself and complete the salvation of victimized humans? The theological discussion about the nonviolent God inevitably falls into its own theological self-contradiction. How can the image of the suffering Father, who cannot save his crucified Son, abruptly change into the powerful God for a nonviolent restoration of the violent world?[126] The nonviolent atonement scholars fail to answer this theological question.

1.6 Constructively Critical Suggestion

There is a hermeneutical common denominator between nonviolent atonement theories and substitutionary ones, namely, God's annihilation of evil.[127] It is indeed impossible to deny that God can and must ultimately execute judgment against sin and evil, beyond an ethical declaration of restoration, in order to essentially restore the suffering world. At this point, we need to remember Weaver's theological tolerance of the active nonviolence of "resistance."[128] By borrowing the hermeneutical definition, both nonviolent and substitutionary atonement theologians may concur that God's own nonviolence in the violent world is his radically active resistance against personal and structural sins that inevitably bring about the victimization of his loving Son, Jesus. God's nonviolence

---

126. Provocatively speaking, the nonviolent God is too vulnerable to save himself. Does God need his own way of self-salvation by nonviolence itself?

127. It may be also the transformation of evil into good.

128. Weaver, *The Nonviolent Atonement*, 9.

can and must deal with the negative guilts and destroying powers in a more absolutely active and positive way than any human can do. The implementation of God's absolutely active resistance against sin and evil ultimately results in his annihilation of them. To illustrate, Brock's feminist healing motif hermeneutically assumes the total destruction of the patriarchal evils experienced by abused women. Schwager's arguments about God's nonviolent forgiveness and restoration are grounded upon a termination of the violent scapegoat mechanism in our world. More significantly, Weaver's belief in God's nonviolent reign confirms that the violent reign of evil is already defeated by God's apocalyptic victory through the resurrection of *Christus victor*. Even if all three nonviolent atonement models declare God to be purely nonviolent, God's sovereign intervention to eradicate sin, guilt, and evil through the atoning death of Christ—what Brock, Schwager, and Weaver disparage as divine violence—is a prerequisite for God's nonviolent salvation. It must be noted that at the heart of nonviolent atonement theories lies God's violent intervention against evil in the actual sense. God is nonviolent, but nonviolence itself is not God himself.[129] We should be alert to how we "project" anthropocentric perspectives "unto the divine being."[130] In order to prevent the misunderstandings of the nonviolent atonement theologians, we should qualify God's own nonviolence as being distinct from any human ideologies. We must be cautious about any understanding of God's being that can be exclusively interpreted by the human-ethical term of "nonviolence." Otherwise, a nonviolent theological interpretation ironically may cause hermeneutical "violence" to "the plain meaning" of the biblical revelation, because the anthropocentric view ignores and distorts the original author's description of God's atoning work in Christ.[131]

---

129. Mangina, *Karl Barth: Theologian of Christian Witness*, 65. My argument is indebted to Mangina's insight that "God is love, but love is not God."

130. Mangina, *Karl Barth: Theologian of Christian Witness*, 65.

131. Packer, *In My Place Condemned He Stood*, 108. Mark Dever observes that according to Stephen Finlan, a doctrine of atonement cannot be a principal idea of Christianity, because its content consists of "only 39 percent of the New Teststament." However, we should not dismiss the enormous volume of scriptural testimonies on atonement. The reason why Finlan strives to remove atonement from biblical soteriology is that he is misled about the continuity between the incarnation, atonement, and deification (*theosis*) of saved sinners, which the Greek Father Athanasius emphasizes. Finlan, *Problems with Atonement*, 120–22. For Athanasius's patristic view of atonement, see Meyer, "Athanasius's Use of Paul in His Doctrine of Salvation," 146–71.

In conclusion, however, I pursue a constructively critical conversation with nonviolent atonement theories. If the nonviolent God is to maintain his own consistency, in which he unconditionally loves sinners and simultaneously resists sin and evil in this violent world, God's own nonviolence must rectify every injustice from eternity to eternity. The divinely active involvement not only removes all the negatives, but restores the fallen world into his own positives.

2

The Nonviolent Jesus

A Functional Christology for the Sake of God's Kingdom

> For it is precisely this "disordered" world that in Christ is reconciled with God and that now possesses its final and true reality not in the devil but in Christ. The world is not divided between Christ and the devil, but, whether it recognizes it or not, it is solely and entirely in Christ, and in this way the false reality will be destroyed which it believes that it possesses in itself as in the devil.[1]

IN THE FOLLOWING DISCUSSION, I will demonstrate that according to Brock, Schwager, and Weaver, the nonviolent Jesus plays a functional role in establishing God's kingdom of nonviolence in a violent world. Rather than describing the ontological implications of the incarnated Son of God, the functional Christology concentrates on illuminating how the human Jesus nonviolently fulfills God's mission to realize his nonviolent reign. Jesus' human victimization on the cross, his revolutionary-prophetic ministry, and his innocent death manifestly reveal structural evils in the violent world. Thus, the resurrection of the crucified Christ is continuously related to God's nonviolent forgiveness and restoration of victimized humankind in a positive and constructive way. Nevertheless,

---

1. Bonhoeffer, *Ethics*, 176.

I will more critically suggest that the nonviolent Jesus has nothing to do with mediating between God and sinners, but can only be identified as a courageous martyr for God's reign in the representative sense. Rather than solving the current issues of violence and evil, the powerlessness of a human Jesus and his inevitable death exacerbate the problems. It is therefore regrettable that due to the absence of Christ's deity and the disregard of his sovereignty, all the functional Christologies—whether feminist, dramatic, or ethical—unavoidably fall into the epistemological projection of the idealistic image of the nonviolent prophet Jesus.

2.1 Brock's Erotic Power-Oriented Christology

The Functional Christology for Feminism

For Brock, the traditional belief in the Son of God, Christ's divine sovereignty, is nothing but a patriarchal ideology that disguises violence and evil. According to Brock, the "passive helplessness" of fallen humans who desperately rely on Christ's supernatural delivery from Satan is "the alter ego of the eco-centric, destructive, and masculine self."[2] The radical appropriation of the military metaphor of Christ's triumph over evil causes a distorted Christological implication, as if Christ's deity and power were exclusively constitutive of his saving work for us. More seriously, given that the Son of God himself saves the whole human race by his almighty power, he does not need to have any solidarity with the suffering victims in a violent world. Rather, as the theological image of the invincible hero, Jesus can be misused to strengthen the human ideologies of prosperity and glory by power. Hence, Brock's feminist critique plays a pivotal role in illuminating the human projection of a corrupt desire to possess absolute power.

> Jesus did not defeat Rome with the armies of God. Instead he died in the hands of Rome. The shock of defeat and loss of messianic hopes seem to have been profound for those who expected deliverance by an omnipotent God and a unilaterally powerful messiah. These disciples are still tempted to worship hierarchal power. They have not fully understood the way of erotic power or the vulnerability of heart.[3]

---

2. Brock, *Journeys by Heart*, 91.
3. Brock, *Journeys by Heart*, 95.

By universalizing her own dichotomous thinking between "exploiter male and exploited female," and "controlling parent and abused child," Brock reaches the conclusion that a power-oriented androcentric society cannot avoid absolutizing a blind submission to power itself.[4] Thus Brock opens a new relational view for a feminist process Christology by asserting that a Christology of "erotic power" is not concentrated on Jesus as a salvific individual, but on "relationship and community as the whole-making, healing center of Christianity."[5] Thus the person and work of Christ are re-interpreted as his participation in "Christa/Community."[6] Even though Jesus never creates "erotic power" in the sovereign sense,[7] the "Christa/Community" is "a lived reality" of salvation that must be described "in relational images."[8] Brock goes on to argue that "the reality of erotic power within connectedness means it cannot be located in a single individual. Hence what is truly Christological, that is, truly revealing of divine incarnation and salvific power in human life, must reside in connectedness and not in single individuals."[9] Following process Christology, Brock states that "the historical Jesus starts a process."[10] She opens the theological possibility that everyone can become Christ, if they follow the divine way.

> Even when Christ is decentralized, Christ refers to individuals within specific communities, to many Christs. I believe that the individualizing of Christ misplaces the locus of incarnation and redemption. We must find the revelatory and saving events of Christianity in a larger reality than Jesus and his relationship to God/dess or any subsequent individual Christ.[11]

On the theological basis of the process Christological view, Brock re-constructs the feminist understanding of salvation beyond the traditional doctrine of Christ-centered reconciliation. Jesus as a savior also needs to be saved, because there is "a fluid interaction" between Christ and believers. The crux of redemption cannot be the person and work of

---

4. Brock, *Journeys by Heart*, 31–33.
5. Brock, *Journeys by Heart*, 52.
6. Brock, *Journeys by Heart*, 52.
7. Brock, *Journeys by Heart*, 52.
8. Brock, *Journeys by Heart*, 52.
9. Brock, *Journeys by Heart*, 52.
10. Brock, *Journeys by Heart*, 64.
11. Brock, *Journeys by Heart*, 68.

Christ himself. But it is the feminist Christian community itself. In this regard, the salvific "once-and-for-all" efficacy in Christ's atoning death should be denied, as the personal identity of Christ is an ongoing process in humankind.[12] The essence of the actual liberation of oppressed women lies in all the community members that create erotic power, not Jesus Christ.

> Christa/Community emerges from, reveals, and recreates erotic power as it moves to include the whole and compassionate being. Even in Jesus' lifetime, Christa/Community is not simply the figure of Jesus combined with an abstract ideal, but the members of his whole community who generate erotic power. Christa/Community involves his community's experience of him, but Christa/community is not limited to the historical Jesus, even in his lifetime.[13]

Thus Brock attempts to re-interpret the whole of Christ's saving ministry in light of feminism's project of deconstructing oppressive paternalism. To illustrate, Jesus' miracle of healing the afflicted woman is not based upon the unilateral transfer of the male Jesus' divine power in the patriarchal hierarchy (Mark 5:21–34). Rather, it is accomplished by the emancipating erotic power in the woman's heart, as "she takes away his patriarchal power as a man. She breaks through the barrier of male privilege and status that separated them."[14] Her courageous act makes public "*kenosis* of patriarchy."[15] In this regard, the healed woman's faith demonstrates "the broken-heartedness of patriarchy and co-creates Christa/Community."[16] For Brock, this healing narrative should be understood as a manifestation of "historical particularity as a *woman*," not as "essential humanness."[17] Brock insists that the narrative reveals the healing dynamics of erotic power in the inner hearts of women, because we do not need a masculine omnipotent savior like Christ. Brock radically goes on to argue that Christian salvation is not essentially accomplished by Christ himself, but by vulnerable women who are directly connected with erotic power.

---

12. Brock, *Journeys by Heart*, 64.
13. Brock, *Journeys by Heart*, 68.
14. Brock, *Journeys by Heart*, 84.
15. Brock, *Journeys by Heart*, 84.
16. Brock, *Journeys by Heart*, 84.
17. Brock, *Journeys by Heart*, 86.

> If feminism can be reconciled with Christianity, such reconciliation is not possible because Jesus, as the heroic figure, reveals a non-patriarchal vision of community in which women may participate. The reconciliation is possible because of the work of women and because feminist insights about erotic power intersect with the Christian confession that divine reality and redemptive power are love in its fullness.[18]

This is the feminist understanding of the functional role of Christ in bringing about human equality and justice. Brock finally develops her own feminist functional Christology with the ultimate goal of realizing God's kingdom, where suffering women can be liberated from patriarchal evil in the world.

> The Markan view of Jesus' death is not that he should suffer alone, but that all true disciples are called to risk a commitment, as a caring community to the promise of the basileia as a dominant-free community . . . The call to discipleship is a call to courage in the face of the shadow of the cross. With such courage, life in the midst of death surfaces through connection.[19]

Feminist Christologies have the common hermeneutical premise that Jesus is understood to be a functional way of accessing the universal truth of God's liberation, because Jesus is not Christ as the Son of God in the objective sense. To be Christ only means to be "the decisive re-presentation of the meaning of ultimate reality for us, of *God* for us," from "an existential-feminist perspective."[20] Thus it is regrettable that Brock's functional understanding of Christology confirms that Jesus is not the eternal Son of God, but a human prophet of feminist emancipation. Given that Jesus is "the healer," his "function" is to "facilitate the recreation" of erotic power through interpersonal "relationships" in his ministry for God's kingdom."[21] He is not the sole savior of sinners, but the divine connector between erotic power and people. It is through a healing-oriented feminist Christology that Christ's hypostatic union of deity and humanity in his own person is replaced by erotic power.

---

18. Brock, *Journeys by Heart*, 67.

19. Brock, *Journeys by Heart*, 96.

20. Stalcup, "What about Jesus? Christology and the Challenges of Women," 128–30.

21. Brock, *Journeys by Heart*, 82.

It is problematic that while Brock herself believes in "the *ontic* framework of erotic power as the most inclusive principle of human existence,"[22] she deconstructs the ontological dimension of the person and work of Christ, who is the functional manifestation of her radical feminist perspective on erotic power. Brock unjustly claims that the restorative events of Christ's healing can take place solely through the interpersonal connection between the human Jesus and suffering women. Thus her own rhetorical terminology regarding erotic power merely functions at the human level of pastoral comfort or existential feminism. Brock overaccentuates the interactive healing motif by emphasizing the erotic power inherent in victimized humans to the extent that it threatens the transcendental relationship between Christ and saved sinners. Moreover, the narratives of Jesus' supernatural salvation dramatically disclose Jesus' hidden deity and his sovereign work of salvation for victimized sinners.[23] Christ's sovereign declaration to the healed woman is the soteriological crux of the miracle story. More seriously, there should have been a hermeneutical distinction between Christ as the objective content of connection and believers as the subjective connectors. Unfortunately, Brock's Christology can neither guarantee the soteriological efficacy of the healing event, nor make possible the realization of a nonviolent Goddess's kingdom in the objective sense.

The Human Victimization of the Prophet Jesus by Patriarchal Evil

It is important to recognize that Brock re-appropriates the prophetic ministry of Christ into her feminist Christology, though she completely rejects Christ's kingship and priesthood.[24] Brock considers Christ's self-sacrificial obedience to God's sovereign will to be non-ethical, because the submission justifies the patriarchal ideology of justifying the abuse of women in a framework of female submission to male dominance. Rather, for Brock, Jesus is the revolutionary prophet "who confronted injustices and risked opposition."[25] Brock objects that in order to justify God's divine violence against an innocent human, it is absolutely necessary for the supporter of substitutionary atonement to argue for Christ's "absolute

22. Brock, *Journeys by Heart*, 26. Emphasis mine.
23. Voelz, *Mark 1:1–8:26*, 373.
24. Brock, *Proverbs of Ashes*, 31.
25. Brock, *Proverbs of Ashes*, 31.

The Nonviolent Jesus

obedience" to the Father.[26] Thus the spirit of protest in Jesus' prophetic and liberating work is overwhelmed by the virtue of submission in his voluntary sacrifice to the Father's justice.[27] Although feminist theologians unjustly deny the classical Christology of the incarnation and the hypostatic union of Christ's deity and humanity, they fairly point out serious problems in the traditional theological perspective. They associate Jesus' crucifixion with a Christian perseverance through sufferings that are mostly attributed to violence and the evil in the present world.[28] As Elisabeth Schussler Fiorenza provocatively insists, the feminist understanding of salvation has nothing to do with the eternal priest's self-giving sacrifice of atonement to appease the wrath of God. Rather, the crucifixion symbolizes the inevitable consequence of his revolutionary prophetic ministry against the evil world.

> Jesus' execution . . . results from his mission and commitment as a prophet and emissary of the Sophia-God who holds open a future for the poor and outcast and offers God's gracious goodness to *all* children of Israel without exception. The Sophia-God of Jesus does not need atonement or sacrifices. Jesus' death is not willed by God but is the result of his all-inclusive praxis as Sophia's prophet.[29]

Likewise, according to Brock, there is no divine necessity for Jesus' being crucified for the salvation of sinners.[30] Christ's death only means that the destructive power of patriarchy is so overwhelming as to crucify him.[31] The human Jesus who nonviolently lives for oppressed women's emancipation inevitably becomes a victim of violent paternalism. Brock states, "his [Jesus'] death is evidence of the power of patriarchy to crush life. In dying he reveals the power of the brokenhearted. He cannot save himself alone. His status as victim of broken-heartedness is a shadow throughout the entire gospel story."[32] Brock underlines the violent manifestation of patriarchal evils at Jesus' death. The crucifixion illustrates the representative case of "broken-heartedness." It is the extremely negative

---

26. Brock, *Proverbs of Ashes*, 31.
27. Brock, *Proverbs of Ashes*, 31.
28. Duff, "Atonement and the Christian Life," 21–33.
29. Fiorenza, *In Memory of Her*, 135.
30. Brock, *Journeys by Heart*, 93.
31. Brock, *Journeys by Heart*, 95.
32. Brock, *Journeys by Heart*, 95.

phenomenon of human victimization by a structural hierarchy that oppresses Jesus' liberation movement.

> The death of Jesus reveals the broken-heartedness of patriarchy. His dying is a testimony to the powers of oppression. It is neither salvific nor essential. It is tragic. The suffering of Jesus reveals the reality of broken-heartedness found in the possessed, oppressed, sick, and wounded in the exorcisms and healings.[33]

Following Mary Daly, Brock even claims that if we venerate Christ's death as his self-giving sacrifice, it would be "necrophilic."[34] However, it is noteworthy that for Brock, Jesus' victimization never ends up as a human tragedy. Even though Brock rejects the objective necessity of Jesus' vicarious death for sinners, Brock indirectly shows the communal implication of the event.

> Jesus in his death calls attention to broken-heartedness. Just as the suffering of those who went before him and those who come after him has done, his suffering compels us not to despair but to remember him and all others who suffer and to seek erotic power by our own action.[35]

How can the victimization of Jesus be salvation for suffering victims in a violent world? Brock never hesitates in answering this theological question. The solution is the erotic power in Jesus and his community. While Fiorenza, who recognizes a hermeneutical "tension" between Jesus' life and death and suggests the "rejection" of the Markan Christology, Brock strives to grasp Jesus' crucifixion in the context of restoration and liberation by erotic power.[36] Brock notes that Jesus' death is already prophesied by a woman's anointing, which symbolizes "the erotic power in their community, a community that would survive his death."[37] As Jesus' death fully reveals "the broken-heartedness of patriarchy," the "tragic" event enables the community of believers to recollect their connection with each other by erotic power.[38] This is "forgiving and empowering *anamnesis*."[39] For Brock, it is through the communal perspective of

---

33. Brock, *Journeys by Heart*, 98.
34. Brock, *Journeys by Heart*, 90.
35. Brock, *Journeys by Heart*, 98.
36. Brock, *Journeys by Heart*, 90.
37. Brock, *Journeys by Heart*, 97.
38. Brock, *Journeys by Heart*, 99.
39. Brock, *Journeys by Heart*, 99.

The Nonviolent Jesus

erotic power that Jesus' liberating miracles of "healing and exorcism" are continuously confirmed, even by the destructive event of Christ's suffering to the point of death.[40]

Here I suggest that we reason inductively about the relationship between Christ's crucifixion and the restoration of his community, following scriptural testimony chronologically. Thus we will reach the conclusion that without Jesus' death, there cannot be such a crucial reversal from broken-heartedness to courage and restoration in the life of the disciples. Therefore, the biblical actuality of Jesus' heartbreaking death paradoxically inspires the broken-hearted disciples to have communal courage against the patriarchal evils that crucified Jesus. In this regard, Brock cannot help admitting the paradoxical necessity of Jesus' death, which has the soteriological effect of healing the broken-heartedness of the disciples and the early church community. At this point, I positively evaluate Brock's paradoxical view of Jesus' courage-giving death, because it can be a substantial common denominator between her own feminist nonviolent atonement theory and the substitutionary perspectives.

Nevertheless, Brock's phenomenological understanding of the victimization of women has to be harmonized with Christ's priestly and kingly ministry against evil. Christ's self-sacrificial death not only means solidarity with enslaved victims, but their salvation from their own sins. It is obvious that broken-heartedness is a subjective phenomenon of victimization and a concrete consequence of sin. Without an objective absolution of sin, there is no way to guarantee subjective healing in human consciousness. More essentially, any kind of domestic violence has nothing to do with the redemptive suffering of Christ for all of us, because there is a personal dissimilarity between abused women and the Savior of sinners.[41] Since Brock completely rejects any divine dimension in Christ's person and work, there only remains human violence and the evil of patriarchalism. Without his sovereignty in his eternal kingship and the priestly-sacrificial atonement, Christ would be nothing but a victimized human who cannot save both himself and humankind from the oppressive power of patriarchy.

More importantly, it is telling that the nonviolent atonement theorist Weaver criticizes Brock's feminist perspective as a modern version

---

40. Brock, *Journeys by Heart*, 90.
41. Duff, "Atonement and the Christian Life," 27.

of Abelard's moral influence theory.⁴² Weaver observes that "in Christa/Community Jesus is one but not the sole representative of erotic power, the basis of the new, non-hierarchal community of healing and hope. In contrast, with narrative *Christus Victor* it was stressed that the fullness of the reign of God was present in Jesus."⁴³ In Brock's feminist theology, there is a confusion between Christology and ecclesiology, as if Jesus' communities and their members could be substituted for his uniquely divine person as a Savior. Thus Weaver corrects Brock's distorted theological view by arguing for the priority of Jesus as the Lord over his church and as a witness of the truth. Jesus is "the full revelation of God," and the feminist community is "the lived manifestation of the rule of God."⁴⁴ For Brock, "salvation happens only when people perceive Jesus and join the interactive relationships of the community."⁴⁵ According to Weaver, in Brock's "Christa/Community" the crucifixion and resurrection of Christ had no fundamental effect on the creation and never brought the apocalyptic establishment of God's kingdom on the earth.⁴⁶ It is also problematic that Brock's "Christa/Community Jesus" is not the one and only savior for sinners. The essence of her feminist Christology is based on an "erotic power" that is not Jesus himself, but the community that he assembled.⁴⁷ Brock's healing-centered soteriology is based on the erotic power of the human heart, not the Triune God's being and act. Her feminist soteriology too optimistically emphasizes the human ability to transform its fallen state, as her theological view fails to recognize the reality of sin and evil in humankind.

The Visualizing and Spiritualizing the Resurrection of Christ

Throughout her theological project, Brock deconstructs the patriarchal ideology of oppression by employing a feminist version of the Trinity as God/dess, Christa/Community, as well as Spirit-Sophia. The key thing is Christa/Community's nonviolent and courageous response to the tragic death of Jesus. The holy courage that never ceases to protest against the

---

42. Weaver, *The Nonviolent Atonement*, 175.
43. Weaver, *The Nonviolent Atonement*, 176.
44. Weaver, *The Nonviolent Atonement*, 176.
45. Weaver, *The Nonviolent Atonement*, 175.
46. Weaver, *The Nonviolent Atonement*, 175.
47. Weaver, *The Nonviolent Atonement*, 176.

injustice of the evil world is the core of her feminist existential interpretation of Jesus' resurrection.

> When the threat of death is refused and the choice is made for justice, radical love, and liberation, the power of death is overthrown. Resurrection is radical courage. Resurrection means that death is overcome in those precise instances when human beings choose life, refusing the threat of death. Jesus climbed out of the grave in the Garden of Gethsemane when he refused to abandon his commitment to the truth even though his enemies threatened him with death. On Good Friday, the Resurrected One was crucified.[48]

Accordingly, Brock never gives any objective meaning to Christ's resurrection.[49] Brock denies the saving power of the risen Christ, because there is no divine dimension in the resurrection itself. She radically insists,

> The resurrection of an abandoned Jesus is a meaningless event; the resurrection comes through the witnesses who saw him die, marked his grave in sorrow, and returned to anoint him. These witnesses refused to let death defeat them. In taking heart they remembered his presence. The resurrection provided a way for Jesus to continue to live in them, and for them to live with and for each other.[50]

Jesus' resurrection plays only a functional role in verifying a spiritual-cognitive bond between Jesus and his followers. At stake is how a Christian actively responds to the event, not the Lordship of the resurrected Christ. Correspondingly, Christ's resurrection never means that he overcomes the power of sin and death by his sovereign work of reconciliation. The event is nothing but a "visionary experience" in which believers are encouraged to remember Jesus and to confirm his erotic power among them.[51] Brock boldly sets forth her own feminist solution, in order to overcome the destructive phenomenon of Jesus' victimization by patriarchal evil.

> The disciples of the Christa/Community at the cross provide the dangerous memory. They transform the defeat of death into a wholeness of vision in the midst of pain and sorrow. Even in the

---

48. Brown and Parker, "For God So Loved the World?," 28.
49. Brock, *Journeys by Heart*, 100.
50. Brock, *Journeys by Heart*, 100.
51. Brock, *Journeys by Heart*, 100.

midst of broken-heartedness, they refuse to give up on erotic power. When Jesus could no longer be with them, they brought him back through memory and a visionary-ecstatic image of resurrection. Despite the brutalness of death under oppression, the community of faithful disciples restores erotic power and the hope of wholeness for their community by not letting go of their relationships to each other and not letting Jesus' death be the end of their community.[52]

In further describing the "visionary-ecstatic" dimension of the resurrection, Brock emphasizes that the event must be understood as "evidence of the presence of the magic of play space" and "a powerful metaphor for connection."[53] Following Nelle Morton, Brock concretely illustrates her own spiritual experience of "the Goddess who brings to her an image of her dead mother."[54]

A similar visionary experience happened to me. When my mother died of a disfiguring and painful cancer in 1983, I found myself so depressed that I could barely function at work. I decided one evening to give in to the depression. I wrote a letter to my mother into which I poured my anger at her for all the wrong things I thought she had done and for all the hurts she had inflicted. As I raged and wept in the deepest parts of myself, I suddenly found myself writing about all the wonderful things she had given me, and everything I would miss because she was gone. Spent from anger and grief, I lay quietly on the floor, eyes open. I felt more than heard a wind at the open doorway to the hall and saw my mother, whole and healed, float into the room toward me. Parallel to my body and several feet above it, she looked into my eyes and said, "It's all right." Her toes touched mine and she entered my body through my feet. I felt a euphoric, peaceful energy return to me.[55]

Regarding the subjective realization of the salvation, I basically agree with the perspective that Christian truth should be holistically experienced and confessed as a matter of the heart. In terms of "lived realty," feminist theologians have striven to overcome a hermeneutical "gulf" between objective doctrines of salvation and subjective experiences of it.[56]

52. Brock, *Journeys by Heart*, 100.
53. Brock, *Journeys by Heart*, 100.
54. Brock, *Journeys by Heart*, 100.
55. Brock, *Journeys by Heart*, 101.
56. Downie, "Discerning Redeeming Communities," 47.

Thus God's living truth that transforms life in Christ should not remain at the level of simply intellectual agreement or dry dogmatic propositions. Nevertheless, Brock cannot justify the absolutizing tendency of feminist subjective experience at the expense of the objective Christ-centered soteriology that the Bible testifies. In this light, Brock' emphasis on subjective experience is nothing but an extreme reaction to the objective doctrines in classical soteriology, which Brock criticizes as masculinizing Christianity. Brock's feminist perspective on resurrection exclusively focuses on humans' awareness of the event, without discussing its objective reality. Brock should have considered the hermeneutical integrity between divine objectivity and the human subjectivity of Christ's salvation.

More seriously, Brock's feminist experience of erotic power has nothing to do with the crucified and resurrected Christ himself. The radically spiritualizing and relativizing tendency of Brock's feminist soteriology culminates in her view of "the resurrected Christa/Community that reveals the presence of Spirit-Sophia."[57] The Spirit, Sophia, not only has life-transforming power in giving life to the dead Jesus, but also empowers everyone in the community to be continuously infused with the erotic power of recreation.[58] The ultimate purpose of Jesus' crucifixion and resurrection is to motivate the church community to "heal life through erotic power" in the manifestation of Spirit-Sophia.[59] The inevitable corollary of Brock's soteriology is that all the Christological implications become objectively unnecessary, because the spirit of erotic power accomplishes the subjective realization of the self-salvation of suffering humanity.[60] Weaver remarks that even though feminist communities "around Jesus" are "restored," according to Brock, "there is nothing about the death and resurrection of Jesus that changes the nature of reality in an objective way."[61] It is therefore regrettable that Brock's process theology indeed gets rid of the "reality" of God's visible kingdom here and now.[62] This fact proves that the personal spiritualization of feminist theology has no space for a cosmic-apocalyptic understanding of Christ's atonement. Weaver points out that due to Brock's "lack of an objective

57. Brock, *Journeys by Heart*, 103.
58. Brock, *Journeys by Heart*, 103.
59. Brock, *Journeys by Heart*, 103.
60. At this point, I am seriously unsure as to whether Brock's feminist theology can still be Christian.
61. Weaver, *The Nonviolent Atonement*, 175.
62. Weaver, *The Nonviolent Atonement*, 177.

accomplishment for resurrection apart from the transformed sinner's own response," her theological stance inevitably falls to the level of moral influence theory.[63]

Lastly, I wonder why Brock considers the notion of Christ's salvation of sinners through resurrection to be an autocratic act that goes against her feminist theological principles of communal relationship and process. Rather, the person and work of Christ are the grounding for the restoration and reconciliation of broken relationships among fallen humankind. "For he himself is our peace, who has made the two groups one and has destroyed the barrier, the dividing wall of hostility, by setting aside in his flesh the law with its commands and regulations" (Eph 2:14). Thus, it is dubious whether Brock assumes that the idealistic feminist community of impeccable women have the same status as Eve's unfallen humanity. Brock should have known that the actual destructiveness in human relationships makes us realize the divine necessity of God's forgiving love in Christ's resurrection.

2.2 Schwager's Dramatically Christological Discussion

The Nonviolent Prophet Jesus and the Kingdom of God

From the dramatic perspective of salvation, Schwager dynamically engages Jesus' public ministry and death with the overarching theme of God's kingdom, to which the Bible testifies as a whole.[64] Thus Schwager is definitely right to claim that "the kingdom of God was seamlessly connected with the person of Jesus" in the sense that Jesus' prophetic ministry was dramatically related to its immanent and historical realization in the world.[65] In this way, Schwager justly places the indivisible wholeness of Jesus' proclamation and God's kingdom in the context of soteriological Theo-drama. The crux of Jesus' gospel is God's gracious "turning toward sinners" and his urgent call for their repentance.[66] God's kingdom encompasses and penetrates Jesus' person and work, because a personal encounter with the Savior is not merely a cognitive event or

---

63. Weaver, *The Nonviolent Atonement*, 176.

64. Kryst, "Interpreting the Death of Jesus," 145. Drawing upon the inner coherence of Scripture, Schwager holds his own hermeneutical presupposition that Jesus himself declares "a new action of God in history."

65. Schwager, *Jesus in the Drama of Salvation*, 115.

66. Schwager, *Jesus in the Drama of Salvation*, 38.

The Nonviolent Jesus   69

ethical decision to turn to God. Rather, after sinners' conversion to God, holistic healing takes place in mind, soul, body, and all of life. Unlike the human prophets of the Old Testament, Jesus can dynamically communicate God's liberating and healing truth into "the innermost heart" of self-deceived sinners, who are unconscious of their enslavement by mimetic violence.[67] Since Jesus' miracles of healing and exorcism function as a "communicative process" for those who are being called into God's kingdom, he is able to bring about "the new gathering of Israel."[68] Therefore, Jesus' person and ministry dramatically confirm that he is the messianic prophet who can lead people into the kingdom of God's truth and peace. If people repent of their inner desires and truly obey Jesus' ethical teachings, they can overcome the external evils of mimetic violence and retributive judgment.[69] In doing so, "the kingdom of God [can] really commence on earth."[70]

With his emphasis on the prophetic office of Jesus, Schwager goes on to explain the innovative nature of Jesus' gospel community. He proposes a qualifying condition for new citizens who are entering into God's kingdom by placing an essential emphasis on their faithful obedience to Jesus' Sermon on the Mount.[71] For Schwager, what is at stake is the inner conversion of the heart or disposition of saved sinners: how they actually follow and imitate Jesus himself, as they practice God's love and forgiveness in the concrete context of their everyday life. Regarding human motivation, Schwager doubtlessly accepts Girard's anthropological perspective in which "people are fundamentally creatures of desire, and their aspirations are not autonomous but are determined, as if by osmosis."[72] Thus to grasp the mimetic desire that influences others "in a quasi-osmotic or nonconscious way" is the crucial key to "make sense of judgments in the Sermon on the Mount."[73] Here Schwager' creativity lies in his own application of Girard's anthropological viewpoint to Jesus' radical re-interpretation on Moses' law in the Old Testament. The practical purpose of Jesus' message is to dispose of the evil mechanism in

---

67. Schwager, *Jesus in the Drama of Salvation*, 41.
68. Schwager, *Jesus in the Drama of Salvation*, 41.
69. Schwager, *Jesus in the Drama of Salvation*, 43.
70. Schwager, *Jesus in the Drama of Salvation*, 43.
71. Schwager, *Jesus in the Drama of Salvation*, 41.
72. Schwager, *Jesus in the Drama of Salvation*, 42.
73. Schwager, *Jesus in the Drama of Salvation*, 42.

mimetic desire.⁷⁴ Without resolving the violent conflict of desires, there is no way to establish God's kingdom in this world. In Schwager' thought, the innermost dimension of human desire is essentially connected with the most external manifestation of the community. The personal subjectivity of desire never remains at a purely spiritual and religious level, but irresistibly emerges in the public and objective dimensions of ethics and law. This evidence leads to the conclusion that how to transform the violent desire of each member is the main point on which the entire community stands or falls. Accordingly, the fundamental solution for controlling desire is that people engage in positive and constructive imitation, not the negative and destructive kind. Thus the new object of human desire must be Jesus himself, because he is the perfect embodiment of "a gracious human goodness which mirrors a preceding divine mercy."⁷⁵ The aim of Jesus' saving work is to reveal the universal problem of violent desire and to announce the urgent need to transform it.

As Schwager emphasizes, I also believe that there is a dramatically interactive relationship between God and humankind. However, in the salvation event, Schwager intends to overlook the asymmetrical relation of God's sovereignty and fallen humanity's free will. The radically anthropocentric view of salvation seems to inevitably fall to the level of Pelagianism, because the establishment of God's kingdom is fundamentally "conditioned by" people's response to the message of Jesus.⁷⁶ Next, Schwager rightly observes that Jesus' proclamation has divine authority starting with the unique expression "I," because he has his own "messianic consciousness" that is completely distinguished from all the human interpreters of God's word.⁷⁷ Yet, for Schwager, Jesus' self-understanding as the Messiah never moves beyond a cognitive dimension, in that there is no objective identification of the person of Christ as the Son of God. Even though Schwager directly refers to Jesus' claim to divine sovereignty, he immediately eliminates the theological probability of the violent actualization.⁷⁸ Yet Jesus says, "do you think I cannot call on my Father, and he will at once put at my disposal more than twelve legions of angels?" (Matt 26:53). Why does Schwager not simply accept the literal meaning

---

74. Schwager, *Jesus in the Drama of Salvation*, 42.
75. Schwager, *Jesus in the Drama of Salvation*, 42.
76. Schwager, *Jesus in the Drama of Salvation*, 43.
77. Schwager, *Jesus in the Drama of Salvation*, 115.
78. Schwager, *Jesus in the Drama of Salvation*, 206.

of Christ's violent power, as he does in the cases of Jesus' moral teaching about nonviolence?[79] This fact shows that Schwager's theological exegesis intends to silence any evidence contrary to his one-sidedness of nonviolence.[80] Unfortunately, the absence of Jesus' deity and sovereignty is attributable to Schwager's obsession with the nonviolent powerlessness of Jesus' humanity. Without a divine-transcendental dimension, there is only an ethical Jesus who perfectly fulfills his teaching of love toward his enemies. It is ironic that the human Jesus in Schwager's dramatically reoriented Christology is indeed equal to the liberal-historical Jesus, who is uncritically projected through the lens of historical-critical research that Schwager himself harshly criticizes.[81]

The Prophet Christ's Substitutionary Victimization by Evil

In contrast to Girard's purely anthropological view of Jesus' death, for Schwager the event has the decisive Christological dimension in which human sin and evil are universally transferred to the crucified Christ as the lamb of God in a divine-particular sense. Schwager theologically modifies the Girardian view of the scapegoat mechanism in order to avoid the deistic criticism that the mechanism functions arbitrarily, apart from Jesus himself. Regarding the human victimization of Jesus, Schwager puts a Christological implication on the event, beyond both the religious tradition of the Old Testament and Girard's purely anthropological interpretation. On the one hand, Jesus is not a "scapegoat" to which a priest imputes sins in a biblical sense, because the Jewish religious elites believe that they "condemn him for his own offences."[82] On the other hand, in contrast to Girard's scapegoat theory, Jesus' persecution and death are not merely a matter to be analyzed in an absolutely passive and

---

79. Brown, "The Dramatic Soteriology of Raymund Schwager," 312–13. Brown asserts that unlike Schwager's naive interpretation, no one can take Jesus' moral instruction of non-retaliation "literally." There are "seeming inconsistencies" between Jesus' ethical teaching and his actual act. While Christ frequently uses violent language—"fools" against the Pharisees and "evil" against his disciples (Matt 23:17)—he warns that anyone who uses an insulting word or curse will be "liable to fiery Gehenna." Thus, Jesus' "focus of the Sermon on the Mount" should be understood as the spiritual-inner matter of "heart, attitudes, thoughts, and dispositions right," not the physical-external practice. Thus no one can take "literally" Jesus' moral instruction of non-retaliation.

80. Brown, "The Dramatic Soteriology of Raymund Schwager," 312–13.

81. Schwager, *Jesus in the Drama of Salvation*, 30.

82. Schwager, *Jesus in the Drama of Salvation*, 91.

irresistible way. Rather, there is the determining cause of Jesus' voluntary and active intention of revealing the evil mechanism.

> Jesus differed from other victims in that the violence which struck him was not *accidental*. Through his message of the basileia he himself had awakened the forces which concentrated against him, and he lured them out of their hiding-place by his judgment speeches. He was not an *accidental* scapegoat, as is usually the case. By his claim expressed in the message of the basileia and by his relentless judgment sayings, he himself set in motion that process which was bound to turn against him.[83]

It is more important to see that, compared to Brock and Weaver, Schwager tries to harmonize a biblical-classical doctrine of Christ's substitution with his own Girardian atonement theory. According to Schwager, the New Testament confirms a doctrine of Christ's substitution for sinners in both an inclusive and exclusive way.

> Christ by his yes in the event of the cross identified himself with all the other people insofar as they are victims of sin. This inclusion of all has an immediate consequence for the exclusivity of his deed: *if he identified himself with all victims of sin, then every offense against a fellow person or against one's self is aimed against him* . . . Condemnation is always leveled against the one who was fundamentally against condemnation, and the persecution of fellow humans strikes that victim who has identified himself with all the victims of every persecution. The universality of the *expulsion* and thus the *exclusive nature of the substitution* are based on the *act of universal inclusion* of the one who stood in for all by making himself one of them.[84]

It is plausible that for Schwager, the "historical" crucifixion of Christ participates in all the victimization events of the entire human history of evil in the "universal" sense.[85] Schwager underlines that Christ's death has its own double "substitutionary" connotations of "exclusion" and "inclusion" because his own particular condemnation by evil embraces the whole of victimized humankind once and for all.[86] In this way, Schwager takes his own theological position by distancing himself from a purely theoretical application of Girard's anthropological ideas.

83. Schwager, *Jesus in the Drama of Salvation*, 92. Emphasis mine.
84. Schwager, *Jesus in the Drama of Salvation*, 192.
85. Schwager, *Jesus in the Drama of Salvation*, 192.
86. Schwager, *Jesus in the Drama of Salvation*, 192.

Likewise, the most insightful contribution of Schwager's Christology is to re-interpret the dynamic character of Jesus' human freedom and decision through an Anselmian lens. It is noteworthy that Schwager effectively relies on Anselm's scholastic concept of God as "something than which nothing greater can be thought" in order to set forth his own dramatic description of Christ's human will to accept the crucifixion for God's plan of nonviolent salvation.[87] In opposition to Maximus the Confessor's traditional view, in which "the choice of the human will" is "a decision between good and evil," Schwager follows Anselm's interpretation of human freedom's "choice between good and better."[88] Drawing upon the Anselmian understanding of human will, Schwager sets forth his own dramatically Christological interpretation of the atonement. Despite the overwhelming power of evil, the human Jesus voluntarily chooses to meet death on the cross by his own free will, because Jesus' human decision opens up the dramatic "possibility of salvation" for sinners to the extent that his sacrificial death prevents the self-destruction of sinful humanity.[89]

After dramatically describing Jesus' tragic destiny, Schwager moves into the cultic dimension of his victimization by evil. Here, the fundamental reason for Jesus' crucifixion lies in the inevitable conflict between Jesus and those who reject his saving truth. The tragic event is not just a historically contingent occurrence but the universal manifestation of hostility between the evil powers that violently dominate the world and God's reign of nonviolence and peace.[90] The victimization that Jesus underwent ultimately pertains to the dualistic perspective between God and evil because, according to Schwager, Jesus' crucifixion has nothing to do with God's divine violence. Thus Schwager re-interprets the substitutionary concept of the once-and-for-all salvific efficacy of Christ's atoning death, transforming it into his own victim-oriented soteriology. Schwager asserts that "the will of Jesus in his passion (Heb 10:10) has appeared to us under a double aspect: (1) as identification with his opponents, insofar as they themselves are victims; (2) as 'conversion' and transformation of evil in surrender."[91] According to Schwager, the human

---

87. Schwager, *Jesus in the Drama of Salvation*, 197.
88. Schwager, *Jesus in the Drama of Salvation*, 206.
89. Schwager, *Jesus in the Drama of Salvation*, 206.
90. Kryst, "Interpreting the Death of Jesus," 156.
91. Schwager, *Jesus in the Drama of Salvation*, 189.

Jesus "radically" directs the way of salvation for his enemies, as he alone suffers the power of sin and death.[92]

> Under the first aspect we can see Christ's love for enemies, insofar as he preferred, faced with his own will to survive, to share their destiny and to suffer in advance on their behalf those consequences of sin which necessarily result from it. This will to identification bore salvation to the extent that it was a presupposition for the second: the conversion and transformation of evil action in love. *He turned the radical delivering of himself to his enemies, as He experienced this in being executed, into a radical surrender to his father.* Christ never consented to the lies and killing which constitutes sin, but rather He dared to suffer the concrete sinful deeds (as being killed by sin) to the point where He was transformed precisely by them into a limitless surrender. Through his identification with his opponents He also infiltrated their world in which their evil will had imprisoned itself and by his transforming power opened it up once again from its new depths to the heavenly Father.[93]

Here we need to see that there is a dualistic perspective between Christ's "opening up" himself toward God and sinners' "closing" themselves in their sinful desire.

> What at first seemed to be something purely negative, as the rejection of love and closing in on oneself, was transformed by Christ into a surrender which bursts all dimensions of earthly existence. He is therefore both scapegoat and lamb of God; he is the one who is the one slain and the bread of life; he is the one made into sin and the source of holiness.[94]

The human nature of Christ must be so violently exploded by evil that God's saving power of nonviolent transformation can take place. The absolute passivity of Jesus' negative victimization paradoxically brings about God's positive salvation, insofar as it transforms evil's violent closure into its nonviolent opening toward himself. The human Jesus' intervention into God's kingdom of nonviolence is parallel to God's divine intervention in the violent world of sin from the substitutionary perspectives. Despite an overtly "negative" dimension in Schwager's theological interpretation of Jesus' crucifixion as victimization by the

---

92. Schwager, *Jesus in the Drama of Salvation*, 189.
93. Schwager, *Jesus in the Drama of Salvation*, 189.
94. Schwager, *Jesus in the Drama of Salvation*, 113.

The Nonviolent Jesus

scapegoat mechanism, Schwager constructively illuminates the positive dimension of how the nonviolent Jesus solely undergoes the evils of "mimetic violence" and "hostility."[95] The veiled truth of the seemingly destructive event is that the crucified Jesus so radically dedicates himself to "the infinite God" of goodness that he provides the breakthrough for those who are being destroyed by the over-competitive relationship of possessing "a finite good."[96] Thus the Girardian perspective affirms that Jesus' innocent victimization "deprives the scapegoat mechanism of its efficacy" by revealing the "hidden" evil of the human desire for violence.[97] From the standpoint of the victimized Jesus in the biblical drama of salvation, Schwager describes forgiving love much more dynamically than any other theologian. The last cry from Jesus' cross shows neither a human rage for violent vengeance, nor the desperate horror of imminent death. Rather, it is an intercessory prayer to God: "Father, forgive them, for they do not know what they are doing" (Luke 23:34). Jesus asks for God's unconditional forgiveness of the sins of communal ignorance and structural violence.

However, for Schwager, God's deity in Christ is overwhelmed by the dramatic role of Jesus as a human, and by his transformative responses to sinners' wills and acts—i.e., his identification with sinners and their conversion from evil. The drama of Jesus' salvation never depends on God's sovereign and eternal plan. Rather, the development of every dramatic stage derives from human actions that exclude any divine intervention or presupposed theological logic. Every decision is made by human actors responding to each other. In fact, there is a discontinuity between God's sovereignty and Christ's saving work in Schawager's anthropological and dualistic framework, as between the human Jesus and the power of sin in the world. All the elements of Schwager's understanding of Jesus' dramatic soteriology are elucidated by "the inner-worldly scapegoat experience and the withdrawal of Jesus' 'Abba' from the Mount of Olives to the crucifixion."[98] Jesus himself, who is persecuted by human sin, has the transforming power to save sinners. This means the nonviolent Jesus unconditionally forgives his adversaries' sin of crucifying him. By doing so, Jesus accomplishes God the Father's divine will to save victimized

---

95. Galvin, "Jesus as Scapegoat?," 182–83.
96. Galvin, "Jesus as Scapegoat?," 183.
97. Galvin, "Jesus as Scapegoat?," 183.
98. Kryst, "Interpreting the Death of Jesus," 257.

humans who mutually deceive and judge each other, as they are enslaved by evil. Insofar as both the Father and Son have nothing to do with divine violence, they nonviolently overcome the power of violence in the world.

Nonetheless, there is an extraordinary circular logic to Schwager's dynamic arguments in his dramatic soteriology. As the Father abandons his Son in the face of evil, the crucified human Jesus is transformed into unlimited submission to God the Father.[99] However, the saving power of Christ in Schwager's nonviolent soteriology is not grounded upon the hypostatic union of deity and humanity and its inner relationship with the Triune God. Rather, God's salvation is based on Jesus' inner, human process in his "radically" nonviolent response to sin.[100] It is odd to see that in place of God's sovereign mystery in the unity of his justice and love in Christ, Schwager argues for the paradoxical power of sin itself in the victimization of Jesus. For Schwager, Christ "dared to suffer the concrete sinful deeds (as being killed by sin) to the point where he was transformed precisely by them into a limitless surrender."[101] Thus the destructive power of sin not only violently judges Jesus in the crucifixion, but also the violent death itself creatively transforms the victim Jesus into the savior for all other victims. The bottom line is that the human violence at the crucifixion is the substantial agent transforming the victimized Jesus into a savior of victims. Consequently, the transforming power of sin motivates and completes the inner human process of Jesus' forgiveness and love towards his evil enemies.

Yet can the mechanism of evil bring about the salvation of sinful humans in the objective sense, without God's sovereign intervention in the event? Hans Urs von Balthasar casts doubt on the hermeneutical appropriateness of the Girardian scapegoat theory, in that "the transferal of the world's guilt to Jesus" in the crucifixion has "only a psychological unloading (as it was in all ritual sacrifice)" and "the power-less God demands nothing in the nature of 'atoning sacrifice.'"[102] Correspondingly, Schwager merely deals with the anthropocentric understanding of the crucifixion, *what* fallen sinners can realize through Christ's death, as if God's saving sovereignty were absent in the substitutionary death of Christ. Schwager narrowly concentrates on illuminating the horizontal

---

99. Schwager, *Jesus in the Drama of Salvation*, 189.
100. Schwager, *Jesus in the Drama of Salvation*, 189.
101. Schwager, *Jesus in the Drama of Salvation*, 189.
102. Balthasar, *Theo-Drama IV*, 310.

dimension of the anthropocentric and subjective reunion between the victimized Jesus and the converted sinners, without confirming the divine and objective reconciliation between God and the fallen sinners. Both Girard and Schwager cannot help acknowledging the divine paradox in Christ's atoning death, in which evil and violence at the temporary and phenomenal level are not incompatible with God's eternal plan and his saving power in Christ's self-sacrificial death.

Next, it must be noted that in order to preserve the divine dimension of the atonement, in place of the hypostatic union of humanity and deity Schwager creatively propounds his own pneumatological Christology. The "human spirit and the divine spirit" are united in the person of Jesus.[103]

> Suffering is here understood unambiguously as surrendering and handing over the Spirit to the Father. Since Luke describes Jesus at the beginning of his ministry as the long-awaited bearer of the Spirit, the return of the Spirit to the Father means at the same time the fulfillment of the mission. The act of dying, the fulfillment of the mission, and the handing over the Spirit to the Father consequently come together in the one event described by the letter to the Hebrews as the sacrifice of Christ.[104]

Here we can see that the Son of God's dialectical movement into human humiliation and divine exaltation is totally replaced by God's sending the Spirit into the human Jesus and the Spirit's return to him at the crucifixion. Jesus' radical self-sacrificial death, beyond human limitation, becomes the crucial reversal to transform human violence into divine nonviolence. In this regard, Schwager makes up for the absence of Christ's deity by positing the unlimited bursting of Jesus' human nature.

At this point, Schwager places an essential emphasis on the subjective application of the Holy Spirit's salvific power to believers. With "the transcendental Christology of Karl Rahner," Schwager believes that the Holy Spirit is "the transcendental love of the eternal Son's human nature for the Father."[105] Just as "the highest act of his concrete human love" happens in Christ's crucifixion, so "the highest form of the 'incarnation' of the Holy Spirit (or of transcendental love) in an act of Christ's human love" takes places in the innermost hearts of all sinful humans.[106] Thus

---

103. Schwager, *Jesus in the Drama of Salvation*, 188.
104. Schwager, *Jesus in the Drama of Salvation*, 188.
105. Schwager, *Jesus in the Drama of Salvation*, 216.
106. Schwager, *Jesus in the Drama of Salvation*, 216.

the Holy Spirit plays a decisive role in communicating eternal freedom to the enslaved victims of evil.[107] As Schwager rightly affirms, the Holy Spirit's dynamic power of salvation should not be underestimated, in that without the Holy Spirit, there is no way for believers to receive the salvific efficacy of Christ's atonement. Nevertheless, the Holy Spirit cannot work apart from the person of Christ himself. Rather, as the Spirit of Christ, the Holy Spirit dynamically communicates the atoning work of Christ himself to fallen humankind, in order to redeem those who believe in Christ. Without the incarnate, crucified, resurrected Christ, the content of the Holy Spirit's saving work would be indeed empty!

Should the reciprocal movement of the Holy Spirit, as Schwager insists, be the main point on which the whole of biblical soteriology stands or falls? As if Christ's atoning work in his own person as God-human were at best functional or even unnecessary? Rather, Schwager should have considered that Christ's free will and sovereignty in atonement is the crux of salvation. The substitutionary perspective is infinitely better than what cannot be planned from any nonviolent understanding of crucifixion.

The Crucified Jesus' Resurrection as God's Nonviolent Forgiveness

With regard to Christ's resurrection, Schwager takes a critical position on historical-critical scholarship. He observes that Bultmann and his followers uncritically claim that there is hermeneutical "separation" between "the Easter kerygma and the historical Jesus."[108] Rather than relying on the "unproved assumption" that truth should be objectively demonstrated in the historical sense, Schwager sees a theological consistency regarding nonviolence in both Jesus' crucifixion and his resurrection. Schwager argues for "the credibility of the Easter message" in the Christological sense.[109]

> What from the historical-critical viewpoint may be felt to be unsatisfying shows itself to be most appropriate at the level of the inner coherence of content. Thus it emerges once more that the cryptic presuppositions of the historical-critical method do not match the reality which came to expression for the first time in the fate of Jesus."[110]

---

107. Schwager, *Jesus in the Drama of Salvation*, 216.
108. Schwager, *Jesus in the Drama of Salvation*, 119.
109. Schwager, *Jesus in the Drama of Salvation*, 119.
110. Schwager, *Jesus in the Drama of Salvation*, 119.

The Nonviolent Jesus

Nevertheless, while Schwager believes in the "transcendent reality" of Christ's resurrection, which takes place beyond the human-immanent dimension of "historical-critical" scholarship, he acknowledges that it is in fact hard to comprehend the accurate character of the risen Jesus' physical presence in human time and space.[111] Rather, Schwager focuses on the actuality of the disciples' visionary experience, just as the early church community is certain of Christ's dynamic presence in the Eucharist.[112] In this light, for Schwager, the objective understanding of the resurrected Christ himself is to be distinguished from the subjective dimension of the disciples' encounter with the living Lord. Since Schwager simply concentrates on the dimension of revelation in Christ's resurrection that corresponds to his crucifixion in the Gospels, the theological validity of the risen Christ merely remains at the cognitive level of his disciples' experienced faith. With this hermeneutical presupposition, Schwager asserts that the ultimate purpose of Christ's resurrection is to awaken God's true image of nonviolence, rather than divine judgment against evildoers. Moreover, the resurrection not only means God's vindication of the victimized Jesus, but it also accompanies God's forgiveness of his enemies, for whom Jesus dies.

> In the resurrection brought about by the Father it is consequently not enough to see merely a verdict for his Son and against those who opposed him. Certainly, this view is correct, as Jesus' opponents are convicted as sinners. But the verdict of the heavenly Father is above all a decision for the Son who gave himself up to death for his opponents. It is therefore, when considered more deeply, also a verdict in favor of sinners.[113]

Thus Schwager places a heavy emphasis on the fact that the resurrection of Christ confirms God's unconditional forgiveness toward those who violently executed his Son. The resurrection as the divine verdict of forgiveness is an inconceivable event beyond the cognitive scope of human judgment, in which judgment sinners always repay evil with evil.

> The heavenly Father in his Easter "judgment" acted differently from the master of the vineyard in the parable. Even the murder of his Son did not provoke in him a reaction of vengeful retribution, but he sent the risen one back with the message "Peace be

---

111. Schwager, *Jesus in the Drama of Salvation*, 137–38.
112. Schwager, *Jesus in the Drama of Salvation*, 137.
113. Schwager, *Jesus in the Drama of Salvation*, 135.

with you!" to those disciples who at the critical moment had allowed themselves to be drawn into the camp of the opponents of the kingdom of God. The judge's verdict at Easter was consequently not only a retrospective confirmation of the message of Jesus, but it also contained a completely new element, namely, forgiveness for those who had rejected the offer of pure forgiveness itself and persecuted the Son . . . A rightly understood doctrine of Easter, not in opposition to Jesus' proclamation of the kingdom of God. On the contrary, it is precisely the peace of Easter which shows how the Father of Jesus willingly forgives, even in the face of people's hardened hearts.[114]

According to Schwager, the Old Testament prophecies the crucified and resurrected Messiah, and the Gospels confirm the historical and biblical actuality of Jesus' Messiahship by his resurrection:[115] "the stone that the builders rejected has become the head of the corner; this was accomplished by the Lord, and it is marvelous in our eyes" (Psalm 118:22; Mark 12:10; Acts 4:11). Accordingly, the nonviolent resurrection of Christ is such a revolutionary event as to function as "the hermeneutical key" to the whole gospel of Jesus' nonviolence and forgiveness.[116] For Schwager, through the nonviolent resurrection both the merciful God and the resurrected Jesus never require any violent satisfaction of retributive justice against self-deceived humans. Schwager argues that "Jesus made the claim, by his proclamation and by his lived decision not to meet the violence of his opponents on their own level, God's action is not identical with action on this earth which brings immediate victory."[117] In this regard, the divine drama of salvation seems to be perfectly complete under the overarching theme of nonviolence.

Nonetheless, Schwager's Girardian perspective on the resurrection of Christ is confined to an affirmation of God's nonviolent forgiveness of self-deceived sinners. Since Schwager concentrates on humankind's epistemic realization of the nonviolent God and Christ, the resurrection has no objective implications. As Kryst notes,

> The effect of the resurrection is to affirm the cross as locus of God's forgiveness of sin and the transformation of evil. Schwager speaks of the event of the cross alone, apart from the event of

114. Schwager, *Jesus in the Drama of Salvation*, 136.
115. Schwager, *Jesus in the Drama of Salvation*, 136.
116. Schwager, *Jesus in the Drama of Salvation*, 136.
117. Schwager, *Jesus in the Drama of Salvation*, 136.

the resurrection, as transformative of evil. There is no indication that the Easter event adds any redemptive significance to the cross, but rather serves simply to interpret the crucifixion event as an unjust act. It unveils the victimage mechanism. Schwager does not affirm any importance to the resurrection aside from its referral to the cross.[118]

Furthermore, uncritically following Girard's understanding of the "universality" of violence in the historical-immanent dimension, Schwager has no hesitation in claiming that Jesus' apocalyptic prophecy simply pertains to "the self-destruction of the whole of humanity," which is "a real possibility" as in world conflict over nuclear weapons.[119] Schwager indiscriminately utilizes the Girardian viewpoint to demythologize all the eschatological implications in the apocalyptic texts of the Gospels. In this way, there cannot be any transcendental intervention of an almighty Christ into the autonomous governing mechanism of evil on the earth. At this point, Schwager seems satisfied with the half-truth that the "apocalyptic" only unveils the self-deceptive and destructive judgment of ignorant humans in a linguistic and cognitive sense. More seriously, although Schwager emphasizes God's forgiveness in a human-cognitive sense, he never argues for the resurrected Christ's apocalyptic victory over the evil powers that dominate the violent scapegoat mechanism. According to Schwager, Jesus' nonviolent "surrender to death" on the cross accounts for the hermeneutical "reservation" of a common misconception of resurrection as "a public victory."[120] It is unfortunate that Schwager's Girardian interpretation of resurrection has no room for the crux of Pauline apocalyptic soteriology. The resurrection manifestly reveals God's judgment against the hostile powers and their annihilation.[121] Given that Jesus is eschatologically identified with the Son of Man, in sharp opposition to Schwager's untenable view, his apocalyptic revelation has the divine content of the final judgment and salvation, especially in regard to the second coming and his power to restore the fallen world

---

118. Kryst, "Interpreting the Death of Jesus," 350.

119. Schwager, *Jesus in the Drama of Salvation*, 133. Here Schwager quotes Girard's argument that "to say that we are in an objectively apocalyptic situation is in no way 'to announce the end of the world.' It is to say that humankind has become, for the first time, capable of destroying itself, something that was unimaginable only two or three centuries ago."

120. Schwager, *Jesus in the Drama of Salvation*, 136–37.

121. Rutledge, *The Crucifixion*, 505.

into the new creation. Schwager should have reflected on Christ's own nonviolence as one that not only forgives sinners but also annihilates sin and evil in a violent world.

2.3 Weaver's Ethically Oriented Christology

The Functional Christology of the Nonviolent Jesus in God's Kingdom.

Unlike Brock and Schwager, Weaver directly sets forth his own functional Christology in his nonviolent atonement theory of the narrative *Christus Victor*. According to Weaver, the violent death of Jesus plays a functional role in establishing God's kingdom of nonviolence.

> The reign of God in Jesus made an ultimate claim, which was confronted by the ultimate claim of the powers of evil. This confrontation of ultimates inevitably resulted in death, but the death was a *function* of Jesus' mission and not the purpose or the goal of the mission. Jesus could have escaped death at the hands of Rome, but that escape would have meant failing his mission. God willed that Jesus face this death rather than abandon his mission.[122]

Here we can see that Schwager's dramatic understanding of the inseparable relationship between Christ's person and God's kingdom has an important influence on Weaver's Christology, in which "the person of Jesus embodies the reign of God."[123]

> Since Jesus' message of the reign of God was inseparable from his person, his deeds—including his nonviolent submission to death—have theological significance . . . Jesus' mission was to make present and visible the reign of God. That mission meant witnessing to and presenting God's unmerited forgiveness and the reconciliation of sinners to God.[124]

Weaver goes on to argue that "the life of Jesus, with its liberationist elements," is "revelatory of the reign of God."[125] This fact proves that Weaver believes Jesus himself to be an ethical activist of nonviolent liberation. In order to vindicate the ethically reoriented Christology, Weaver

---

122. Weaver, *The Nonviolent Atonement*, 92. Emphasis mine.
123. Schwager, *Jesus in the Drama of Salvation*, 115.
124. Weaver, *The Nonviolent Atonement*, 43.
125. Weaver, *The Nonviolent Atonement*, 295.

emphasizes the practical dimension of the Christian life.[126] He is convinced that throughout the history of Christian doctrine, "the accommodation of violence" has unfortunately become "the self-evident norm."[127] Hence, his theological project is to offer a critical reassessment of violent atonement theories through "the biblical interpretation that presumed nonviolence."[128] The reason Weaver censures Anselmain satisfaction theory is that saved sinners only play a "passive role" in the drama of Jesus' salvation, without their "active participation" in the atonement.[129] Weaver demonstrates the theological and ethical dissimilarity between substitution and his nonviolent model.

> Narrative *Christus Victor* pictures humankind actively involved in history as sinners against the rule of God, and as actively involved in salvation as the transformed individual participants in witnessing to the presence of the reign of God in history. In contrast, for satisfaction atonement, the sinner is passive observer of a divine transaction between the Father and Son that occurs outside history. As a result of the transaction, the sinner's legal status before God changes, but beyond that change in status there is no transformation of the life of sinner qua sinner who lives in history.[130]

Weaver underlines that "satisfaction atonement in its several forms features an essential separation of salvation and ethics. The atonement image changes the sinners' legal status before God but says nothing about a transformed life."[131] I basically support Weaver's ethical emphasis on nonviolence. Both traditional evangelical and modern progressive camps believe in Jesus' nonviolent public ministry, life, and death as well as the Christian life and discipleship that conform to the ethical teachings of nonviolence. According to the Sermon on the Mount, Jesus lived a perfect nonviolent life, showing his unconditional and embracing love

---

126. Weaver, *The Nonviolent Atonement*, 14. John Howard Yoder's Christian ethics of nonviolence has an essential influence on Weaver' nonviolent atonement theology. Weaver humbly confesses that his atonement theory, narrative *Christus Victor*, is nothing else than the theological reconstruction of Yoder's Christian ethical vision of nonviolence. See Yoder, *The Politics of Jesus*.

127. Weaver, *The Nonviolent Atonement*, 99.

128. Weaver, *The Nonviolent Atonement*, 99.

129. Weaver, *The Nonviolent Atonement*, 98.

130. Weaver, *The Nonviolent Atonement*, 99.

131. Weaver, *The Nonviolent Atonement*, 99.

towards fallen sinners. Following Walter Wink, Weaver persuasively addresses the historical Jesus' ethics of "nonretaliation," as follows.

> The teaching and the life of Jesus show that the objectives of the reign of God are not accomplished by violence. Rejection of violence, however, ought not be interpreted as passivity . . . Far from counseling passivity, Jesus' statements about turning the other cheek, giving the cloak, and going the second mile (Matt 5:39–41; Luke 6:29) actually teach an assertive and confrontation nonviolence that provides an opponent with an opportunity for transformation. With suggestions such as these the oppressed person has the potential to seize the initiative, shame the offender, and strip him of the power to dehumanize.[132]

This is the ethical and practical strength of Weaver's model, in which the contemporary followers of Jesus can not only protest evil but also actively awaken the guilty consciousness of evildoers. By sacrificing their rights and relinquishing interests, Christians are able to actually demonstrate Jesus' self-giving love towards the fallen world, where people incessantly conflict with each other to gain profits and powers. As a messenger of Christ's gospel, the Apostle Paul insists "do not repay anyone evil for evil" and "do not be overcome by evil, but overcome evil with good" (Rom 12:17, 21). It is undeniably what the Bible commands us to do. Weaver leads us to Christian discipleship, to follow what we can learn from the life and ministry of Christ, including his crucifixion and resurrection, with the ethical stance of nonviolence.

Nevertheless, I criticize Weaver's theory insofar as it unfairly presumes the absolute ethical priority of nonviolence over God's atoning work in Christ. According to Balthasar, what is lacking in the theology of nonviolence is a Christian "realism" in the yet-violent world, because there is a practical necessity for violence. Balthasar even acknowledges the inevitability of the abuse of violence if it is realistically involved with governmental power to protect society.[133] Moreover, it must be noted that unlike Weaver, Yoder warns of the absolutization of nonviolence itself by claiming that Christian "pacifism simply as rejection of violent means" is unrealistic in a real world.[134] Thus we should not absolutize a human standard of nonviolence, apart from God's being and work in Christ. The

---

132. Weaver, *The Nonviolent Atonement*, 37.
133. Balthasar, *Theo-Drama IV*, 484.
134. Yoder, *The Politics of Jesus*, 239.

divine dimension of God's saving work must not be squeezed into the ethical manifestation of nonviolence itself. Thus, a nonviolent God must not be an impotent God in the face of violence and evil.

Likewise, since Weaver's theology is grounded upon Yoder's theology of peace, his narrative *Christus Victor* theory exclusively emphasizes an ethical and epistemological dimension of God's work of nonviolence through Jesus' life and death.[135] In other words, according to Yoder, "pacifism as an epistemology" essentially "shapes how a person knows," because "the commitment to nonviolence is a life-shaping, mind-shaping kind of conviction—a conviction that shapes all other convictions."[136] Thus nonviolence itself is an ethically oriented epistemology. In this regard, it is through "an epistemology of vulnerability" that we can realize God's persuasive power through his self-sacrificing love in the crucifixion of Jesus.[137] God's suffering in his Son's death becomes the epistemological actualization of his nonviolence in the world. Likewise, the core ideas of Yoder's epistemology of nonviolence permeate Weaver's theological arguments about nonviolent atonement.

However, I cannot but raise an objection to Yoder's unconvincing philosophical assumption that epistemology—*how* to know reality—can be effectively pursued without discussing ontology—*what* the nature of being or reality is. Theologically speaking, an ethical epistemology cannot be the sole norm by which Christ's person and work are judged in the ontological sense. It is thus regrettable that in Weaver's theology there is no objective dimension in the person and work of Christ. Weaver exclusively focuses on the ethical value of Jesus' humanity by overlooking his deity. Weaver's radical denial of the theological language and interpretation of the Chalcedonian definition threatens to collapse the hermeneutical boundary that distinguishes an ecumenically orthodox Christology from the Christological heresies in the history of the church.[138]

---

135. Yoder, *A Pacifist Way of Knowing*.

136. Grimsrud, "Pacifism and Knowing," 404–5.

137. Grimsrud, "Pacifism and Knowing," 407.

138. For a constructive and critical evaluation of the Chalcedonian Definition, see Coakley, "What Does Chalcedon Solve and What Does It Not?" Sarah Coakley challenges three different perspectives of theological interpretation: "linguistically regulatory," "metaphorical," and "literal." She insists that while the ancient ecumenical discussion sets a hermeneutical "boundary" around the person of Christ as God-human, excluding all the Christological heresies, its own "apophatic" character fails to express the dynamic actuality of Christ's hypostatic union of deity and humanity for his atonement and resurrection in the Scripture.

> While our worldview does not generally use the categories and world picture of Nicea and Chalcedon, another dimension of these formulas actually present a more problematic dimension from a nonviolent perspective. Recall that Nicea's central claim is that Jesus is "one substance" or "one being" with the Father. Recall that the formula of Chalcedon proclaimed Jesus as "fully God and fully man." With awareness of the nonviolent character of the reign of God made visible in the narratives of Jesus and expressed in narrative *Christus Victor*, I simply ask, "What is there about the formulas of Nicea and Chalcedon that expresses the character of the reign of God, in particular its nonviolent character?" "What is there about these formulas that can shape the church that would follow Jesus in witnessing to the reign of God in the world?" Answer: virtually nothing. If all we know of Jesus is that he is "one substance with the Father," and he is "fully God and fully man," there is nothing there that expresses the ethical dimension of being Christ-related, nothing there that would shape the church so that it can be a witness to the world. When these formulas serve as the summary touchstone of Christian faith, there is nothing of the particularity of Jesus to enable the Christ-related person to shape the church as the extension of Jesus' presence in the world.[139]

Rather than ruling out the doctrinal as non-biblical and non-ethical in an indiscriminate way, Weaver should have acknowledged the doctrinal-historical context of the Christological discussion and its necessity for protecting the biblical truth of Christ's unique identity from heretical interpretations such as Apollinarianism and Nestorianism. Why does Weaver refuse to construct his nonviolent Christology within the doctrinal "safe space" allowed by the universal and catholic church as the body of Christ? Given that the Hellenistic philosophical language of nature or *hypostasis* is not to be absolutized in grasping the reality of the Son of God, the doctrinal concept is not incompatible with the biblical narratives of Jesus. Rather, Christological reflection and biblical truth are mutually beneficial, as if they were bones and muscles.

More seriously, Weaver assumes that catholic Christology lays a theological foundation for the violent satisfaction theory, as if God were an absolute emperor maintaining the universal order of his reign. We should attend to how Weaver describes the person of Jesus within the dichotomy of violence and nonviolence. Weaver definitely prefers the

---

139. Weaver, *The Nonviolent Atonement*, 121.

phrase "human Jesus" to "Christ," which is rarely used in the narrative *Christus Victor*. For Weaver, the deity of Christ is a stumbling block, because his divinity not only means sovereignty but also obviously contradicts the human inevitability or unexpectedness of the crucifixion. Weaver's nonviolent Jesus is equal to the nineteenth-century liberal portrait of Jesus as the ethical teacher, because Weaver thinks that the intrinsic value of nonviolence in Jesus' life is the absolute ethical norm for contemporary Christians. Without understanding the dynamic principle between Christ's person and work, Weaver deals with the Gospel narratives of Jesus as if Jesus were a human being rather than the incarnate God, fully God and human. The Christ of Weaver's narrative *Christus Victor* is nothing but the Christ of adoptionism or the moralistic and exemplary Jesus of nineteenth-century liberal theology. Thus, Weaver's theological project attempts to confirm that Jesus' entire life, crucifixion, and resurrection, as well as God's kingdom, solely target the actualization of nonviolence in our world.

The Cultic Dimension of Jesus' Victimization by Evil

For the sake of nonviolence-centered biblical hermeneutics, Weaver reinterprets the sacrificial language in Scripture in order to remove the substitutionary connotation in Christ's atoning work. Weaver's chief aim is not to reject the Levitical sacrifice rituals themselves, but any legal and commercial idea of God's violent satisfaction in them or in Christ's eternal priestly work in Hebrews. Since Weaver believes in the correlation between atonement and sacrifice, he agrees that the biblical theme of sacrifice can be attributed to Jesus' atoning death.[140] As Weaver confirms that "the life of the flesh is in the blood" (Leviticus 17:14), he defines the essence of sacrifice through the lens of nonviolence as "a ritual self-dedication and self-giving of the worshippers to God."[141] Here, Weaver intends to exclude the holy violence of God commanding a priest to kill an innocent animal, because according to Weaver, only the blood in the sacrifice could be directly dedicated to God without the mediating process of the sacrificial death.[142] This is Weaver's spiritual and symbolic

---

140. Weaver, *The Nonviolent Atonement*, 70–71.
141. Weaver, *The Nonviolent Atonement*, 70.
142. Weaver, *The Nonviolent Atonement*, 70.

understanding of the biblical sacrifices, and he unjustly disregards the divinely sanctioned violence in Scripture.

Likewise, following Loren L. Johns, Weaver believes that the sacrificial death of Christ is "exemplary," not "substitutionary."[143] It is more problematic that Weaver understands the essence of Christ's atoning death as a holy martyrdom. Weaver supports Stephen J. Patterson's "martyrological" interpretation of Christ's death in Romans 3:26.[144] Patterson says, "The martyr's death is expiatory, and so satisfies God, but it is vicarious also by its exemplary nature; it shows the kind of faithfulness that is pleasing to God."[145] Although Patterson argues for an exemplarism in Jesus' self-giving sacrificial death, he believes that the crucifixion has the "expiatory" and "vicarious" character of atonement.[146] Patterson claims perplexingly to Weaver that "now Jesus is the perfect sacrifice, unblemished, without sin, as must be all victims offered to *satisfy God's anger*."[147] Here, Weaver's eclectic method of biblical exegesis, which seems to be tailored to his narrative *Christus Victor*, cannot avoid an internal contradiction.

The nonviolent God never requires any satisfaction to appease his wrath, because the death of Jesus is completely attributable to evil powers. Yet surprisingly, according to Patterson, the death of Jesus demonstrates the propitiation of God's wrath. Rather than vindicating the puzzling issue of divine violence, Weaver himself goes on to argue that Jesus' sacrificial death is "expiatory," because "it removed the stain of sin from those who participated in the new community."[148] However, without God's divine intervention in Christ's atoning death, how can Weaver argue for the expiation of sins by Jesus' blood, brought about by evil? If Weaver honors the expiating power in Jesus' death, it means the theological justification of the violence that causes the death. Does the evil power produce good? Not at all! Otherwise, it must be God's violent intervention in Christ's

---

143. Weaver, *The Nonviolent Atonement*, 80. Cited from Johns, "'A Better than Sacrifice' or 'Better Than Sacrifice'?, 123.

144. Weaver, *The Nonviolent Atonement*, 80. Cited from Stephen J. Patterson, *Beyond the Passion*, 80.

145. Weaver, *The Nonviolent Atonement*, 76. Cited from Patterson, *Beyond the Passion*, 80.

146. Weaver, *The Nonviolent Atonement*, 76. Cited from Patterson, *Beyond the Passion*, 81.

147. Weaver, *The Nonviolent Atonement*, 76. Emphasis mine.

148. Weaver, *The Nonviolent Atonement*, 76.

atoning death in the paradoxical sense. At this point, Weaver makes a self-contradictory argument.

Although Weaver rejects any kind of satisfaction motif in the atonement, he accepts the literal meaning of propitiation and expiation in the death of Christ. What Weaver never wants to lose is the nonviolent aspect of Christ's self-sacrificial death for his people. The bottom line is that for Weaver, Christ's sacrifice itself never appeases God's wrath, but God is nonviolently pleased with Jesus' exemplary obedience as the holy victim killed by evil powers. God is not the sovereign agent of Jesus' death, as if he were a sacrifice for human sins.

It is obviously unjust that although Weaver criticizes human centrality in Abelard's moral influence theory of atonement,[149] he argues for the hermeneutical validity of exemplarism in Christ's death for the purpose of rejecting God's sovereign involvement. In line with Girard's nonviolent approach to the scapegoat mechanism in culture and religion, Weaver believes Girard's view that "there is nothing in the Gospels to suggest that the death of Jesus is a sacrifice, whatever definition (expiation, substitutionary, etc.) we may give that sacrifice."[150] Nonetheless, as was mentioned above, Weaver acknowledges all the sacrificial concepts in the Bible, except substitutionary doctrine. Weaver insists that as the eternal Mediator, Christ is the high priest in the essential sense, rather than the Lamb of God.[151] It is more striking to see that even though Weaver accepts the theological application of the Girardian perspective, in which Jesus is nothing but an innocent victim, Weaver supports Hardin's claim that Jesus sovereignly sacrifices himself, fulfilling the plan of God.[152] Yet does this simply mean that Christ violently kills himself, in order to satisfy God's requirement? Indeed, Weaver cannot get out of the hermeneutical framework of satisfaction theory. Jesus' death is orchestrated by God's sovereignty, though Weaver relies on an eclecticism in which he selects the nonviolent aspects of Christ's atoning work by obscuring the direct meaning of the sacrificial language in the Bible. Therefore, Weaver's cultic reconstruction of Jesus' death fails to maintain theological integrity, because Weaver merely borrows the external and nonviolent form of sacrifice but never concedes its inner logic, namely that of the

---

149. Weaver, *The Nonviolent Atonement*, 19.

150. Weaver, *The Nonviolent Atonement*, 51. Cited from Girard, *Things Hidden Since the Foundation of the World*, 180.

151. Weaver, *The Nonviolent Atonement*, 78.

152. Weaver, *The Nonviolent Atonement*, 78–79.

Son's self-giving under God's sovereignty. More significantly, according to Weaver the dualistic confrontation between God's kingdom and the power of violence causes the human inevitability of Jesus' death.[153]

> In carrying out that mission, Jesus was killed by the earthly structures in bondage to the power of evil, his death was not a payment owed to God's honor, nor was it divine punishment that he suffered as a substitute for sinners, Jesus' death was the rejection of the rule of God by forces opposed to that rule. In fact, this review of Jesus' life as narrative *Christus Victor* exposes how incongruous it is to interpret this story as one whose ultimate purpose was to produce a death in order to satisfy divine justice. Far from being an event organized for a divine requirement, his death reveals the nature of the forces of evil that opposed the rule of God. It poses a contrast between the attempt to coerce by violence under the rule of evil and the nonviolence of the rule of God as revealed and made visible by the life, death, and resurrection of Jesus.[154]

Jesus is an inevitable victim of the dualistic confrontation between the nonviolent God and violent evil. As a Mennonite, Weaver's dualism between violence as a deconstructive evil and nonviolence as a revealing and transformative power is the paradigm that drives his reinterpretation of the traditional Anselmian atonement theory. It is important to understand Weaver's view of dualistic conflict in his narrative *Christus Victor*. This dualistic concept is originally attributed to Gustaf Aulén's *Christus Victor* model, which dramatically describes God's victory over evil powers in the framework of a cosmic battle.[155] In a similar way, Weaver asserts

---

153. Weaver, *The Nonviolent Atonement*, 91–92. Borg, "Executed by Rome, Vindicated by God," 161. Weaver's nonviolent interpretation of the crucifixion of Jesus accords with the prominent Jesus Seminar scholar Marcus Borg, who offers a political interpretation of Jesus' life and death. According to Borg, the fundamental reason why Jesus was crucified by the Roman Empire was that since Jesus himself was the revolutionary advocate of God's "justice" and his kingdom, he threatened the "domination system" of "injustice" in the socio-political sense. Like Weaver, Borg underlines the "human inevitability" of Jesus' death, because the tragic event is "the collision between the passion of Jesus and the domination system of his time." Therefore, there is no salvific efficacy in Jesus' atoning death for sinful humans, because Jesus never died for sins of the world or according to God's plan, but for the structural sins of the world. Evil violently executed him.

154. Weaver, *The Nonviolent Atonement*, 47.

155. Aulén, *Christus Victor*, 4–5. Aulén claims that "the background of the idea is dualistic. God is pictured as in Christ carrying out through a victorious conflict against powers of evil which are hostile to his will." In spite of Aulén's revival of the

that there is "a confrontation between good and evil, between the forces of God and the forces of Satan, between Christ and anti-Christ in the entire narrative of Revelation."[156] Beyond the mythological perspective on the cosmic battle, Weaver views this dualism through the concrete historical conflict between God's good reign in the life of Jesus and Satan's evil reign in the Roman Empire in time and space. Thus Weaver summarizes the core of the Gospels as the dualistic struggle between evil's reign by "violence" and "the nonviolence" of Jesus in his historical embodiment of God's reign.[157] The inevitable death of Jesus is ultimately attributed to the conflict between God's reign of nonviolence and evil's reign of violence.[158]

Weaver's overarching theme of dualism between God's nonviolence and the devil's violence in Revelation and the Gospels dangerously overlooks God's sovereignty in a series of devastating catastrophes. Weaver assumes that there are demonic dominating powers and areas where God's reign could not reach before his triumph in the resurrection of Jesus.[159] But to take this position is to see not so much the God revealed in the Bible as the good god depicted in Zoroastrian dualism. Moreover, Weaver forces us to interpret God's victory over evil, symbolized as the Roman Empire, in a nonviolent way. He denies a variety of violent images such as wrath, judgment, army, and the sword of God, as well as the wrath of the seemingly nonviolent lamb in Revelation (14:19; 14:7; 19:19; 6:16).

Weaver never takes into consideration that if the victory of God over evil is radically reduced to serve the purpose of moral ethics like nonviolence, it becomes merely a human projection of an ethical ideology that undoubtedly detracts from God's transcendent sovereignty in Christ.[160] It is crucial to acknowledge "the *penultimate* dualism of the Apocalypse" for the sake of a holistic interpretation of the relationship

---

victory motif in Christ's atonement, Aulén completely rejects the vicarious humanity of Jesus as "a discontinuous divine work" in the objective type. He unfairly concentrates on Christ's deity as "a continuous divine work" in the classic model. Thus I insist that because of the unbalanced relation of Christ's deity and humanity, it would be fair to say that Aulén's *Christus Victor* is a modern version of Docetism.

156. Weaver, *The Nonviolent Atonement*, 21.

157. Weaver, *The Nonviolent Atonement*, 47.

158. Weaver, *The Nonviolent Atonement*, 21.

159. Weaver, *The Nonviolent Atonement*, 46. Weaver understands the demons' reign as the "not-yet-reign-of-God."

160. Sherman, *King, Priest, and Prophet*. Robert Sherman illustrates the case of Immanuel Kant's ethical reinterpretation of Christian doctrines from the standpoint of human reason.

between human suffering, the demonic powers, and the ultimate sovereignty of God.[161] The exercise of the demonic powers is "permitted" to take place in the world by the sovereign will of God, who orchestrates his hidden and final triumph over the visible and temporary victory of evil.[162] The biblical testimony confirms that nothing can happen outside God's sovereign reign, no matter what it is.

Correspondingly, Michael Root points out that the biblical concept of "God's sovereignty" can be contradicted by a radical dualistic thought between God and the evil powers, as if evil could reign beyond God's ruling power.[163] Thus Root argues that "liberation" from evil and suffering cannot be the overarching topic in Scripture, because we are not only the victims of evil but also sinners who are still involved with evil.[164] Rather, we need "reconciliation," in which Christ forgives our sins through his self-sacrificial death on the cross.[165] Even though evil brings about human suffering and violence, its power is controlled by God's sovereignty (Rev 6:7).[166] At the heart of Revelation lies the wholly paradoxical combination of the two images of Christ as the slain lamb and victorious lion. At a literal level, the passion narrative of the Gospels seems to illustrate the ultimate conflict of God and the evil powers that persecuted Jesus.[167] Yet at a hermeneutical level, assuming biblical integrity on God's sovereignty over evil, Jesus' submission to death as the enemy of God confirms the divine mystery that God intended the event to happen. Christ voluntarily fulfilled God's will, and the enemy paradoxically accomplished God's plan of reconciliation.[168] The story of Gethsemane shows that Christ's seemingly inevitable submission to death means, in a very real sense, his voluntary acceptance of God's plan of reconciliation.[169] Root affirms that it is through "the double-sidedness" of the relationships between God and Christ, God and the evil enemy, and Christ and the enemy that Christ's submissive passivity to death becomes his sovereign

161. Mangina, *Revelation*, 124.
162. Mangina, *Revelation*, 124.
163. Root, "Dying He Lives," 157.
164. Root, "Dying He Lives," 157.
165. Root, "Dying He Lives," 157.
166. Root, "Dying He Lives," 158.
167. Root, "Dying He Lives," 159.
168. Root, "Dying He Lives," 160.
169. Root, "Dying He Lives," 159.

act over the evil power of sin and death.[170] Jesus Christ is not only the liberator of victims from the evil powers, but also the reconciler between "death-invoking" sinners and "the loving righteousness of God."[171] In this regard, the Anselmian approach to reconciliation is interrelated with the *Christus Victor* model of liberation.[172]

Likewise, Weaver's narrative *Christus Victor* contradicts the biblical testimonies that "he [Christ] must go to Jerusalem and suffer many things at the hands of the elders, the chief priests and the teachers of the law, and that he must be killed and on the third day be raised to life," and that "This is my blood of the covenant, which is poured out for many for the forgiveness of sins" (Matt 16:21; 26:28). Christ not only predicted his crucifixion but proclaimed the purpose of his vicarious death for sinners. Thus the crucifixion cannot be interpreted as an inevitable event. The Christ revealed in the Gospels is neither a human victim of a political or religious power game nor a holy martyr in a doomed situation. Weaver distorts the God-human Jesus Christ and his voluntary obedience to the crucifixion into the human Jesus' inevitable decision to avoid failing his task.

Weaver seems satisfied with his claim that the death of Christ plays a functional role in manifesting the intrinsic value of nonviolence to a world of violence. If there is no divine necessity in Christ's crucifixion, Weaver's theory is indeed nearer to moral influence theory. According to Robert W. Jenson, the subjective theories of atonement in liberal theology fail to guarantee the biblical actuality of God's reconciliation through Christ's atoning death, because the liberal perspectives focus on the ethical application of Christ's life and death to believers' lives in the ecclesiastical community.[173] As a result, "there is no real difference between redemption as a whole and reconciliation in particular."[174] Even the event of Christ's atonement does not necessitate that it be a crucifixion of sacrifice and judgment, insofar as his death ultimately fulfills God's mission of love and forgiveness towards his opponents.[175] Thus it is hypothetically possible that even if Jesus had "died in bed," he would have accomplished God's mission of establishing his kingdom of peace and

---

170. Root, "Dying He Lives," 160.
171. Root, "Dying He Lives," 158.
172. Root, "Dying He Lives," 158.
173. Jenson, *Systematic Theology I*, 187.
174. Jenson, *Systematic Theology I*, 187.
175. Jenson, *Systematic Theology I*, 187.

nonviolence.[176] Moreover, according to George Hunsinger, since Weaver does not consider the essential role of Jesus' eternal deity, his theological position unescapably falls into "Arianism":[177]

> Those who would disparage Nicaea, while wishing to take apart in the ecumenical movement, are going to have to explain why their Trinitarian and Christological alternatives do not degenerate into Arianism. We need this explanation from the critics of Nicene Christianity. While the Christological picture in their writings is not unmixed, it often displays definite Arian undercurrents. After paying lip service to what they may call "ontological" questions—which they seem to regard as fairly worthless—the only thing that seems left for them is an exemplarist Christology in liberationist dress. What they regard as the "meaning" of the incarnation and of faith would be unrecognizable to most of the ecumenical church on account of its being so reductionist. It is of course laudable, as all Christians would agree, to want to stand with the victims of injustice and alleviate their suffering. No doubt liberation theology has much to teach us here. There is a big difference, however, between Jesus as God incarnate and Jesus as merely "incarnation" (i.e., symbolic presence) of God's reign. If critics of Nicene Christianity cannot upgrade their Christologies to meet Nicene standards, their ecumenical prospects are not bright.[178]

I believe that "the presence of God" cannot replace Christ's deity in the ontological sense. In Weaver's theory, the deity of Christ becomes unnecessary for the reason that the nonviolent Jesus is nothing but the human most ideal for demonstrating the new relationship with the loving God. As we have seen, from Weaver's nonviolent perspective the atonement is understood as Jesus' compassion on and solidarity with victims of violence, as well as Jesus' nonviolent termination of evil by the crucifixion. In practice, the nonviolent atonement theory replaces the four biblical concepts of sin, sinners, the God-human Christ's substitutionary death, and God's sovereignty over the event. The last has its own contextualizing issues of suffering, victims, the human Jesus' solidarity with them in the crucifixion, and the evil causing the event. In fact, the nonviolent atonement theory attempts to explain Christ's death in the context of theodicy, not soteriology. This is at best a victim-oriented soteriology

---

176. Jenson, *Systematic Theology I*, 187.
177. Hunsinger, *The Eucharist and Ecumenism*, 288–89.
178. Hunsinger, *The Eucharist and Ecumenism*, 288–89.

in which all humanity is not fallen but deprived from the socio-political point of view. On a hermeneutical level, nonviolent atonement theories reject a Christology "from above" in order to get rid of God's sovereign will in the death of Christ. Instead, from a perspective of low Christology, Weaver's nonviolent atonement theory exclusively seeks to interpret the crucifixion in terms of Jesus' human suffering. Due to his anthropological perspective, Weaver fails to grasp the core of Christ's atonement. I believe that the human Jesus' "horizontal" nonviolent conflict with evil in the violent world co-occurs with Christ's divine obedience—in an ethically nonviolent way—"vertically" when he sacrifices himself to atone for fallen humans from the standpoint of a righteous and merciful God.

The Apocalyptic Resurrection: Discontinuity between Crucifixion and Resurrection

Weaver is right to criticize the one-sidedness of crucifixion in Anselmian satisfaction theory. Anselm and his uncritical followers fail to do justice to the dynamic and biblical motif of God's conquest over the hostile powers by Christ's resurrection. They miss the apocalyptic perspective of the Apostle Paul.

> Anselm's satisfaction atonement has no necessary role for resurrection. In satisfaction atonement, the focus is on the penalty-paying death, and the resurrection occurs at an entirely different place in the theological outline. In contrast, resurrection is the foundation of Paul's thought . . . Since satisfaction atonement lacks a role for resurrection in salvation, it is not apocalyptic in orientation, and therefore is incompatible with Paul.[179]

For Weaver, Christ's resurrection is the objective corollary of atonement, because "resurrection constitutes the basis of the new creation, transformed life lived under the power of the reign of God."[180] It is through the lens of Pauline apocalyptic theology that Weaver theologically resurrects the dynamic motif of Christ's resurrection, which is inseparable from his atoning death. Here Weaver opens the conversation with the New Testament scholar J. Christiaan Beker:[181]

---

179. Weaver, *The Nonviolent Atonement*, 56–57.
180. Weaver, *The Nonviolent Atonement*, 56.
181. Beker, *Paul the Apostle*, 210. According to Beker, a Christocentric interpretation "divorces the death and resurrection of Christ from God's redemptive purpose

> It is the apocalyptic orientation of narrative *Christus Victor*, with the proleptic presence of the reign of God (or the future reign of God breaking into the present) that makes narrative *Christus Victor* the motif that supports confrontation of the *status quo* by the church as representative of the reign of God. Here is the basis of the Christian's commitment to life in Christ and to continue Jesus' mission to witness to the presence of the reign of God in history. In contrast, lacking a proleptic presence of the reign of God via resurrection, satisfaction atonement features an image of salvation outside of history, which means that it lacks any impulse of confrontation with and witness to the social order, which orients it toward accommodation and support of the *status quo*.[182]

This is Weaver's contribution to the nonviolent view of atonement. He connects Jesus' nonviolent death with his apocalyptic resurrection, which transforms the old world of violence as the reign of evil into the new world of nonviolence as the reign of God. More importantly, Weaver highlights the socio-political implications of his nonviolent atonement theory, in that the apocalyptic dimension of Jesus' resurrection guarantees his nonviolent conquest over the structural evils in the violent world. Since the narrative *Christus Victor* emphasizes the historical-immanent aspect of Jesus' confrontation with evil, the ethically reoriented *Christus Victor* based on the vulnerable humanity of Christ effectively overcomes the mythological-transcendental limitation of Aulén's *Christus Victor*, grounded upon Christ's eternal deity.

It is, however, problematic that Weaver radically separates the crucifixion and resurrection of Christ by denying the continuity of the two events. Weaver claims that the basis of the nonviolent atonement is not crucifixion but resurrection. He selectively quotes Beker's argument entirely out of context. The citation indicates that Jesus' death is brought into his resurrection as "the apocalyptic-cosmic event that inaugurates

---

for his creation so that it inevitably individualizes and privatizes the Christ-event." Yet it is regrettable that in order to avoid a functional understanding of Christ's atoning work, Beker hastily argues for "the theocentric focus" on Christ's death and resurrection without fully considering the Mediatorial Christological implication that is the crux of the Pauline soteriology (1 Tim 2:5–6). For an evangelical review of apocalyptic literature and the theological implications of atonement, see Rutledge, "The Apocalyptic War," *The Crucifixion*, 348–94.

182. Weaver, *The Nonviolent Atonement*, 57.

the cosmic triumph of God."[183] Consequently, Weaver affirms that even God's judgment of sin and his absolution of guilt in Christ's atoning death cannot proclaim "the new ontological state of life."[184] Rather, according to Weaver, it is solely Christ's victorious "resurrection" that not only destroys the power of sin itself, but also establishes God's reign in the eschatological creation.[185] Weaver indeed puts the crucifixion event into the inevitable process of human death, which is ultimately transformed into the life of resurrection. This means that Weaver exclusively focuses on illuminating the temporal-phenomenal transition from Jesus' crucifixion to his resurrection without realizing the paradoxical dimension of atonement in Pauline soteriology. Christ's death is "the death of death," for the event is his own eternal life-giving death for us.[186] It is the substitutionary *death* that kills sinners' *death* in the apocalyptic sense. Weaver unfairly presupposes that Paul's apocalyptic understanding of Christ's cross excludes God's forensic judgment against sinful humanity, because it is the intrinsic violence of God. Weaver believes that the resurrection of Christ is related to God's positive affirmation of his yet-suffering creation, in that Christ's apocalyptic victory confirms its liberation from the hostile powers of sin, death, and the devil.

By contrast, according to Beker, the Apostle Paul himself tries to avoid any dualistic understanding of crucifixion and resurrection. He "refrains from assigning death and resurrection to distinct spheres, as if the death of Christ refers only to judgment and his resurrection only to life."[187] While Paul's apocalyptic theology dramatically distinguishes the annihilation of the old world from the re-creation of the new world in the temporal sense, his own unique "accentuation" of the different stages of salvation never brings about the separation between crucifixion and resurrection. Rather, the Pauline doctrine of atonement confirms the continuity of the two events as Christ's saving work, through his own person as God-human. Just as Anselm over-accentuates crucifixion apart from resurrection, so Weaver goes to the other extreme and over-emphasizes resurrection at the expense of crucifixion. Weaver's dualistic perspective on death and life is unable to grasp Christ's apocalyptic crucifixion and

183. Weaver, *The Nonviolent Atonement*, 56.

184. Weaver, *The Nonviolent Atonement*, 56.

185. Weaver, *The Nonviolent Atonement*, 56.

186. For a Protestant scholastic understanding, see Owen, *The Death of Death in the Death of Christ*, 1852.

187. Beker, *Paul the Apostle*, 198.

resurrection as the whole that the Apostle Paul declares. In contrast to Weaver, who radically separates Jesus' death and the failure of his mission to establish God's kingdom in the resurrected Christ's life and victory, Beker argues that the crucified Jesus himself already reveals "the hidden victory" in the atonement.[188]

> The bleakness and the lonely forsakenness of the man on the cross, the total breakdown of the Jewish religious establishment, and the final apocalyptic judgment on Judaism are as striking here as the insight of the gentile centurion that the suffering figure on the cross is truly the King of the Jews and the Son of God. The cross has no need, as it were, of the confirmation of the resurrection. It is itself both the judgment of the world, and the victory over the world.[189]

Since the crucified human Jesus is identified with the second person of the Trinity, the three distinctive themes of God's verdict, Jesus' human victimization, and the divine victory—as I add up Weaver's crucial issues in Beker's theological interpretation—are to be holistically superimposed on the apocalyptic crucifixion of Christ himself. The powerless victim crucified by evildoers is the same as the omnipotent Savior, the Son of God who takes the sin of the whole world upon himself. Here and now, the crucified Christ himself is the eternal truth, life, and saving righteousness of God, so that he needs no further human justification or even a divine one. Accordingly, there is a principle of correspondence between the person of Christ and his work of atonement. As the Son of God, Christ accomplishes his apocalyptic salvation throughout both crucifixion and resurrection; simultaneously, as the human Jesus, he had to be inevitably victimized by evil, but with his own sovereign decision to obey God's plan.

What Weaver skillfully avoids acknowledging is that the crux of Pauline apocalyptic theology is the crucifixion of Christ himself. Paul's most distinctive idea from the Jewish apocalyptic heritage is his "theology of the cross," how to proclaim the saving righteousness and power in Christ's death.[190] Beker insists that "the inauguration of the new age with the resurrection is contingent on the radical end of the old age in the cross, and Paul's reinterpretation of the Jewish-Hellenistic tradition

---

188. Beker, *Paul the Apostle*, 201.
189. Beker, *Paul the Apostle*, 201.
190. Beker, *Paul the Apostle*, 191.

must be understood in this light."[191] Unlike Weaver, Paul never removes the sacrificial language and juridical dimension of Christ's atoning death, but declares the cultic-penal substitution at the apocalyptic dimension, as a whole. Any kind of dualism between God and evil or an exclusive choice of one motif among several for Christ's atonement are impossible in Paul's theology. As such, Paul maintains his own theological integrity on the understanding of Christ's death and resurrection. There is no question that for Beker, the core of Pauline soteriology is God's judgment in Christ's death.

> He [Paul] transforms Jewish-apocalyptic thought by radicalizing not only God's wrath, but also the powers of sin and death ("the last enemy"). The death of Christ becomes the focus of God's judgment, and faith in Christ's death for us will be the norm for the future last judgment. Because all have sinned, all must die. The death of Christ signifies the apocalyptic judgment on all humankind, and his resurrection signifies the *sola gratia* of the new life in Christ for all . . . For the death of Christ signifies God's universal judgment on all: "Since all have sinned and fall short of the glory of God" (Rom 3:23). Thus, all fall under God's wrath and judgment and all are justified in Christ (Rom 5:18)."[192]

Here we can see that, in contrast to Weaver's rejection of any hermeneutical views involving God's violent intervention in the atonement, the Apostle Paul declares the positive and re-constructive power of God's judgment against sinful humankind in Christ's vicarious death. Without the judgment of sin in Christ's death, there cannot be a justification of sinners in Christ himself. In this way, Weaver's theological dualism between the God of nonviolence and the evil powers of violence, as well as his view of human inevitability in Christ's death, are brought into question by Paul's apocalyptic theology of the cross. However, with his own nonviolence-centered assumptions, Weaver claims that "the saving element of the narrative *Christus Victor* is resurrection and God's call that reconciles the sinner to the reign of God."[193] If, as Weaver claims, the crucifixion has no vital value for the salvation of sinners, I argue that the real content in his atonement theory would be empty, in that the consequence of atonement unfairly substitutes for its foundation. Against Weaver's denial of saving efficacy in the crucifixion, Martin Hengel confirms that

191. Beker, *Paul the Apostle*, 191.
192. Beker, *Paul the Apostle*, 193.
193. Beker, *Paul the Apostle*, 340.

the ancient Christian communities believed in the radical uniqueness and universality of Christ's atoning death, because his death as the eternal sacrifice once-and-for-all terminated all the cultic rituals of animal sacrifice in the Jewish temple, and the power of Christ's atoning work had been revealed in his resurrection.[194] We can see that the substitutionary and cultic dimension of Christ's death is manifestly attested in the New Testament. The nonviolent atonement theory, without the saving power of Christ's death as the actuality of atonement, would be in fact "no-atonement."

However, I do not want to make one-sided criticisms of Weaver's narrative *Christus Victor*. Rather, I assess his apocalyptic view of resurrection much more positively than any other nonviolent atonement theory. I believe that Weaver's resuscitation of the apocalyptic view of Christ's resurrection is a hermeneutical bridge for mutual understanding between the nonviolent perspectives and the substitutionary ones. Therefore, I constructively suggest that Weaver needs to consider the apocalyptic continuity of God's saving righteousness in both Christ's crucifixion and resurrection, in order to move forward to a holistic comprehension of Jesus' nonviolence in both an ethical and divine sense.

2.4 Systematic Theological Review

Here I will summarize what we have observed from the nonviolent Christologies of Brock, Schwager, and Weaver. The Christological core is the functional role of Jesus for God's kingdom and saved victims.

1. The notion of the nonviolent Jesus in God's reign of nonviolence in a violent world implies a functional Christology. The essence of Jesus' life, ministry, death, and resurrection is the human-ethical manifestation of his nonviolence.

2. Jesus' nonviolent resistance against evil, forgiveness for evildoers, and salvation for victims is the functionally decisive means through which God's kingdom of nonviolence is established in the world.

3. Regarding the three classical categories of Christ's ministry (prophet, priest, and king), rather than being a triumphant king or a holy priest, Jesus himself is considered to be a revolutionary prophet revealing social, religious, and political evils in the fallen world. The

---

194. Hengel, *The Atonement*, 51.

narratives of Jesus in the synoptic Gospels confirm Jesus' protest against the power of vested interests. Jesus' radical message of God's kingdom threatens an evil *status quo* that justifies exploitation and domination over the poor and women.

4. The crucifixion of Jesus should be directly attributed to malicious religious and political powers that violently suppress his revolutionary movement of justice and liberty. Any transcendental and violent motif involving the divine necessity of atonement, or the Father's wrath against sinners and the Son's obedient death to satisfy it, is to be eliminated. The violent view of atonement is nothing but a justification for socio-political ideologies that require sacrifice and submission.

5. The nonviolent Christologies concentrate on the vulnerable humanity of Jesus, who is inevitably victimized by evil, instead of the transcendent and unassailable deity of the Son of God. Evil has such an overwhelming power that it can ruthlessly crush Jesus to the point of a cruel death. Thus there is a dualistic and even asymmetrical relation between the seemingly omnipotent evil powers and the vulnerable human Jesus.

6. The Christological implication of Jesus' human victimization by evil is the core of a victim-oriented soteriology, because only the victimized Jesus can have solidarity with victimized humankind. As Jesus is raised from the dead by God's restorative power, the victims will be saved by God in the same way. In this regard, Jesus himself is the personal representative of all the saved victims, not the impersonal substitute for their personal identities.

7. In order to fill out the absence of Christ's deity, the nonviolent atonement scholars seek to undergird their functional Christologies by re-illuminating a multifaceted dimension of God's own restorative power—i.e., Brock's feministic erotic power, Schwager's pneumatological application, and Weaver's apocalyptic view of Jesus' resurrection.

8. There is a Christological paradox in which the helpless Jesus, who had to be violently executed by evil, ultimately has life-giving power for his community and God's kingdom of nonviolence. The human Jesus in his crucifixion is a nonviolent savior of restoration in the resurrection. In other words, the crucified and resurrected Christ is a "wounded healer" for all victimized humankind.

The benefit of having a functional Christology is that the concrete identity of the historical Jesus underlines his solidarity with suffering humans in a violent world. The person of Christ as a true human being, just like other helpless victims, is consolation for people under structural evils and increases their courage to protest the overwhelming power of evil. Jesus' ministry, crucifixion, and resurrection not only have the historical actuality of God's nonviolent resistance against evil, but they also encourage Christians to participate in the suffering of Jesus and to cooperate with God's nonviolent restoration of a violent world.

What about the ontological and epistemological analyses of Christ's crucifixion and resurrection? The nonviolent atonement theories indicate that there is neither a positive epistemology of God's revelation of saving righteousness nor an ontological implication of reconciliation and restoration in Jesus' death. The victimization shows the negative epistemology of revealing structural evils in the name of religion and politics and the human victimization of Jesus by them. By contrast, Jesus' resurrection confirms the complete opposite situation. There is a positive dimension of nonviolent restoration in both an epistemological and ontological sense, because the resurrected Christ is the visible realization of God's restorative reign of nonviolence. We can conclude that at the crux of nonviolent salvation lies an epistemologically dualistic perspective between the negativity of Jesus' victimized humanity and the positivity of God's restorative power. The epistemological frame essentially corresponds to an ontological discontinuity between Jesus' resurrection and his crucifixion.

However, the functional Christologies of Brock, Schwager, and Weaver expose a serious weakness. Their entire Christological thinking is radically limited by a human-ethical standard of nonviolence. As the nonviolent atonement theories remove all the violent motifs of Christ's atoning death, they unjustly throw out the actual content of atonement, the person and work of the crucified Christ himself.[195] At the moment of atonement, God disappears from Christ. In order to fill the gap, the nonviolent atonement scholars focus on the historical Jesus' socio-political

---

195. Love, *Love, Violence, and the Cross*, ix. According to Love, "Some critics of the idea that God reconciles us through the event of Jesus' death reject not only certain models of atonement but the need for atonement altogether. They keep salvation but not atonement, and the locus of salvation is moved off the cross back onto the power of Jesus' life and ministry, or forward to his resurrection and to our roles as partners with God in healing the world."

protest against hierarchy, or the post-resurrection church communities as the courageous followers of Jesus. Yet, without God's being and act in Jesus Christ as God-human, no one can guarantee the salvation to which Holy Scripture testifies. If these functional Christologies radically focus on the human Jesus' nonviolent ministry, life, and death, apart from his eternal deity, it would not be unfair to argue that the new Christological perspective inevitably falls into "Arianism."[196] Thus, according to George Hunsinger, nonviolent atonement scholars such as Weaver should have objectively confirmed the deity of Christ.[197] It is ambiguous whether Jesus himself is merely a divine example of nonviolence for humankind or the sole Savior of the fallen world. Rather, the incarnate Son of God whom we "worship" should be the same one whom Christians, as his disciples, must "follow."

> How could Christ be worshipped if he were not fully God? Yet how could he be followed if he were not fully human? In the high mystery of the incarnation, these affirmations could only remain in tension. Some aspects of Christ's saving office belonged uniquely to his person alone, while others were such that his disciples were invited to emulate them. Christ could not be worshipped without being followed, or followed without being worshipped. To drive a wedge between worship and discipleship, or between Christ's deity and his humanity, disparaging the one while affirming the other, could only wreak havoc on the gospel.[198]

It is no accident that a functional emphasis on Jesus' nonviolence itself distorts the hermeneutical integrity between the person and work of Christ. The human Jesus as the personal embodiment of nonviolence does not necessarily mean the divine Mediator between God and humankind, though the opposite is the biblical case.

2.5 Constructively Critical Suggestion

The common Christological denominator is Jesus' self-sacrificial death for God's kingdom of nonviolence. At stake are the Christological implications of Jesus' death. The nonviolent atonement theologians protest

---

196. Hunsinger, *The Eucharist and Ecumenism*, 288.
197. Hunsinger, *The Eucharist and Ecumenism*, 288–89.
198. Hunsinger, *The Eucharist and Ecumenism*, 285.

with one accord that the crucifixion of Jesus has no salvific efficacy, because the tragic event simply means his human victimization by the evil that violently rules the world. Jesus' crucifixion as a revolutionary prophet symbolizes the inevitable death caused by nonviolent resistance to violence and evil. At this point, I surmise that substitutionary atonement theologians are willing to accept the anthropological reinterpretation of Jesus' crucifixion, unless it is made the be-all and end-all of Jesus' passion narratives. But they would critically ask whether there should be no divine and positive dimension to the crucified Christ himself.

Regarding the person of Christ, nonviolent atonement theologians seem to concede at least that since Jesus himself is a divine figure, he has divinity in a more qualitative sense than other people. Jesus' crucifixion for God's kingdom has a relatively representative character, even if not absolutely and objectively. Thus a Christological corollary is that Christ's death far exceeds the level of human Christian martyrdom, because the divine example provides those who follow him with boundless courage to protest evil in the world. In this regard, why do the nonviolent atonement scholars avoid re-illuminating a positive dimension of Jesus' agony and his decision to accept the death in the passion narratives? According to both the synoptic Gospels and John's, while Jesus himself seems unexpectedly terrified during the prayer in the Mount of Olives, already predicting his tragic destiny of crucifixion, he does not hesitate to publicly confess himself as the Son of God in front of the chief priest, elders, and teachers.[199] The biblical testimony proves that as Jesus himself confesses himself the eternal Son of God; he is voluntarily willing to sacrifice himself for the realization of God's kingdom. It must be noted that Jesus' human weakness facing the crucifixion is inseparable from his own divine determination to dedicate himself to God's kingdom.

For Brock, even if Christ is not the only savior of the world, he still takes the communicative role for restorative salvation. We may assume that Jesus' death is his own self-sacrificial activation within the erotic power network that connects suffering humankind with God. More positively, Schwager describes Jesus' crucifixion as a nonviolent opening of himself against the evil in that self-sacrifice. The self-giving sacrifice of Jesus finally brings about God's nonviolent forgiveness and restoration. Furthermore, we should note Weaver's indirect implication of Christ's deity in the apocalyptic victory of the resurrection. The person of Christ

199. Matt 26:57–68; Mark 14:53–65; Luke 22:66–71; John 19:7.

as God-human in his self-giving death is the objective ground for nonviolently overcoming violence and evil. Considering the indivisible oneness between the crucified Christ and the resurrected one, the nonviolent atonement theologians should have acknowledged the Christological implications of the Son of God's self-sacrificial death for the salvation of sinners. Provided that Brock, Schwager, and Weaver constructively pursue a simultaneity in which the crucified Jesus is both a human victim of evil and the self-dedicating Christ, their functional Christologies would provide a more biblical, catholic, and reasonable grounding for sharing the gospel of Jesus with modern people.

3

God's Sovereign Purpose in Christ's Crucifixion

Violence or Restoration?

He [Second Isaiah] speaks of an idealized righteous person who suffers because he is righteous, challenging all the normal concepts, and claims that was both God's intention ("It was the will of the Lord to crush him," 53:10) and the servant's own choice ("He poured out himself to death," 53:12). He claims that those who were truly guilty finally came to the realization that they had been healed, forgiven (vv. 5b, 11b, 12b) because of what he suffered. Those sufferings led to death itself (vv. 8–9) and apparently to life beyond death (vv. 10–12). This may be the prophet of the future, carrying the work of his predecessors far beyond anything one of them could do—suffering worse and accomplishing more because *God is present in him* to an extent never before imagined.[1]

NONVIOLENT ATONEMENT THEOLOGIANS CLAIM that the classical understanding of God's divine intervention in Christ's substitutionary death is nothing but God's violent satisfaction by his justice, not by love. Yet in this section, I will elucidate how Anselm, Calvin, and Barth understand God's being and act in the atonement, in order to defend their

---

1. Gowan, *Theology of the Prophetic Books*, 161.

theological thought on God's sovereign satisfaction, which accomplishes the restoration of the fallen creation in Christ. More constructively, I will demonstrate that there is common ground between Weaver and the three substitutionary atonement theologians. Firstly, Anselm's satisfaction theory is basically in line with nonviolent atonement theories, because the divine purpose of atonement is the recreation of the fallen world by God's restorative justice. Next, Calvin's seemingly violent doctrine of atonement has both the objective dimension of punishment by God's retributive justice and the subjective implication of God's unconditional love for sinful humankind. Finally, I will prove that by creatively employing a biblical metaphor for God as a consuming fire, Barth puts the two contradicting motives of Anselmian restoration and Calvinistic punishment into the integrative concept of God's restorative judgment, because he argues for the dynamic union of God's justice and love in his own being. In this way, Barth's holistic atonement theology indicates that God's divine satisfaction is his own active and sovereign reconciliation with humankind, not a passive and conditional event.

3.1 Anselm: God's Honor and his Restorative Satisfaction

The Necessity to Restore God's Honor

For nonviolent atonement scholars, the most serious problem in the substitutionary perspectives is the doctrine of God's violent satisfaction, which originated from Anselm's honor-based atonement model.[2] Here we will critically review whether the divine satisfaction in which Anselm, Calvin, and Barth believe is a theological justification for violence under the name of God or not. Above all, it is important to understand Anselm's commercial analogy of sin as debt to God and God's restorative satisfaction by Christ's compensating death.

> He who does not render this honor which is due to God, robs God of his own and dishonors him; this is sin. Moreover, so long as he does not *restore* what he has taken away, he remains in fault; and it will not suffice merely to *restore* what has been taken away,

---

2. Weaver, *The Nonviolent Atonement*, 219–320. Weaver contends that although there are various modern satisfaction theories with theological modifications, all of them without exception are still under the accusation of divine violence. See *The Nonviolent Atonement*, Chapter 7, "Conversation with Anselm and His Defenders and Detractors."

but considering the contempt offered, he ought to *restore* more than he took away. For as one who imperils another's safety does not do enough by merely restoring his safety, without making some compensation for the anguish incurred; so he who violates another's honor does not enough by merely rendering honor again, but must, according to the extent of the injury done, make *restoration* in some way satisfactory to the person whom he has dishonored. We must also observe that when any one pays what he has unjustly taken away, he ought to give something which could not have been demanded of him, had he not stolen what belonged to another. So then, everyone who sins ought to pay back the honor of which he has robbed God; and this is the satisfaction which every sinner owes to God.[3]

Humankind's "debt" to God means their stealing what belongs to God himself, in that "as a rational creature" they disobey God's perfect "will."[4] Yet we need to avoid overestimating the "commercial" meaning of "debt" beyond Anselm's theological intention, because the term implies an ethical obligation that created humans must observe.[5] Moreover, Anselm claims that the original sin occurs as an objective problem to God's entire creation, because a sinner "disturbs the order and beauty of the universe."[6] In terms of God's satisfaction, Anselm obviously indicates that "the payment of honor" from the human side goes beyond a "proportionate compensation" of "the offence committed."[7] The infinite dignity of God's being is dishonored by the seriousness of sin within a dominant-subordinate relationship between God and humankind. Anselm emphasizes that in terms of divine satisfaction, sinners must consider what is beyond a financially full payment to God as a creditor, because their sins unjustly impinge upon the honor of God himself. At this point, we may critically concur with Anselm's theological presuppositions about restorative atonement. Though written in medieval times, they still seem persuasive to modern people. For instance, sinners in a human court have to pay all-inclusive compensation, including both physical and emotional injury, to those who are harmed by their crimes. The original purpose of jurisdiction is not only to inflict punishment on offenders, but also to

---

3. Anselm, "*Cur Deus Homo*," *Basic Writings*, 202. Italics mine.
4. Anselm, "*Cur Deus Homo*," *Basic Writings*, 202.
5. McIntyre, *St. Anselm and His Critics*, 73.
6. Anselm, "*Cur Deus Homo*," *Basic Writings*, 223.
7. McIntyre, *St. Anselm and His Critics*, 94.

rehabilitate victims from dishonor and pain. What Anselm theologically pursues is the restoration of fallen humankind, which was originally the perfect creation of God himself. God mercifully cannot fail to restore the fallen humanity that he creates. The restorative atonement for human sin is the sovereign actualization of God's original and irrevocable plan of creation.[8] By accentuating God's restorative atonement for the fallen creation, Anselm is able to emphasize that God's eternal "compassion" for sinners is no less than God's infinite "holiness" against their sins.[9]

Anselm stipulates two decisive factors that must be required for the restorative satisfaction of God's honor. One is "the immutability of his [God's] honor," which corresponds to God's eternal being of perfection.[10] The other is God's sovereign will to maintain the order of his perfect creation.[11] Anselm's doctrine of atonement is aimed at demonstrating the harmony of God's perfect being and his will to maintain the whole of creation. With regard to the necessity of atonement, Anselm qualifies divine sovereignty as fundamentally different from a sort of "necessity" that amounts to "compulsion," or a kind of "impossibility" that means "restraint" in the dimension of human inevitability.[12] Rather, Anselm argues for God's self-determination of atonement by his own free will.

> Since, then, he [God] does what he chooses and nothing else, as no necessity or impossibility exists before his choice or refusal, so neither do they interfere with his acting or not acting, though it be true that his choice and action are immutable. And as, when God does a thing, since it has been done it cannot be undone, but must remain an actual fact; still, we are not correct in saying that it is impossible for God to prevent a past action from being what it is. For there is no necessity or impossibility in the case whatever but the simple will of God, which chooses that truth should be eternally the same, for he himself is truth.[13]

---

8. Anselm, "Cur Deus Homo," *Basic Writings*, 256. It cannot be exaggerated that we may consider Anselm's emphasis on God's restorative atonement for fallen creation to be a sort of incipient stage in God's apocalyptic recreation, which modern theologians re-illuminate.

9. Anselm, "Cur Deus Homo," *Basic Writings*, 300.

10. Anselm, "Cur Deus Homo," *Basic Writings*, 286.

11. Anselm, "Cur Deus Homo," *Basic Writings*, 258.

12. Anselm, "Cur Deus Homo," *Basic Writings*, 288.

13. Anselm, "Cur Deus Homo," *Basic Writings*, 287–88.

God's self-determining character is revealed in the biblical testimony on Christ's death, in which "he offered because it was his own will." Anselm accurately considers "a subsequent necessity arising from the thing itself" to be the case of God's necessity, in lieu of "an antecedent necessity" that is "the cause of a thing."[14] Since "no necessity" can exist before God's own eternal will, Anselm logically proves that God's divine necessity is grounded upon his own inner being.[15] It must be noted that unlike the misunderstanding of his later critics (such as Abelard), Anselm's theological insight on the divine necessity means that God is never forced to do anything by "any alien necessity."[16] Rather, God himself sovereignly wills his own necessity for the purpose of continuing to preserve his perfect being and doing the divine work of creation and salvation. God's restorative will in his being precedes any kind of external necessity. The atonement means God's own self-decision to preserve God's creation and to restore his honor, which is impaired by human sin as moral irresponsibility. It can be concluded that, unlike the nonviolent atonement scholars' misconstruction, Anselm's theological concept of God's honor is a restorative justice for saving sinners, not retributive justice against them.

Anselm and Weaver's Restorative Soteriology as God's Non-Punishment

In contrast with a Calvinistic doctrine of penal substitution, Anselm's restorative view of God's satisfaction by Christ's sacrifice has more substantial similarities with the nonviolent atonement theories.[17] Anselm insists that "the punishment of the sinner" fails to give "honor to God," because "when the sinner does not repay what he took away, but is punished, if the punishment of the sinner is not to the honor of God, then God loses his honor and does not regain it." This "seems contrary" to the fact that God constantly preserves his honor.[18] According to Anselm, God's satisfaction by Christ's compensatory death never necessitates

14. Anselm, "*Cur Deus Homo*," *Basic Writings*, 290.
15. Anselm, "*Cur Deus Homo*," *Basic Writings*, 291.
16. Weingart, *The Logic of Divine Love*, 90.
17. For constructive research, see Reesor-Taylor, "Anselm's *Cur Deus Homo* for a Peace Theology," 180–81. Reesor-Taylor contends that Anselm never justifies divine violence in the crucifixion of Christ. Rather, the crucial motif of atonement is God's restorative justice, which is essentially in line with the theology of nonviolence.
18. Anselm, "*Cur Deus Homo*," *Basic Writings*, 221.

his punishment of creation. For Anselm, the absolute necessity of God's satisfaction is not so much "legal" as "moral."[19] According to Rachel Reesor-Taylor, Weaver totally misconstrues the necessity of God's satisfaction as divinely sanctioned violence.[20] Yet, regarding the justice of God's salvation, Anselm himself believes that restorative satisfaction is a much better option than unconditional forgiveness or retributive punishment.[21] Anselm presumes "the necessity of punishment" as a hypothetical possibility, but only so as to highlight the alternative God has in fact chosen: satisfaction.[22] Christ's compensatory death for God's honor, and his punishing of sinners, are mutually exclusive. The former achieves the restoration of the fallen creation, whereas the latter merely causes the destruction of the entire world. For Anselm, God's punishment of a sinner cannot bring about his satisfaction, in that the retributive event simply causes either "the annihilation of the sinner" or "the eternal torments of hell."[23] Thus God's satisfaction cannot be fulfilled by his punishment. In a forensic image of atonement, Aulén fails to distinguish Anselm's concept of satisfaction and that of the later Protestant theologians, who develop the juridical formulation of God's vindicatory justice by punishment.[24] Anselm never argues for God's forensic satisfaction through punishment. Dániel Deme rightly observes that divine satisfaction as "the restoration of God's honor" denies any possibility of God's punishment of sinful humankind as the destruction of his creation.[25]

> The punishment of the sinner cannot have the last word in the restoration of the honor of God and the order of the universe, since it does not answer the demand of God's original plans with humankind, which is to bring it to the state of eternal blessedness and a perfect communion with his divine self.[26]

While God's forensic judgment seems to fit with his vindicatory justice, violent judgment itself contradicts God's restorative will to maintain his perfection creation. Therefore, it is remarkable that compared

19. McIntyre, *St. Anselm and His Critics*, 93–94.
20. Reesor-Taylor, "Anselm's *Cur Deus Homo* for a Peace Theology," 173.
21. Anselm, "Cur Deus Homo," *Basic Writings*, 180.
22. McIntyre, *St. Anselm and His Critics*, 97.
23. McIntyre, *St. Anselm and His Critics*, 196.
24. McIntyre, *St. Anselm and His Critics*, 199.
25. Deme, *The Christology of Anselm of Canterbury*, 91.
26. Deme, *The Christology of Anselm of Canterbury*, 91.

to Calvin and Barth, Anselm sets himself closer to the nonviolent perspectives on atonement, because Anselm denies the absolute necessity of God's forensic judgment against his fallen creation. In this way, Anselm theologically separates the restorative-commercial dimension of atonement from God's destructive-juridical verdict at the crucifixion of Christ. It must be noted that Anselm's dualistic distinction between the positive aspect of restoration and the negative one of punishment is in line with the nonviolent atonement theories in the epistemological sense. God's satisfaction is solely achieved by the nonviolent restoration of fallen creation, not a violent punishment that means the annihilation of God's creation. Here there is a decisive affinity between Anselm and Weaver. Just as Anselm strives to prove that God's work of salvation as recreation has nothing to do with his destructive punishment, so Weaver believes in a separation between divine judgment and human restoration. It is noteworthy that although Weaver criticizes the violent motif of satisfaction in the Anselmian doctrine of atonement, he fundamentally follows Anselm's theological assumption that punishment cannot bring about restoration. According to Weaver, nonviolent atonement is grounded upon the absolute necessity of God's forgiveness.

> Forgiveness is true and should be practiced by Christians first of all because it emerges from the story of Jesus and what that story reveals to us about the character of God. Forgiveness works and it is true because it is of God. The intersection of psychology and theology at the juncture of forgiveness is important. Theology does touch the world of human experience, and in this case evidence from empirical science validates a theological claim. The idea of a lived theology that expresses the nonviolence of Jesus has points of appeal in human experience as well as in biblical material and theological logic. The exercise of restorative justice is an area where insights derived from the narrative of Jesus intersect with evidence derived from human experience.[27]

With his own theological presupposition that God's being and work can be explained and validated by the anthropocentric view of nonviolence, Weaver indeed seems to believe that God's saving righteousness only consists of "restorative justice" by forgiveness. A loving God should not execute vindicatory justice against sinners, because retribution is a kind of violent destruction that both humankind and God must not commit. Rather, God reveals himself in the nonviolent life of Jesus, in

---

27. Weaver, *The Nonviolent God*, 215.

order to teach humans his saving truth of restoration, which is a practical application of nonviolence to their human life.

> Restorative justice is an alternative to retributive justice. Whereas retributive justice focuses on the end goal of administering punishment fairly, restorative justice has the end goal of restoring the relationship broken by the offense. Although obviously some or even many shattered relationships can never be fully restored, the goal remains to restore them as far as possible. For restorative justice, justice is being done when the relationship between victim and offender is being restored, which involves healing of both victim and offender. This approach addresses needs not dealt with by the justice system, which focuses on determining guilt and meting out retribution as punishment.[28]

Anselm claims that his restorative atonement model underscores "how great a burden sin is" in front of God.[29] From the human side, there must be an infinitely valuable offering to restore God's eternal honor. Without the satisfaction of God, who is offended by sinful humans, there cannot be any objective reconciliation between the two parties. In the same way, according to Weaver's nonviolent atonement theory, a sinner must "recognize" the seriousness of sinning against a victim and "take responsibility for his or her actions," which ethically corresponds to "the punishment of retributive justice.[30] At this point, we can see how the divine necessity of restoration, which Anselm argues for in *Cur Deus Homo*, is theologically transposed into the human perspective in Weaver's nonviolent atonement. The vertical perspective on a destructive problem between God and fallen humanity in Anselm's doctrine of atonement is horizontally represented in Weaver's interpersonal concern for "victim and offenders." Therefore, Anselm's restorative satisfaction theory represents an intersection between nonviolent theories and substitutionary theories. In terms of God's ultimate purpose in atonement, nonviolent restoration lies at the heart of both Anselm and Weaver's theological discussion on God's saving work in Christ. While there is a doctrinal dissimilarity regarding whether God's intervention in the crucifixion of Christ is sovereign or inevitable, Weaver and other nonviolent atonement theologians should be aware of the common denominator of restoration.

---

28. Weaver, *The Nonviolent God*, 215.
29. Anselm, "*Cur Deus Homo*," *Basic Writings*, 242.
30. Weaver, *The Nonviolent God*, 216.

However, I cannot but a raise a hermeneutical question about both Anselm and Weaver's restorative atonement models. Without any implication of negative ontology—God's annihilation of sin and evil through his divine judgment—could there be a purely nonviolent restoration of the fallen creation? The seemingly nonviolent process of transforming fallen creation into perfection must be preceded by God's obliteration of the sin that impairs the beauty of God's creational order, or the evil itself that violently destroys humankind. Anselm and Weaver's dualistic perspective between God's *positive* work of restoration and evil's *negative* work of destruction cannot offer a practical solution for getting rid of sin itself. Weaver overestimates the cognitive dimension of "restorative justice" too much to see God's sovereign intervention in annihilating sin by his own vindicatory justice, which is the negative side of God's saving righteousness.[31] Likewise, as we have critically observed in the nonviolent atonement theories, Anselm's restorative perspective on God's nonpunishment in his atoning work totally disregards how God annihilates sin and evil in the fallen creation.

Anselm's constructive motif of restoration seems to contradict the destructive phenomenon of Christ's death. We cannot but witness the fact that God's violent intervention takes place in the atoning death of Christ. Why does Anselm believe that God never punishes human sin and the evil powers that victimize the suffering world? Are they a sort of disorder or pollution that cannot affect God's perfect being? Anselm answers the relationship between sin, evil, and God's honor as follows.[32] Concerning God's being himself, God's honor is inviolable in the eternal sense. Yet regarding the disorder caused by Adam's sin of disobedience, his honor is violated in the temporal sense. In the scholastic reasoning, there is no objective necessity for God's judgment against sin and evil. Although Anselm rightly observes that God's eternal aseity is never damaged by humanity's fall and their sins, Anselm's honor-based view of atonement fails to recognize the destructive power of evil on humans themselves. The almighty and righteous God is simply satisfied with the eternal restoration of his own transcendental honor, without solving the urgent and immanent problems of sin in human time and space. Regrettably, there seems to be no hermeneutical room for the biblical revelation of God's righteous judgment against sin in Anselm's scholastic doctrine of atonement.

---

31. Weaver, *The Nonviolent God*, 217.
32. Anselm, "*Cur Deus Homo*," *Basic Writings*, 222–23.

More seriously, Anselmian satisfaction theory assumes that God's honor is a sort of separate and independent standard that controls the atoning work of God himself.[33] Anselm's commercial understanding of God's honor is so effective as to reveal his restorative justice for the fallen world. Yet, in terms of the cause of Christ' death, Anselm over-accentuates the absolute necessity of the atonement for the sake of restoring the Father's honor. The Anselmian God seems to be inevitably obliged to observe the external standard of commercializing honor that radically impairs the divine integrity of God's compensating justice and his free grace in his own inner being. Despite Anselm's emphasis on God's salvation "for our sakes,"[34] his scholastic concept of atonement is based on the asymmetrical relation between God as the merciful feudal Lord and fallen humans as rebellious tenants in economic insolvency. Without the restoration of God's honor through the death of Christ, there is no forgiveness of our sins and reconciliation with God.

It is impossible to deny that Anselm's scholastic reflection on God's being and work is grounded upon a medieval feudal social system in which an honorable Lord should take responsibility for what his tenants had done wrong. If Christ must make the atonement of compensation for sinners' debts, for the sake of the eternal maintenance of God's inviolable honor, then the atoning death must be primarily necessary for God's honor, not for sinful humans. Thus it would not be unfair to say that for Anselm, the salvation of sinners is the concomitant consequence of God's restoration of the honor violated by their sins. Regarding God's honor being satisfied by Christ's compensating death, I would like to raise a question on whether Anselm's scholastic God can sacrifice his infinite honor in order to save sinners. The Anselmian God focuses on maintaining his perfect being and the cosmological order of his entire creation. However, Anselm should have biblically considered that God's atonement in Christ not only reveals the perfect harmony between God's eternal being and his infinite justice in himself, but also actualizes his self-sacrificial Fatherly love towards sinners in Christ.

33. Yet my theological evaluation also tolerates a charitable reinterpretation of Anselm's honor-based theology of atonement. For thoughtful research on the issue, see Sonderegger, "Anselmian Atonement." According to Katherine Sonderegger, while the "theological Anselm's" scholastic reflection on the satisfaction of God's honor is criticized for its necessity of violent atonement, the "historical Anselm's" original intention is to maintain that God's honor is his divine and unchanging love and restorative justice for the entire world created by himself.

34. Anselm, "*Cur Deus Homo*," *Basic Writings*, 158.

3.2. Calvin's Paradoxical View on the Simultaneity of Judgment and Salvation

God's Forensic Satisfaction

Calvin humbly confesses that the atoning death of Christ is "a singular mystery" beyond the scope of human reason and experience.[35] Calvin focuses on describing Christ's atonement according to three biblical concepts: penal substitution, vicarious sacrifice, and victory over sin and death.[36] Nevertheless, Calvin's doctrine of atonement has been typically classified as one of "the Latin type"—that is, a variation on Anselm's satisfaction view.[37] Aulén points out that "the Latin type" fails to connect the incarnation with the doctrine of objective satisfaction, wherein Christ's human obedience and death are overemphasized as penal punishment, without taking into consideration the dynamics of the deity and sovereignty of God in Christ.[38] Importantly, although Calvin is emphatic about the forensic aspect of Christ's crucifixion, he never attempts to systematize the forensic logic of atonement, unlike later Calvinists.[39] According to Louis Berkhof, Reformed orthodoxy argues for "the Anselmian doctrine of *absolute* necessity of atonement," based on God's eternal justice, whereas Calvin believes in "a relative or hypothetical necessity of atonement" grounded upon God's free sovereignty.[40] While Calvinism doctrinally reinforces the Anselmian claim that the incarnation is absolutely necessary for God's retributive justice, Calvin himself answers *Cur Deus Homo* by referring to God the Father's "heavenly decree"—"Immanuel, that is God with us" (Isa 7:14; Matt 1:23).[41] Calvin goes on to argue for God's eternal choice to fulfil the reconciliation in, through,

---

35. Calvin, *Institutes* II.16.6.

36. Peterson, *Calvin and the Atonement*, 69–100. Robert A. Peterson defines the three major themes "Christ the Victor," "Christ Our Legal Substitute," and "Christ Our Sacrifice" in a balanced way. However, he is reluctant to choose the key concept in Calvin's doctrine of atonement.

37. Aulén, *Christus Victor*, 128–33.

38. Aulén, *Christus Victor*, 152.

39. For an excellent essay on the difference between the theology of Calvin and Calvinism, see Muller, "Was Calvin a Calvinist?" Muller insists that "unique or individualized doctrinal formulation was not Calvin's goal."

40. Berkhof, *Systematic Theology*, 406.

41. Calvin, *Institutes* II.12.1.

and with Christ, because "God solely of his own pleasure appointed him Mediator to obtain salvation for us."[42]

Calvin places a heavy emphasis on the biblical truth that God's divine love takes the initiative to bring about the atonement (John 3:15, 1 John 4:10).[43] While Christ's atoning death itself is "the second and proximate cause," the love of God is "the highest cause or origin" of God's reconciliation in Christ.[44] He even states that "apart from God's pleasure Christ could not merit anything."[45] Regarding the relation of God's love and his justice, Calvin believes that for God, "the beginning of love is righteousness."[46] God's love towards sinners is not opposed to his justice against sin. The two attributes of God are not in a relationship of conflicting opposition in God's being, but inter-complementing harmony. God takes the initiative for atonement, because God is eternal love, and he eternally loves sinners in Christ. Yet the divine love of God for sinners is not without his justice against sin. Rather, God's saving love accomplishes his righteousness of salvation. God saves sinners by imputing the saving righteousness of Christ to them. For Calvin, the righteousness of Christ's merit is distinguished from God's love. God's love and Christ's grace are a unity, but with "distinction," because God's love needs to be satisfied with Christ's saving work as his merit for us.[47] Rather than scholastically inferring how Christ's atoning death infinitely restores God's honor, Calvin directly illuminates the scriptural testimonies on God's eternal love by his free will in Christ. God is the Savior whom the Bible testifies is not an abstract deity of honor who is passively satisfied with Christ's death as the offering. The sovereign subject of atonement is God the Father, who reveals himself and reconciles the fallen creation to himself in Christ. In this way, Calvin theologically distances himself from Anselmian satisfaction theory, in which God's being and his atoning work must be involved with an absolute condition or external standard apart from God himself.

Yet there is no doubt that Calvin believes in Christ's penal substitutionary death, in which "He bore the weight of divine severity since he was 'stricken and afflicted' (cf. Isa 53:5) by God's hand, and experienced all the

---

42. Calvin, *Institutes* II.17.1.
43. Calvin, *Institutes* II.17.2.
44. Calvin, *Institutes* II.17.2.
45. Calvin, *Institutes* II.17.2.
46. Calvin, *Institutes* II.17.2.
47. Calvin, *Institutes* II.17.2.

signs of a wrathful and avenging God."[48] Although Calvin has a strong theological affinity with Anselm's concept of sin as personal and direct guilt before God, Calvin's idea of sin never remains at the relational level. Calvin claims, "by the fall of and revolt of Adam, the whole human race was delivered to the curse, and degenerated from its original condition."[49] We need to notice that Calvin's doctrine of sin directly relates the personal iniquities of sinners to the negative effect of the sins as guilt that brings about their eternal destruction under the evil powers. Calvin insists that "so great was the disagreement between our uncleanness and God's perfect purity! . . . without a Mediator. What, then, of man: plunged by his mortal ruin into death and hell, defiled with so many spots, befouled with his own corruption, and overwhelmed with every curse?"[50] Since original sin immediately enslaves humans to the evil powers and brings death to sinners, no one can escape from universal ruin and God's righteous wrath. Thus Calvin goes on to argue that the atoning work of Christ is to forensically take the punishment of God upon himself in order to satisfy the requirement of "God's righteous judgment."[51] Calvin insists that "our Lord came forth as true human and took the person and the name of Adam in order to take Adam's place in obeying the Father, to present our flesh as the price of satisfaction to God's judgment, and, in the same flesh, to pay the penalty that we had deserved."[52]

Here Calvin arrives at the crux of his penal substitutionary interpretation of the doctrine of atonement. Above all, God must satisfy himself by punishing sin and evil through Christ's atoning death. According to Calvin, "no common assurance is required, for God's wrath and curse always lie upon sinners until they are absolved of guilt. Since he is a righteous Judge, he does not allow his law to be broken without punishment, but is equipped to avenge it."[53] Without God's satisfaction as the "righteous Judge" in atonement, there is no way to guarantee objective reconciliation between God and fallen creation. Here Calvin justifies God's violent intervention by qualifying his vindicatory justice against sin, because "it is rebellion against the will of God, which of necessity

48. Calvin, *Institutes* II.16.11.
49. Calvin, *Institutes* II.1.1.
50. Calvin, *Institutes* II.12.1.
51. Calvin, *Institutes* II.12.3.
52. Calvin, *Institutes* II.12.3.
53. Calvin, *Institutes* II.16.1.

provokes God's wrath, and it is a violation of the law, upon which God's judgment is pronounced without exception."[54] Nevertheless, although God should judge the rebellious sinners, he determines to reveal himself as "Redeemer in the person of his only-begotten Son."[55] Calvin highlights the fact that God's atoning work solely takes place in Christ, for apart from the Mediator, there is no knowledge and power of salvation. How can God in Christ reconcile himself with sinners?

> However much we may be sinners by our own fault, we nevertheless remain his creatures. However much we have brought death upon ourselves, yet he has created us unto life. Thus he is moved by pure and freely given love of us to receive us into grace. Since there is a perpetual and irreconcilable disagreement between righteousness and unrighteousness, so long as we remain sinners he cannot receive us completely. Therefore, to take away all cause for enmity and to reconcile us utterly to himself, *he wipes out all evil* in us by the expiation set forth in the death of Christ . . . Therefore, by his love God the Father goes before and anticipates our reconciliation in Christ.[56]

For Calvin, the core of atonement is not God's violent execution of his Son, but his objective removal of sin and evil through Christ's atoning death. God's judgment in the crucifixion is the annihilation of what is detestable in his beloved humankind, which God himself created by love in Christ. The historical reality of atonement corresponds to the merciful Father's eternal love before the foundation of the world.

Moreover, for Calvin, God's judgment is inseparable from Christ's self-sacrificial death for us. There is a simultaneity in Calvin's theology of Christ's penal and cultic substitution. Jaeseung Cha rightly observes that due to "the externality of death," "punishment" cannot be the sole actuality to communicate "the internal reality of God's self-sacrifice" to fallen humans in Calvin's doctrine of atonement.[57] Yet it does not necessarily follow that to avoid absolutizing the forensic motif is to nullify the reality of Christ's penal substitutionary death for sinners. Rather, the biblical truth that Christ became "a curse" in the crucifixion means, for Calvin, his taking "the reality of human sin" upon his own vicarious humanity

---

54. Calvin, *Institutes* II.8.59.
55. Calvin, *Institutes* II.6.1.
56. Calvin, *Institutes* II.16.3. Emphasis mine.
57. Cha, "Calvin's Concept of Penal Substitution," 127.

in the place of God's holy judgment.[58] Furthermore, defining God as the righteous judge, Calvin believes that Christ stands not as an innocent victim but as the priest, for the purpose of propitiating God's wrath. Calvin places Christ's priestly work in the center of the forensic context, in order to describe what can appease the wrath of God and how the work can be done. According to Calvin, "advocate" and "high priest" are interchangeable concepts for Christ's atoning ministry.[59]

> At this point, Christ interceded as his advocate, took upon himself and suffered the punishment that, from God's righteous judgment, threatened all sinners; that dominant he purged with his blood those evils which had rendered sinners hateful to God; that by this expiation he made satisfaction and sacrifice duly to God the Father.[60]

Calvin comprehends the relational concept of Christ's crucifixion as his vicarious suffering of God's "punishment" of sinners, from the throne of "God's righteous judgment." Calvin accentuates the content of the atonement, in which the "blood" that Christ shed from the cross made "expiation" for sinners, for the sake of "satisfaction and sacrifice" to God.[61] In this regard, Calvin's doctrine demonstrates a solid biblical and theological rationality, in which a gracious God righteously judges sin and evil, in order to save sinners and the fallen world.

Nonetheless, it is somewhat regrettable that in a number of exegeses of texts on Christ's crucifixion (Isa 53:9; Rom 3:24; Gal 3:13), with few exceptions, Calvin directly applies the human logic of legal retribution into God's judgment. According to Colin E. Gunton, if one interprets "too *literally*" what the Scripture says about atonement, one cannot grasp "the metaphorical nature of the language."[62] Due to a literal understanding of a specific metaphor, the dynamic character of the metaphor not only disappears, but also becomes a fixed theory at the static level of logic. In this regard, Calvin often goes too far beyond the hermeneutical boundaries of the biblical metaphors about God's judgment. Robert S. Paul accurately

---

58. Cha, "Calvin's Concept of Penal Substitution," 125.
59. Van Buren, *Christ in Our Place*, 69.
60 Calvin, *Institutes* II.16.2.
61 Calvin, *Institutes* II.16.2.
62. Gunton, *The Actuality of Atonement*, 64. Gunton illustrates that "it is as if, when Mark reports Jesus as saying that he had come to give his life as a ransom for many, we were to speculate about how much money was to be handed over and to whom (Mark 10.45)."

God's Sovereign Purpose in Christ's Crucifixion

indicates that "the theory of penal substitution" is the essence of Calvin's view of the atonement "in the sacrificial context" of "the Bible's plan for salvation."[63] Calvin's interpretation gives the impression that Christ's sacrifice and his victory are nothing but the means and result of his penal substitutionary death. In contrast with Anselm, Calvin is deductively inclined to concentrate on God's vindicatory justice against sin rather than his restorative righteousness for the fallen creation.

For those in favor of penal substitution, God's judgment is an essential motif of atonement in Scripture, because the divine judgment against sin and evil is the objective grounding for the restoration of the fallen world. Yet at a fundamental level, the biblical motif of God's judgment heavily relies on human analogy. On the one hand, the metaphorical approach is uncritically inclined to claim that, just as a king or a feudal Lord, God must observe the divine law of justice in an external way.[64] On the other hand, the apologetic presuppositions of evangelical doctrine depend on humankind's inner "conscience" in front of the holy God.[65] I firmly agree with the basic principle of penal substitution in which sin must be punished by the holy Triune God on the judgment seat.[66] That is the undeniable biblical truth. Yet I am deeply concerned with the way in which God's atoning act is deductively and directly explained by a human concept of law and the forensic logic in penal substitution theory.

It is remarkable to note that according to the modern Reformed theologian Hans Boersma, there is a hermeneutical one-sidedness in the

---

63. Paul, *The Atonement and the Sacraments*, 102–3.

64. Holmes, "Can Punishment Bring Peace?," 114. Holmes compares God's law to the Magna Carta, which "is still celebrated, because it codifies the revolutionary idea that there are some things that even kings cannot do: there is a law that is not merely the decree of fiat of whoever happens to hold sovereignty, but which is somehow, within the nature of things, binding on all human beings." I basically agree with the conclusive truth, but not with the intuitive approach.

65. Packer, *In My Place Condemned He Stood*, 82–83. According to Packer, God's judgment in penal substitution presupposes that the divine principle of forensic retribution works against our guilt in the past, present, and future, such that our "conscience" proclaims God's law of "retribution" to be just. I believe that our repentant faith confirms Christ's penal substitutionary death.

66. "I [*God*] will punish the world for its evil, the wicked for their sins" (Isa 13:11); "For we must all appear before the judgment seat of *Christ*, so that each of us may receive what is due us for the things done while in the body, whether good or bad" (2 Cor 5:10); "When he [*the Holy Spirit*] comes, he will prove the world to be in the wrong about sin and righteousness and judgment" (John 16:8). The Holy Trinity judges the sins of the world!

overaccentuation of God's juridical violence in the Augustinian and Calvinistic understanding of the crucifixion of Christ.

> The problem with the development of atonement theology does not lie with the notion of punishment as such. Punishments are based on laws, and the concept of law obviously plays an important role in the biblical witness. To affirm a juridical element in the atonement does not mean, however that we should *reduce* the atonement to juridical elements, to law court scenes, or to notions of personal forgiveness of sins. When I speak about the juridicizing of the atonement, I have in mind a form of reductionism that limits the divine-human relationship to juridical categories, and that views the cross solely in terms of laws, infractions, judicial pronouncements, forgiveness, and punishments.[67]

It is evident that at the heart of the Reformed tradition, from Calvin and even to Barth, lies a strong tendency to explain atonement through the lens of penal substitution in the primary sense. It overaccentuates the penal dimension of substitutionary doctrine, as if Christ's saving work could be solely confirmed and explained in terms of forensic logic. The overemphasis on one aspect of Christ's atoning work rather than Christ himself unavoidably distorts the theological integrity of Christ's person and work.[68] Consequently, the absolutizing of atonement's specific dimension separates Christ's saving work from Christ himself. Therefore we need to be alert to the absolutization of the retributive logic of God's satisfaction, in that the death of Christ for God's satisfaction cannot be the be-all and end-all of his atonement. As the theological founder of penal substitution theory, Calvin neglects to consider that God's judgment of sin by Christ's death is a penultimate method through which God achieves his ultimate goal of saving sinners in Christ.

Likewise, what is yet unresolved in Calvin's theology of atonement is the relationship between God's love and justice in his being. Calvin humbly confesses that there is indeed "some sort of contradiction" on the issue: "(A) We were enemies of God until we were reconciled to Christ,

---

67. Boersma, *Violence, Hospitality, and the Cross*, 163–64.

68. Similarly, Roman Catholicism overemphasizes the sacrificial effect of the Mass, as if it were only through participation in the sacrifice of Christ that we can be reconciled to God in Christ. Matthew Levering, *Sacrifice and Community*, 115. However, salvation is possible for us, not because Christ offered himself to God in the form of "sacrifice," but because Christ gave himself for us as the eternal sacrifice.

and (B) God had already embraced us with his free favor."⁶⁹ In order to solve the dilemma, Calvin strives to emphasize that God's love towards sinners precedes his wrath against sin in Christ's atonement.⁷⁰ However, Calvin hardly gets out of the doctrinal impasse regarding the fact that the unconditional love of God must be satisfied with the absolute condition of his penal justice. Thus it cannot be denied that Calvin's theology tends to separate God's penal justice against sin and Christ's vicarious love towards sinners. The hermeneutical integrity of God's noetic and ontic aspects in his atoning work becomes inscrutable in Calvin's phenomenal and temporal analysis of God's satisfaction by Christ's substitution.⁷¹ Nevertheless, even if Calvin's theological issue of contradiction or paradox between God's unconditional love and his penal justice seems to be a dilemma on the human plane, we must keep in mind that from the ontological standpoint of God's being and will for us from eternity, there is a dramatically consistent harmony between God's saving righteousness and his eternal self-sacrificial love in Christ. Calvin's biblical-revelation-centered perspective on atonement inductively confirms that saved sinners who were the enemies of God finally come to realize God the Father's eternal love, which recreates their sinful beings in Christ, and the divine justice that annihilates sin and evil.⁷²

Calvin and Weaver on the Cognitive Dimension of the Crucifixion

It is interesting to see that Calvin's substitutionary atonement theology has a subjective and epistemic approach that the nonviolent atonement theologian Weaver can share. We should take notice of Calvin's dramatic reinterpretation of Christ's penal substitution, in light of Pilate's illegal

69. Helm, *John Calvin's Ideas*, 392. Cited from Calvin, *Institutes* II.16.2.

70. Calvin, *Institutes* II.16.4.

71. According to Bruce L. McCormack, if we uncritically follow Calvin's cognitive logic of "divine accommodation," it follows that "the way God reveals himself to be is not finally commensurate with what he is in himself." Bruce L. McCormack, "For Us and our Salvation," 302.

72. "But God demonstrates his own love for us in this: While we were still sinners, Christ died for us. Since we have now been justified by his blood, how much more shall we be saved from God's wrath through him! For if, while we were God's enemies, we were reconciled to him through the death of his Son, how much more, having been reconciled, shall we be saved through his life!" (Rom 5:8–10). In his theological exegesis, Calvin dramatically describes the core of Pauline soteriology, though there seems to be a theological over-accentuation of God's penal justice.

verdict in an evil world. Stephen Edmondson rightly observes that the clause in the Apostles' Creed that "Christ suffered Pontius Pilate" plays a pivotal role in Calvin's view of educating believers on the biblical truth of substitution.[73]

> The curse caused by our guilt was awaiting us at God's heavenly judgment seat. Accordingly, Scripture first relates Christ's condemnation before Pontius Pilate, governor of Judea, to *teach* us that the penalty to which we were subject had been imposed upon this righteous man.[74]

We should note that, beyond an objective discussion of atonement, Calvin's biblical narration includes subjective implications.

> We could not escape God's dreadful judgment. To deliver us from it, Christ allowed himself to be condemned before a mortal man—even a wicked and profane man. . . . we may *learn* what Isaiah teaches: "Upon him was the chastisement of our peace, and with his stripes we are healed" [Isa. 53:5]. To take away our condemnation. To take away our condemnation, it was not enough for him to suffer any kind of death: to make satisfaction for our redemption a form of death had to be chosen in which he might free us both by transferring our condemnation to himself and by taking our guilt upon himself.[75]

Calvin recapitulates the very crux of penal substitution that Weaver criticizes. Yet Calvin never explains the logic of Christ's penal substitution from the transcendent and timeless dimension of a heavenly seat of righteous judgment. Rather, Calvin attempts to concretely describe the historical process of Jesus' death for sinners through the lens of the biblical testimony of Pilate's unfair judgment.

> If he had been murdered by thieves or slain in an insurrection by a raging mob, in such a death there would have been no evidence of satisfaction. But when he was arraigned before the judgment seat as a criminal, accused and pressed by testimony, and condemned by the mouth of the judge to die—we know by these proofs that he took the *role* of a guilty man and evil doer.
>
> Thus we shall behold the person of a sinner and evildoer represented in Christ, yet from his shining innocence it will at the

---

73. Edmondson, *Calvin's Christology*, 99.
74. Calvin, *Institutes* II.16.5. Emphasis is mine.
75. Calvin, *Institutes* II.16.5. Emphasis is mine.

same time be obvious that he was burdened with another's sin rather than his own. He therefore suffered under Pontius Pilate, and by the governor's official sentence was reckoned among criminals. Yet not so—for he was declared righteous by his judge at the same time, when Pilate affirmed that he "found no cause for complaint in him" (John 18:38). This is our acquittal: the guilt that held us liable for punishment has been transferred to the head of the Son of God (Isa 53:12). We must, above all, remember this substitution lest we tremble and remain anxious throughout life—as if God's righteous vengeance, which the Son of God has taken upon himself, still hung over us.[76]

By underlining the "role" of sinful humankind, Calvin goes on to accentuate humanity's dramatic participation in Jesus' passion narrative in front of Pilate. It is through the theological exegesis that Calvin emphasizes the subjective-existential realization of saved sinners in Christ. The paradoxical truth of Pilate's unrighteous verdict against Christ and his public testimony of Christ's sinlessness dramatically shows that we cannot avoid God's condemnation against our sinful being; simultaneously, we are also freely justified by the righteousness of Christ in our sinful place. Calvin's intention in his dramatic description of the judging Pilate and the judged Christ is to subjectively apply the divine mystery of penal substitution—why the innocent Son of God must be crucified—to the heart of believers in Christ. Hence Calvin's biblical soteriology confirms that God's objective atonement must correspond to a subjective human awareness for the sake of assurance of salvation.

At this point, let us turn to Weaver's nonviolent atonement theory, narrative *Christus Victor*. Regarding God's nonviolent love in the crucifixion, Weaver, like Calvin, takes an epistemic approach to biblical revelation. It is remarkable to see that unlike other nonviolent scholars, Weaver is right to emphasize the biblical identity of humans as sinners. Weaver underlines that we are accomplices of the same evil that killed Jesus on the cross.[77] According to Weaver, sinful humankind's "role" was to crucify the innocent Jesus against the dualistic background of the evil powers and God's kingdom.[78] Weaver accurately points out that the traditional soteriological views focus on believers' "collective" act of participation in Christ's saving atonement, by "bypassing" their reflective process

---

76. Calvin, *Institutes* II.16.5. Emphasis mine.
77. Weaver, *The Nonviolent Atonement*, 93.
78. Weaver, *The Nonviolent Atonement*, 93.

of "identification" with "sin."[79] By employing the term "identification," Weaver vividly describes the seriousness of our sins in the event of Jesus' crucifixion.[80] It is to be noted that Weaver's hamartiology is much more scripturally based than other nonviolent scholars'.

> To confess to being a "sinner" is not merely an abstract concept involving a debt owed to the divine honor. Being a sinner means to acknowledge our identification with those who killed Jesus and our bondage to the powers that enslaved them. Every human being, by virtue of what human society is, participates in and is in bondage to those powers and is therefore implicated in the killing of Jesus . . . When Jesus died "for us," on "our behalf," we are implicated in his death as partners with and as captives to the forces of evil that killed him.[81]

It is of great importance to note that Weaver dares to employ a theological formula for substitutionary atonement—Christ dies for sinner—from an anthropocentric and cognitive perspective. In fact, Weaver acknowledges that Jesus' death is the consequence of sin. The crucifixion implies the co-involvement of both human sin and evil powers. Humanity has a double identity: we are not only passive victims but also active sinners in persecuting Jesus. In this regard, Weaver's nonviolent atonement model holistically modifies a victim-oriented soteriology in which humans are nothing but victims of evil. Moreover, Weaver's theological discussion of sin agrees with Schwager's dramatic comprehension of God's salvation. Sinful humans' identification with evil characters in Jesus' drama of salvation play a pivotal role in his saving work.

> Before participating in the saving act of Jesus, we (sinners) need to acknowledge participation and identification at another point. In the drama of salvation, we need first to identify with sin. And that identification is more than an abstract confession of sinfulness and guilt. In particular, we need to acknowledge our enslavement to the powers that killed Jesus, to confess our place on the side of those who opposed the reign of God. We are identified with the Roman imperial leaders who had ultimate authority for his death, with Jewish leaders who cooperated to condemn Jesus, with the rabble who acquiesced to his condemnation, with the disciples who slept rather than praying with

79. Weaver, *The Nonviolent Atonement*, 93.
80. Weaver, *The Nonviolent Atonement*, 93.
81. Weaver, *The Nonviolent Atonement*, 93–94.

him as he struggled in the garden, with Judas who betrayed him, with Peter who denied him.[82]

Likewise, Weaver suggests that there is a human conversion of sinners from God's enemies to his followers in his narrative *Christus Victor*.[83] In order to solve the ethical dilemma between God's justice and love, Weaver heavily relies on Schwager's Girardian reflection on God's indirect judgment, which means "turning people over to their own wickedness, which continues to bind them." As I mentioned above, and as Schwager contends, this is self-deceiving sinners' judgment on themselves.

> The wrath of God and the love of God represent the two stances from which we view the salvation drama, the two perspectives from which we view the act of God in Christ—as an act of judgment as long as we continue in bondage to the powers of evil that enslave us, and as an act of love that frees us from the powers of evil. These are not consecutive stages in God's attitude toward humankind but differing stages in humankind's perception of God.[84]

In order to solve the ethical problem of how God allows the violent death of Christ, Weaver takes advantage of the "epistemic turn" in humanity's knowledge of God's atoning work. Although it seems as if an angry God punishes his own Son, according to Weaver, this is a hermeneutical illusion from the cognitive perspective. According to Weaver, if our eyes are truly open to the resurrection of the crucified Christ, we can confess that atonement is God's nonviolent salvation for sinful humankind.

Correspondingly, Calvin is not unaware of the hermeneutical problem of atonement in which God's eternal love towards sinners seems to be incompatible with his righteous wrath against their guilt. In order to move beyond the contradiction between God's hospitable love and vindicatory justice, Calvin insists that God only temporarily appears to be a wrathful judge, before humans realize the Father's eternal love towards them as his elected children in Christ.[85] Finally, both Weaver and Calvin have a theological common denominator. It is the cognitive demonstration of how God himself is nonviolent. The two representative atonement theologians share the saving truth of God: He loves and saves sinners in

---

82. Weaver, *The Nonviolent Atonement*, 93–94.
83. Weaver, *The Nonviolent Atonement*, 97–98.
84. Weaver, *The Nonviolent Atonement*, 98.
85. Calvin, *Institutes* II.16.2.

Christ. This is God's nonviolent hospitality hidden in the violent event of Christ's crucifixion. Weaver neglects to consider the positive content of salvation through the negative phenomenon of Christ's substitutionary death *pro nobis*. While Weaver naively understands Christ's atoning death and structural evil in a human-immanent dimension, Calvin dramatically presents a holistic view of atonement that embraces both God's sovereignty and the human inevitability of Pilate's judgment in the crucifixion.

3.3 Barth's Unifying Perspective on God's Being and His Work of Atonement

The Theological Dynamics of the Doctrine of God

Barth believes that there is neither a hidden revelation nor actual reconciliation apart from Jesus Christ, in that God reconciles the world to himself in Christ (2 Cor 5:19). The truth that God is in Christ reveals and actualizes the dynamic fullness and oneness of God's justice and mercy, beyond the static and limited comprehension of humans. Since God's being and act are inseparable, Barth's own dynamic definition of God's being in his act demonstrates that all the attributes of God and his work never cease to be harmonized into Christ's person in his work *pro nobis*. Barth argues that if we let God be God beyond the scope of human reason, he is so "in his own perfection," and that God himself exists "in the multiplicity of his perfections."[86] God's mercy and righteousness are neither separate nor independent but inseparable from each other in Christ. Since God in Christ is righteous, he is also merciful in Christ. The inter-Triune relationship of *perichoresis* is related to the indivisible oneness of the two attributes of God's righteousness and his mercy in his being.[87]

> We shall have to emphasize the righteousness of God no less than his mercy. If possible, we shall have to emphasize it even more. But we cannot do this, we cannot speak at all of the righteousness of God which is so much emphasized in the Bible, if we do not proceed from a consideration of God's mercy. The relationship between God's mercy and righteousness will also present itself to us as a relationship of mutual penetration and consummation, but here again it will receive its characteristic stamp from the fact that divine mercy necessarily precedes. For only in this way

86. Barth, *Church Dogmatics* II/1, 376.
87. Barth, *Church Dogmatics* II/1, 376.

does it correspond to the economy of the revelation and therefore the being of God, which must always be respected and never replaced by any arbitrarily introduced symmetry.[88]

God's mercy is righteous and his justice is merciful. Yet, since the decisive revelation of God in Christ is his reconciliation with the entire fallen creation, Barth believes that "the mercy of God must precede his righteousness, just as his grace had to precede his holiness."[89] In order to overcome the Reformed orthodox tendency of portraying arbitrariness in God's will and the separation between God's justice and mercy, Barth emphasizes the unity of God's will and his being.[90] In this regard, Barth attempts to overcome the tendency to separate God's attributes from his being—i.e., the contradicting relationship between mercy and justice in both Anselmian satisfaction theory and the penal substitutionary doctrine—in the classic dogmatic approaches to God's atoning work. Rather, God's full presence and work in Christ is dynamically represented as God's being in his saving act.

At this point, we have to deal with Barth's theological actualism, the dynamic understanding of God's saving work in Christ. Barth says,

> God actually made and executed the necessity of the fact that the being of God, the omnipotence of his free love, now has this concrete determination and is effective and revealed in this determination and no other, that God wills to magnify and does in fact magnify his own glory in this way and not in any other, and therefore to the inclusion of the redemption and salvation of the world.[91]

The eternal will of God decides his own act of salvation. Barth further claims that the fact that "God's being is event, the event of God's act, necessarily (if, when we speak of it, we turn our eyes solely on his revelation) means that it is his own conscious, willed, and executed decision. It is his own decision."[92] However, the actualistic ontology should not be misunderstood along the lines of McCormack's provocative claim that

---

88. Barth, *Church Dogmatics* II/1, 376.

89. Barth, *Church Dogmatics* II/1, 376.

90. Barth, *Church Dogmatics* II/1, 379. Barth claims that just as "the will of God is revealed as righteous *eo ipso*," so "it is also righteous *eo ipso* in God himself."

91. Barth, *Church Dogmatics* IV/1, 213.

92. Barth, *Church Dogmatics* II/1, 272–73.

God's will to elect humanity is constitutive of the Triune being.[93] This is the revisionist position in which God's will precedes his being. Nonetheless, Barth's actualistic understanding of the atonement has nothing to do with the revisionist interpretation of Anselm's *Cur Deus Homo*, as if the necessity of atonement were God's primal decision to determine his own being.[94] Revisionists seriously misconstrue Barth's theological intention to move beyond the traditional understanding of the relationship between God's being and his act. Rather, what Barth seeks is not to throw away all static terms such as being and essence, but to confirm the dynamic unity in the distinction between God's being and act.[95] The subject of salvation, the Triune God, is accomplishing his own act of atonement in Jesus Christ.[96] At the heart of Barth's dynamic understanding of the relationship between God's being and his act lies the truth that God's being in his act is nothing other than the Triune God from eternity to eternity. God's being in his act is the eternal uniqueness of God's mode of existing and acting, and it has nothing to do with any kind of humanizing concept of God.

More essentially, in order to overcome the theological limitations in the classical dogmas of atonement—i.e., Anselm's scholastic arguments about God's honor and Calvin's forensic perspective on the satisfaction of God's justice—Barth presents his own revolutionary understanding of God's being in his act by integrating the doctrine of God into that of reconciliation. Thus Barth simultaneously places the doctrine of Christ's substitutionary death in both God's being (II/1) and his work of

---

93. McCormack, "Grace and Being," 92–110. However, Barth himself argues for the existence of the Triune God from the eternity. "The whole being and life of God is an activity, both in eternity and in worldly time, both in himself as Father, Son, and Holy Spirit, and in his relation to the human being and all creation" (IV/1, 7). "Godhead is always the Godhead of the Father, Son, and Holy Spirit" (II/2, 115).

94. Jones, "Barth and Anselm," 260–261. Uncritically following McCormack's revisionist position, in which God's election of humanity is constitutive of the Triune being, Paul Dafydd Jones unfairly engages Anselm's task-oriented interpretation of God in *Cur Deus Homo*, reading it into the election and atonement in the theology of Barth. Yet Anselm believes the Triune God has eternally existed before Christ's atonement (Anselm, "Cur Deus Homo," *Basic Writings*, 204–6).

95. Barth, *Church Dogmatics* II/1, 375.

96. See Hunsinger, "Election and the Trinity," 188. Against McCormack's position, George Hunsinger claims that for Barth there is no such will constituting the Triune being, because from all eternity God exists as the Trinitarian God. God's being cannot be constituted by his decisions, because we cannot think of God's will apart from his being. Logically, the will of God is preceded by his being.

reconciliation (IV/1). On the other hand, Barth more dynamically unifies Anselm's commercial motif with Calvin's forensic understanding of the divine punishment of sin and evil in §30.2, "The Mercy and Righteousness of God." For Barth, with the dynamic unity in distinction between God the Father and the Son, it is God himself who bears sin and judgment in Christ.[97]

> 1. The fact that it was God's Son, that it was God himself, who took our place on Golgotha and thereby freed us from the divine anger and judgment, reveals first the full implication of the wrath of God, of his condemning and punishing justice. It shows us what *a consuming fire burns against sin*. It thus discloses too the full implication of sin, what it means to resist God, to be God's enemy, which is the guilty determination of our human existence.[98]

Contrary to Weaver's denial of the violent motif of God's judgment in the atonement, Barth positively engages the juridical concept in God's atoning work in Christ. Here we should pay attention to Barth's theological application of the biblical metaphor of "a consuming fire" in his doctrine of atonement.[99] In Holy Scripture, fire not only negatively symbolizes the physical annihilation of sinners,[100] and even the eternal damnation of hell,[101] but also positively means God's purifying work.[102] I argue that Barth assimilates both the destructive and restorative meaning of the divine fire revealed in the Bible, in order to describe the paradox of God's salvation, in which God's fire annihilates sin and evil but at the same time restores sinners into the image of God.

97. Barth, *Church Dogmatics* II/1, 399.

98. Barth, *Church Dogmatics* II/1, 399. Emphasis mine.

99. "To the Israelites the glory of the Lord looked like a consuming fire on top of the mountain" (Exod 24:17). "For the Lord your God is a consuming fire, a jealous God" (Deuteronomy 4:24). "For our God is a consuming fire" (Heb 12:29).

100. "See, the Name of the Lord comes from afar, with burning anger and dense clouds of smoke; his lips are full of wrath, and his tongue is a consuming fire" (Isa 30:27).

101. "Then death and Hades were thrown into the lake of fire. The lake of fire is the second death" (Rev 20:14).

102. "This third I will put into the fire; I will refine them like silver and test them like gold. They will call on my name and I will answer them; I will say, 'They are my people,' and they will say, 'The Lord is our God'" (Zech 13:9). "These have come so that the proven genuineness of your faith—of greater worth than gold, which perishes even though refined by fire—may result in praise, glory, and honor when Jesus Christ is revealed" (1 Pet 1:7).

In addition, Barth creatively employs the phenomenological contrast between "negative" judgment as God's "No" against sin and the "positive" content of the fulfillment of God's covenant as his "Yes" towards the entire creation.[103] By doing so, he proves his own divine teleological argument of God's reconciliation with humankind in Christ. This is a dialectical perspective.[104] Yet Barth does not overlook the seriousness of human sin, as if God's "No" of judgment were mechanically negated (*Aufheben*) into his "Yes" of reconciliation at a noetic level.[105] We have to remember Barth's own warning: a Hegelian dialectical perspective on God's being and act may cause a hermeneutical absolutization that seriously infringes the divine freedom of God, who elects and saves sinful humankind. In other words, God's saving work can be described by dialectical logic, but logic itself cannot explain why God loves sinners by grace in Christ.

> Hegel, in making the dialectical method of logic the essential nature of God, made impossible the knowledge of the actual dialectic of grace, which has its foundation in the freedom of God. Upon the basis of this dialectic the attempt to speak of a necessity to which God himself is supposed to be subject would be radically impossible.[106]

Barth's Ontologically Modified Version of Satisfaction Theory: God as a Consuming Fire

With these theological presuppositions of God's gracious sovereignty and his atoning work, Barth proposes a modified view of satisfaction in Anselm's doctrine of atonement. Barth basically agrees with the divine necessity of Christ's incarnation, as well as the motif of God's satisfaction by Christ's vicarious death in Anselm's *Cur Deus Homo*.[107] Barth says that

---

103 Barth, *Church Dogmatics* IV/1, 257.

104. For an excellent research on Barth's dialectical perspective, see Baark, "Seeking Out the Enemy on His Own Ground," 54. For Sigurd Baark, the uniquely divine event of Christ's crucifixion is "the absolute negativity" of "the infinite judgment."

105. Webster, *Barth's Ethics of Reconciliation*, 5–7. According to Webster, Alister McGrath misconstrues Barth's theology as focusing only epistemologically on what God has already accomplished from eternity. See McGrath, *The Making of Modern German Christology*, 104–16.

106. Barth, *Protestant Theology in the Nineteenth Century*, 406.

107. Watson, "A Study in St. Anselm's Soteriology and Karl Barth's Theological

"in his own Word made flesh, God hears that satisfaction has been done to his righteousness, that the consequences of human sin have been borne and expiated, and therefore that they have been taken away from man—the man for whose sake Jesus Christ intervened."[108] Nonetheless, Barth distances himself from the traditional satisfaction theory. The vulnerable point in Anselm is that without the restoration of God's honor through the compensatory death of Christ, there is no forgiveness of our sins and reconciliation with God. The death of Christ has infinite meritorious value to restore God's honor rather than vicarious power to save us. For Barth, God's sovereign will in his eternal freedom takes the divine initiative in Christ's atonement, because he rejects *"an abstract conception of right which is superior to* [God] *himself"* in Anselm's satisfaction theory.[109] Barth's decisive objection to Anselm's absolutization of God's justice here is "to oppose any attempt to separate revelation as God's action from the action of the atonement, as if the sovereignty and effectiveness of God's action were conditioned by a prior claim of justice."[110] Furthermore, in order to avoid the theological tendency of arbitrariness in God's will and the separation between God's justice and mercy in Protestant scholasticism, Barth emphasizes the unity of God's will and his being.[111] Barth underscores that even the justice of God cannot overwhelm the sovereignty of God. According to Barth, since the righteousness of God is not only preceded by his mercy, but is also the integrated decision of God's love and mercy,[112] I can deduce the statement that God's righteousness is loving righteousness for us, not retributive justice against us. In Anselmian satisfaction theory or penal substitution, God's grace and justice are juxtaposed in a paradoxical relationship, whereas for Barth, righteousness and mercy are resituated in the principle of integrity and harmony in God himself. In the event of God's reconciliation with all humanity and the evil world, "the mystery of his mercy" is identified with "the mystery of his righteousness."[113] Accordingly, God's righteousness against our sins

---

Method," 493.

108. Barth, *Church Dogmatics* II/1, 403.

109. Barth, *Church Dogmatics* II/1, 401. Emphasis mine.

110. Watson, "A Study in St. Anselm's Soteriology and Karl Barth's Theological Method," 495.

111. Barth, *Church Dogmatics* II/1, 379.

112. Barth, *Church Dogmatics* II/1, 376.

113. Barth, *Church Dogmatics* IV/1, 237.

and his mercy towards sinners are not contradictory to each other, but harmonized into the person and work of Christ.

More significantly, the Barthian perspective on the substitution aims at eliminating the dualistic background of the divine violence between God the wrathful judge and Christ the innocent victim punished by the Father. According to Barth, God's judgment never means the destruction of creation, i.e. the failure to satisfy God's honor.[114] Christ's substitutionary death is God's cancellation of his direct punishment of sinful humankind, which cannot endure it. Rather, the divine simultaneity of God's justice and mercy fully reveals that the merciful God takes the condemnation of sin and death upon himself at the crucifixion of his own Son.[115] The element that most distinguishes Barth's forensic understanding from the traditional "penal substitutionary atonement"[116] is that beyond a purely penal logics of retribution, God in Christ comes into the world and gives himself, in order to take our human sins, and accomplishes his divine judgment in himself.[117] Barth is never ashamed of declaring "the reflexive action of God in the atonement,"[118] because God becomes "the object of his own severity, his own righteous condemnation

---

114. Barth, *Church Dogmatics* II/1, 400–401.

115. Barth, *Church Dogmatics* II/1, 401.

116. Holmes, "Penal Substitution," 295. According to Stephen R. Holmes, "Penal substitutionary atonement assumes the logic of the law court. Sin is understood as law-breaking, and so necessarily attracts a penalty, which is inevitably death. In dying on the cross, Jesus pays the penalty of death for all those who are saved, and so they are freed from their deserved punishment. God's justice is satisfied by Jesus' death." Here we need to be aware of the theological misidentification of "forensic" and "penal" in the direct sense, for it must be noted that "not all forensic doctrines are penal in emphasis." In contrast to Calvinistic and modern-evangelical understandings of penal substitution, Barth strives to minimize the theological implication that punishment plays in sinful humankind's reconciliation with God. Barth believes that rather than being punished instead of sinners, from a human perspective on criminal justice, Christ as the judge was judged in our place in the divine dimension. The issue at stake is not that someone must be punished for sin, but that the sinner must be reconciled, made righteous, and become a new creation, and that can only happen if the old self dies and the new self comes alive in Christ. In this regard, Barth's substitutionary doctrine of atonement should not be confined to nor explained by a penal view of vicarious punishment itself, but it can be apocalyptically described by the forensic dimension of Christ's substitutionary death. Regarding the distinction between "penal" and "forensic" approaches to substitutionary atonement, my arguments are essentially indebted to a conversation with Dr. Mangina.

117. Barth, *Church Dogmatics* II/1, 401.

118. Williams, "Karl Barth and the Doctrine of the Atonement," 241.

and punishment in our stead."[119] Yet God's act of reflexive judgment should not be misunderstood, as if God executed himself—"death in God" in a Hegelian formula, because the incarnate God overcame death by dying as a human Jesus.[120] Barth denies the Father's punishment of his own Son at the level of "human experience" and "individuation," but Barth resituates the ontological foundation of forensic judgment into the God-human Jesus Christ himself as the "second mode" of the unified being and work of God the Trinity.[121] Barth accurately points out the limitations of traditional penal substitutionary atonement theory, in which the wrathful God seems to be violently satisfied with the punishment that Christ suffers at the cross.[122] While Barth believes that Christ takes God's judgment upon himself instead of sinful humankind, he underlines that the divine purpose of Christ's penal substitution is not only our exemption from punishment at the cross, though it is still crucial for us, but also the definitive revelation of the "negation" of fallen humanity and their sins and the "cancellation" of God's wrath.

> The decisive thing is not that he has suffered what we ought to have suffered so that we do not have to suffer it, the destruction to which we have fallen victim by our guilt, and therefore the punishment which we deserve. This is true, of course. But it is true only as it derives from the decisive thing that in the suffering and death of Jesus Christ it has come to pass that in his own person he has made an end of us as sinners and therefore of sin itself by going to death as the One who took our place as sinners. In his person he has delivered up us sinners and sin

---

119. Barth, *Church Dogmatics* II/1, 398.

120. Bruce McCormack, "The Ontological Presuppositions of Barth's Doctrine of the Atonement," 361.

121. McCormack, "The Ontological Presuppositions of Barth's Doctrine of the Atonement," 364. McCormack says that "The Triune God pours his wrath out upon himself in and through the human nature that he has made his own in his second mode of his being—that is the ontological significance of penal substitution."

122. Barth, *Church Dogmatics* IV, 253. Barth claims, "He [Christ] has suffered this punishment of ours. But we must not make this a main concept as in some of the older presentations of the doctrine of the atonement (especially those which follow Anselm of Canterbury), either in the sense that by his suffering our punishment we are spared from suffering it ourselves, or that in so doing he 'satisfied' or offered satisfaction to the wrath of God. The latter thought is quite foreign to the New Testament. And of the possible idea that we are spared punishment by what Jesus Christ has done for us we have to notice that the main drift of the New Testament statements concerning the passion and death of Jesus Christ is not at all or only indirectly in this direction."

> itself to destruction. He has removed us sinners and sin, negated us, cancelled us out: ourselves, our sin, and the accusation, condemnation, and perdition which had overtaken us.[123]

The juridical formulation of Christ's vicarious death itself is inclined to absolutize the violent penal motif, though the original intention is to declare God's judgment against sin through Christ's substitutionary death. The doctrine of penal substitution highlights retribution against sinners, whereas Barth's own forensic description of atonement concentrates on God's restorative judgment against sin itself. By recognizing the hermeneutical weakness, Barth properly distinguishes a biblical concept of God's restorative judgment from a human ideology of retributive punishment.[124] With the modified assumptions of God's judgment through the crucifixion, Barth finally reaches his theological reinterpretation of God's satisfaction by Christ's atoning death.

> Not out of any desire for vengeance and retribution on the part of God, but because of the radical nature of the divine love, which could "satisfy" itself only in the outworking of its wrath against the man of sin, only by killing him, extinguishing him, removing him. Here is the place for the doubtful concept that in the passion of Jesus Christ, in the giving up of his Son to death, God has done that which is "satisfactory" or sufficient . . . For this reason the divine judgment in which the Judge was judged, and therefore the passion of Jesus Christ, is as such the divine action of atonement which has taken place for us.[125]

We can see that for Barth, the concept of satisfaction is still essential for God's reconciliation with sinners. It does not stand for God's retributive justice, but for the "radical nature of the divine love."[126] His

---

123. Barth, *Church Dogmatics* IV, 253–54.

124. Terry, *The Justifying Judgment of God*, 120. Justyn Terry correctly explains Barth's theological distinction between punishment and judgment. "The punishment he [Christ] suffered does indeed deliver us from the punishment that we deserve, but this is not to be seen as the mechanism by which we are freed from our sin. Punishment is, for Barth, a consequence of a judgment that yields condemnation, not a process that must be undergone in its own right."

125. Barth, *Church Dogmatics* IV/1, 254–55.

126. Barth, *Church Dogmatics* IV/1, 254–55. Here, Barth's theological accentuation of God's self-satisfaction by his love reiterates Aulén's reinterpretation of Luther's atonement theology in *Christus Victor*. "His [Luther's] concept of the wrath of God and the way in which it is overcome shows that there is no thought here of a satisfaction of the legal claims of the divine justice, for it is God himself, the divine blessing,

righteous love never condones sin but consumes sinful humanity itself. What is at stake is how the love of God dynamically works, "killing," "extinguishing," "removing" our sinful existence. God's love of salvation is like a holy fire, from the stance of the divine wrath. At the crucial point of exposing God's atoning work in Christ (IV/1), Barth brings up the specific motif of a consuming fire again. It is the biblical metaphor that he highlights as God's own being (II/1). It is no accident that the whole of Barth's theological argument proceeds like a sort of theological symphony of harmony and correspondence. What Barth is eager to repeatedly emphasize is God's self-sacrificial love for sinners. As the eternally consuming fire, God himself reveals his own self-sacrificial substitution in our sinful place. Yet the divine love is to be actualized in the form of righteous wrath. Bearing the condemnation and curse of our iniquities and the evil of the fallen world upon his own being of mercy and justice, the eternal fire, God himself, consumes sin and evil itself, in order to recreate sinful humankind and the fallen world.

With the theological simultaneity of God's justice and mercy revealed in the dynamic metaphor of God's consuming fire, Barth confirms that since God loves sinners in Christ, he judges their sins through the crucifixion of his own Son, in order to save all of them. Barth represents the biblical motif of judgment as fire in his exposition of the Heidelberg Catechism.

> For he himself is the one on whom God's wrath has been revealed. He is the man who has borne and suffered under this burden. Jesus Christ did not "get by." And if we Christians belong to this Christ, we also cannot get by, for we cannot get around him. He stands before us as the rejected one. "Upon him was the chastisement that made us whole" (Isa 53). And

---

which in Christ prevails over the wrath and the curse. Thus the term 'satisfaction' in Luther's mouth exhibits the strength of the Divine Love, which could go in under the punishment that impended upon men. The satisfaction is made by God, not merely to God," Aulén, *Christus Victor*, 118. In addition, regarding Barth's engagement with evangelical theology, it is of great significance that Barth's doctrine of ontologically modified atonement influences the twentieth-century evangelical Stott's vindication of God's self-satisfaction, sacrifice, and substitution in Christ. "The theological words 'satisfaction' and 'substitution' need to be carefully defined and safeguarded, but they cannot in any circumstances be given up. The biblical gospel of atonement is of God satisfying himself by substituting himself for us. The concept of substitution may be said, then, to live at the heart of both sin and salvation. For the essence of sin is man substituting himself for God, while the essence of salvation is God substituting himself for man . . . Perhaps no twentieth-century theologian has seen this more clearly, expressed it more vigorously, than Karl Barth." Stott, *The Cross of Christ*, 159.

because it lies on him, we are bound in him to take it seriously. It is only at this one place where God's wrath has burned as *a consuming Fire-Golgotha*. There is where the judgment of God on man is revealed.[127]

Barth believes that God's consuming fire is the "No" at the cross. But it never ends up annihilating sinful humanity, because from the cross of God's judgment ultimately comes the restorative salvation of fallen creation as "the deep hidden Yes" of God himself *pro nobis*.[128] This is the essence of Barth's own constructive unification of Anselm's feudal emphasis on God's satisfaction and Calvin's penal formulation of the substitutionary death of Christ *pro nobis*.

Barth's Theological Understanding of Nonviolent Atonement

Barth's substitutionary atonement theology is marked by a holistic perspective that illuminates God's nonviolence as restorative judgment. Barth's emphasis on God's self-substitution and self-giving in the crucifixion of Christ is related to the crux of Weaver's nonviolent atonement theory. According to Hunsinger, Barth confirms the divine nonviolence of God's atoning work in Christ by paradoxically describing the mystery of God's self-sacrificial "suffering love" towards sinful humanity as his enemies.

> In the cross God does not meet his enemies with malice, retaliation, or crushing force. He meets them with the mystery of suffering love. He not only treats them with restraint, but offers himself up for them all. He presents himself as a living sacrifice, saving them from their self-inflicted destruction by suffering the condemnation they deserve. He does not repay evil for evil, but overcomes evil with good, even to the point of setting at stake his own existence. The politics of God thus reveals itself as the politics of nonviolent love.[129]

Hunsinger underlines that for Barth, "it was not God who needed to be reconciled to the world, but the world that needed to be reconciled to God."[130] With the nonviolent qualification of reconciliation, Barth argues

127. Barth, *Learning Jesus Christ through the Heidelberg Catechism*, 46. Emphasis mine.
128. Barth, *Learning Jesus Christ through the Heidelberg Catechism*, 46.
129. Hunsinger, *Disruptive Grace*, 35.
130. Hunsinger, *Disruptive Grace*, 35. Hunsinger further explains that "The New

that the crux of reconciliation is not God's violent and passive satisfaction by Christ's death, as Anselm and Calvin are often inclined to overaccentuate, but his sovereign and positive "fulfillment of the broken covenant" with humankind in Christ.[131]

Barth claims that substitution is not God's violent execution, in which he punishes Christ instead of sinners, but the nonviolent salvation in which God in Christ takes the place of his hostile enemies. God's substitution for fallen sinners in Christ is the objective grounding for their justification by divine grace. For Barth, God's penal substitution in Christ implies his own nonviolent salvation, because God never punishes sinners but takes our sin upon himself.

Here we need to remember that Weaver justifies his human-ethical reinterpretation of nonviolent atonement in the name of the doctrinal heritage of his denomination. The Mennonites actively promote the pursuit of peace. Nevertheless, it is thought-provoking that Amy L. Barker and Ben C. Ollenburger, two Mennonite theologians, disapprove of Weaver's argument that there is no salvific meaning in Christ's vicarious death by God's sovereign judgment, though they faithfully follow the same ethical cause of non-violence in their theological tradition.[132] In contrast to Weaver, Barker and Ollenburger acknowledge Barth's doctrine of Christ's substitutionary atonement through God's judgment. They insist that the integrity of the biblical gospel should not be confined to the human-ethical dimension of nonviolence. Apart from the divine dimension of God's judging work in Christ, there is no way to comprehend and declare God's love and salvation *pro nobis*.

> We have proposed Hosea 11 as an expression of God's history with Israel, a history of judgment and salvation, in which God enclosed his wrath within himself for Israel's life and for God's own. The New Testament continues this history, but with a

---

Testament does not speak of the atonement as having removed a divine hostility toward humankind. 'God does not need reconciliation with human beings,' observes Barth, 'but they need reconciliation with him' (IV/1, 74). The New Testament 'tells us that God has made this reconciliation, and how he has made it' (IV/1, 74). It tells us that he has made it by becoming incarnate in Jesus Christ, dying in the place of his enemies that they might live. Although human beings are unfaithful, hostile, and antagonistic to God, God is not so toward them. However, neither the depth and seriousness of God's love nor the depth and seriousness of human sin can be known for what they are apart from the cross."

131. Barth, *Church Dogmatics* IV/1, 67.

132. Ollenburger and Barker, "The Passion and God's Atonement."

> rupture. This rupture, which takes place in and through Christ, opens the whole world to God's history and to God's life—God's intra-Trinitarian life. Because of God's holiness in and as justice/righteousness, and the injustice, the evil, the sin of the world, this opening involves divine judgment . . . The bearer of God's judgment is Jesus Christ, who is also its subject and the end of Israel's exile. As Karl Barth put it, the passion of Jesus Christ is the judgment of God in which the Judge himself was the judged. By no means was Jesus God's victim; he was ours, the world's, and both the author and embodiment of God's suffering love.[133]

At this point, we have to take notice of "rupture" as God's radical and unconditional embracing of the sinful world at the sacrifice of his beloved Son. It is the unremitted divine intervention in the violent issues of sin and evil that culminates in Christ's vicarious death. The holy and righteous God never remains a passive, powerless, and irresponsible spectator to the pressing problem of humans who not only rebel against the true God but also destroy each other. Rather, the sovereign God is infinitely active, powerful, and responsible for his loving creation beyond the limited spectrum of human ethics. Even though his saving work seems to be violent, God the Father reveals his eternal love and justice through the reconciling death of Christ, who is judged in place of sinners. Above all, Weaver would have benefited from considering that his judgment against sin and evil proceeds from the Triune God's being and act. And then, because of the asymmetric relation of God to human beings, Weaver would realize that God's reconciling work in Christ sheds light on the ethical perspective of nonviolence as God's self-sacrificing love for sinful humankind. The merciful God never avenges himself on sinners but judges their sin in Christ's atoning death, in order to prevent the annihilation of his entire creation by the infinite guilt and the hostile powers.

However, Barth's theological interpretation of the crucifixion seems to focus on the vertical dimension of God's sovereignty from above, without taking full consideration of the problem of pain in the yet-suffering world. According to Barth, all the historical sufferings and victimizations in time and space no longer have any substantial weight, when compared to God's absolute judgment in Christ's substitutionary death. It is his most wrathful punishment in the whole of world history.

> This event is the judgment which reduces to insignificance the seriousness of all the other judgments which from the beginning

---

133. Ollenburger and Barker, "The Passion and God's Atonement."

of the world have been seen to sweep over peoples and individuals—from the great catastrophes of nature and history which have and will come upon thousands and even millions, to that which we all have sooner or later to bear in the deprivation of health, wealth, and opportunities in consequence of our own and others' folly or wickedness, and finally in the unique form of our death. It can, again, be more effectively expressed the other way round. The meaning of illness and want, of the mental and physical suffering of each individual, of war, hunger, tyranny, and revolution in the life of peoples, of the winding sheet of death spread unceasingly over everything and everyone, is revealed in its true frightfulness only on Good Friday. For we can always relativise and soften and finally forget the pain and suffering, not only of others but also our own.[134]

While it is correct that Barth points out the objective and universal implication of the divine judgment that the Bible testifies as a whole, he seems to absolutize the forensic/judicial motif of God's saving work at the cross of Christ. As Jenson rightly puts it, the academic mainstream has a theological tendency to overemphasize the decisiveness of Christ's crucifixion, as if the centrality of the cross were the be-all and end-all of God's salvation for us.[135] In order to avoid this absolutization, I modestly suggest that, with the objective implication of God's universal judgment at the cross, Barth also needs to meticulously distinguish innocent people's victimization by oppressors from the actualization of God's justice against structural sin and evil. As Barth claims, given that God's righteous judgment accomplishes his restorative salvation in Christ, the crux of the event is the sovereign hospitality of God, who universally embraces sin, evil, suffering, and the death of the entire fallen creation, in order to make all things new in Christ.

3.4 Systematic Theological Review

Here I will summarize Anselm's, Calvin's, and Barth's different dogmatic approaches to God's being and his atoning work. The theological common denominators are as follows.

---

134. Barth, *Church Dogmatics* II/1, 394.
135. Barth, *Church Dogmatics* II/1, 179.

1. The righteous and gracious God has the sovereignty and ability to accomplish the whole atonement.[136] God himself is eternal justice and love for humankind. The everlasting life and restorative power of salvation can and must originate from the holy God himself, who self-exists from eternity to eternity. In sharp contrast to all the human ideologies that need external proof in the fallen world, God is God in himself.[137]

2. In terms of soteriology, the God of justice never lets injustice and evil go in a violent world, because he can and must save it. It must be noted that while the fall of humankind inevitably causes the violent death of Jesus, it is *contingent*. God's atonement in Christ is the omnipotent and omniscient God's *eternal* self-determination to be gracious to sinful humans in Christ. God's sovereign involvement in the crucifixion is neither arbitrary nor violent. Rather, it is through Christ's death that God reveals his own righteousness for sinners' salvation by disclosing the self-deceptive evil of the fallen world. God's divine intervention in the crucifixion of Christ has the corollary of the annihilation of sin as guilt and evil as power, the forgiveness of sinners, and the restoration of those who suffer.

3. The tragic event of the fall and Christ's crucifixion by evildoers occur in a world that God creates and reigns. There is no such dualistic conflict between God and evil, as if the hostile powers arbitrarily execute the Son of God beyond the scope of God's sovereign reign of justice and grace.[138] In spite of the negative and destructive phenomenon of Christ's violent death in the substitutionary atonement models, the omnipotent and merciful God himself brings about the positive and constructive work of his own life-giving salvation through the atoning death of Christ. In this way, any dualistic view

---

136. Balthasar, *Theo-Drama IV*, 317. According to Balthasar, the history of the doctrine of atonement shows that "the whole process is shown to be the result of an initiative on the part of divine love."

137. Dorner, *History of Protestant Theology*, 319. Isaak August Dorner insists that "there is in Christianity an *inward truth*, which *being self-testifying*, can dispense with all other kind of evidence." Emphasis mine.

138. It is noteworthy that for Barth, God's judgment must deal with a dualistic confrontation between human sin and God's eternal righteousness in Christ. Yet God sovereignly takes "the inevitable conflict" in Christ himself to the violent point of crucifixion, because the "faithful" God never abandons "unfaithful" humankind to the tragic destiny of eternal self-destruction. Barth, *Church Dogmatics* II/1, 397.

of death and life is overcome within the inner being of God, who satisfies his own justice by sacrificing his own Son as the eternal love in himself.

4. The theological perspective on God's atoning work confirms God's attributes as justice and love for the restoration of the world and reconciliation with it. Thus, the substitutionary atonement theologians believe that the righteous God who judges sin is the same as the gracious one who saves sinful victims. From the human perspective, the subjective, epistemically experienced turn from God's anger to his mercy corresponds to his objective work of satisfaction in the restoration of the fallen world.

5. There is a divine paradox in God's attitude toward and relationship with the crucified Son of God. From an anthropological perspective, although it appears that a merciless and violent God decides Christ's crucifixion for the sake of the salvation of the world, the loving God never abandons his own Son throughout the atonement. The gracious and righteous Father declares the saving efficacy in his own Son's death for sinful humankind in the objective dimension.

The greatest contribution of substitutionary atonement theories is the objective understanding of the crucifixion of Christ. Beyond an anthropological-ethical perspective, the crucifixion reveals and achieves God's saving work in Christ himself. The inductive reasoning of the substitutionary perspectives accords with God's restorative justice, which nonviolent atonement scholars overaccentuate in lieu of vindicatory justice.[139] More importantly, the theological dimension of God's being and act through Jesus' atoning death is the grounding for perfect healing and restoration of victims in the violent world.

Correspondingly, Anselm, Calvin, and Barth are in one accord with the biblical truth that God achieves the positive content of salvation in the negative phenomenon of Christ's atoning death for sinners. First is a positive epistemology: God's saving power and righteousness is hidden to human reason and experience, but revealed to us by faith in the crucifixion of Christ. Second is a positive ontology: God never fails to complete his original plan of perfect creation, because God's being and act in the atoning death of Christ brings about the restoration of the fallen

---

139. Even the heart of Calvin's theology of atonement is God's restorative satisfaction of his justice viz the divine judgment, not the punishment itself.

world and objective reconciliation between God and sinful humankind. Additionally, in contrast to Anselm, who rejects God's violent punishment of the sinner, both Calvin and Barth believe that God's righteous judgment has the power to save sinners, because the seemingly negative and destructive event of Christ's atoning death has the positive and constructive efficacy to annihilate sin and evil.

3.5 Constructively Critical Reflection

The substitutionary atonement theologies rightly place the divine purpose of the seemingly destructive event of Christ's death within the objective context of God's being and act. They dynamically illuminate the paradoxical relationship between God's justice and love in Christ. Yet the Theo-centric understanding of atonement exposes the hermeneutical limitation of divine violence, insofar as God the Father decides on the crucifixion of his Son. It is noteworthy that substitutionary atonement theologians are not unaware of the controversial issues surrounding divine violence. They never want to make God an arbitrary and violent tyrant who requires the innocent blood of his own Son, the crucified Christ. Anselm's dialogue partner, Boso, provocatively asks,

> For what justice is there in *his* suffering death for the sinner, who was the most just of all men? What man, if he condemned the innocent to free the guilty, would not himself be judged worthy of condemnation? And so the matter seems to return to the same incongruity which is mentioned above. For if he could not save sinners in any other way than by condemning the just, where is his omnipotence? If, however, he could, but did not wish to, how shall we sustain his wisdom and justice?[140] . . . For it is a strange thing if God so delights in, or requires, the blood of the innocent that he neither chooses, nor is able, to spare the guilty without the sacrifice of the innocent.[141]

Anselm shows no hesitation in answering this critical inquiry by concentrating on the relationship of mutual trust and eternal love between the Father and the incarnate Son. Anselm would reply to his modern critics by arguing that God is neither a sadist nor a criminal charged with domestic violence.

---

140. Anselm, "*Cur Deus Homo,*" *Basic Writings*, 205.
141. Anselm, "*Cur Deus Homo,*" *Basic Writings*, 214.

God's Sovereign Purpose in Christ's Crucifixion

> Since, therefore, the will of the Son pleased the Father, and he did not prevent him from choosing, or from fulfilling his choice, it is proper to say that he wished the Son to endure so piously and for so great an object, though he was *not pleased with* his suffering.[142]

We may argue that Anselm's doctrine of atonement should be understood from the immanent perspective of the Triune God, because "the self-oblation of the Son on the cross proceeded out of God's eternal, triune inner being."[143] Likewise, a modern criticism of penal substitution is that the event in fact seems to break the essential unity between God the Father and the Son.[144] If Christ takes vicarious punishment upon himself, how can his unity with the Father be maintained? Calvin paradoxically contends that the Father loves his own Son even at the critical moment of the crucifixion.

> We do not suggest that God was ever inimical or angry toward him. How could he be angry toward his beloved Son, "in whom his heart reposed" (cf. Matt 3:17)? How could Christ by his intercession appease the Father toward others, if he were himself hateful to God?[145]

For Calvin, although the dereliction of Christ by God means that he takes God's wrath upon himself, there is no eternal separation between God and Christ in the crucifixion because the Son of God cannot be abandoned by the Father.[146] Calvin lays great emphasis on the fact that Christ's forsakenness by God is a historical and spiritual event, not an eternal and physical one. However, it is odd to see that both Anselm and Calvin strive to offer a Christological solution to the Theo-centric problem of violence. Anselm stresses that the Son's divine obedience is

---

142. Anselm, "*Cur Deus Homo*," *Basic Writings*, 213. Emphasis mine.

143. Rutledge, *The Crucifixion*, 162–63.

144. Williams, "Penal Substitution," 72. Since Socinus, a number of liberal theologians have criticized the doctrinal concept of God's retributive justice and penal substitution, in that it contracts the biblical integrity between what God does and what he commands us to do: Packer, *In My Place Condemned He Stood*, 89. Against the divine mystery of Christ's substitution in our sinful place, the Socinian "rationalistic criticism" assumes a reductionist view in which God's work should be judged by the human ethical standard of nonviolence and love.

145. Calvin, *Institutes* II.16.11.

146. Balthasar, *Theo-Drama IV*, 251. According to Balthasar, Augustine also had the view that "the Son could not be abandoned by the Father."

voluntary, whereas Calvin emphasizes the person of Christ, who can endure God's judgment. Although the two great Christian theologians literally confirm that God is never violent in the substitutionary death of Christ, their theological defense merely remains at the level of symbolic declaration. More seriously, nonviolent atonement scholars can misunderstand that both Anselm and Calvin assume God's satisfaction as a sort of conditional cause of atonement in a negative sense. They criticize that without divine satisfaction in the form of restorative or vindicatory justice, there is no atonement. From deductive reasoning, it is indeed inevitable that, as nonviolent atonement scholars object, the Anselmian and Calvinistic doctrine of God seems to be hermeneutically involved with divine violence, though Anselm and Calvin strive to describe God's compassionate love for both Christ himself and sinful humankind as lying at the heart of satisfaction theory. Targeting the hermeneutical weakness, Weaver indiscriminately censures that the Anselmian and Calvinistic doctrines of atonement are inclined to indiscriminately project their own socio-cultural image of God as feudal Lord or righteous judge into the biblical metaphors of God's restoration and judgment in his own eternal being *pro nobis*. In my view, both Anselmian satisfaction theories and Weaver's nonviolent atonement model rely too much on human reasoning about atonement, in order to justify their theological logic. If evangelicals overstress the literal understanding of God's commercial or penal satisfaction itself, although the biblical metaphors imply the salvific reality of atonement event, it may become merely a theological ideology that guarantees the assurance of salvation. Yet it is much more misleading to absolutize the ethical concept of nonviolence by disregarding all the divine implications of God's being and act in Christ.

And then how can the substitutionary atonement theologians be faithful to the biblical testimony of God's righteous judgment in the crucifixion, without being involved with the modern accusation of divine violence? At this point, rather than explaining the doctrine of God's judgment by anthropological analogies to criminal jurisdiction or personal conscience, we need to keep in mind the properly theological dimension of the coherence between God's justice and God's love.

Barth clarifies "a relationship of mutual penetration and consummation" of "God's mercy and righteousness" in the being of God and his atoning work *pro nobis*.[147] Barth's theological insight on this point

---

147. Barth, *Church Dogmatics* II/1, 376.

is greater than Anselm's and Calvin's. With the dynamic unity of God's seemingly contradictory attributes in Christ himself, I suggest that the issue of divine satisfaction in the substitutionary atonement models should be positively understood from the perspective of God's being—his self-sacrificial love that *satisfies* his eternal justice—and his active reconciliation with sinful humankind at the cross. The subject of reconciliation is God in Christ. Atonement is not God's passive response to the crucifixion of Christ, as if the Father were separated from the Son. God's unfailing love and saving righteousness never depend on the human merit of Jesus' death itself in a commercial and conditional way.[148] Here I am not denying the historical reality of Christ's crucifixion as God's divine satisfaction or saving righteousness. Rather, the historical event itself should be preceded by God's eternal will of reconciliation and his objective achievement in Christ. With the divine consistency of God's being and work, there is a corresponding relationship between God's eternal covenant of salvation in heaven and the incarnate Christ's historical actualization on the earth. God the Father and Christ actively achieve the salvation of sinful humankind, which they determine "before the creation of the world" (Eph 1:4). Here, I fundamentally agree with Fleming Rutledge's holistic view of atonement from the perspective of both eternity and history.

> The event of the cross is the enactment *in history* of an *eternal* decision within the being of God. God is not changed by the historical event but has always been going from God's self in sacrificial love. The being of God also includes his opposition ("wrath") to all that stands against his love. God's "wrath," or his "violence," if you will, is not to be understood literally, as though he were choosing specific moments to unleash his rage and other specific moments to withdraw it. God's judgment on sin and death—incarnated in the Son's life, death, and resurrection—is in place within his being from before all time. God is against all that is not part of his purpose; that is the meaning of his "wrath."[149]

---

148. Calvin rightly observes that "in discussing Christ's merit, we do not consider the beginning of merit to be in him, but we go back to God's ordinance, the first cause. For God solely of his own good pleasure appointed him Mediator to obtain salvation for us," Calvin, *Institutes* II.17.1.

149. Rutledge, *The Crucifixion*, 500. Yet Rutledge needs to correct the argument in which "God is not changed by the historical event," because it may cause miscomprehension, as if the crucifixion were unnecessary or extravagant. Rather, the eternal purpose of God's atonement in Christ or the best plan of salvation for us had never been changed by the historical and human violence that was inflicted upon Jesus.

Given that God is the sovereign subject of atonement, the substitutionary atonement theologians neglect to fully clarify that God's satisfaction in Christ's atoning work reveals his own active and positive achievement of his eternal covenant of righteousness and love with humankind in Christ. Therefore, God's atoning work of restoration or judgment cannot be described apart from the person and work of Christ, because there is a dynamic unity between God the Father and the Son. Hence, in the next chapter, we will move to Anselm, Calvin, and Barth's Christological reflection of Christ's self-giving death for atonement.

4

Christ the Mediator's Self-Sacrificial Atonement *Pro Nobis*

In this form he was offered, because it is under this form that he is the Mediator, in this form he is the Priest, in this form he is the Sacrifice.[1]

Jesus' death and resurrection, in other words, function as the moment of the new exodus, of the "return" from the long exile of sin and death, of the overthrow of all the powers that enslaved the world . . . This can only mean that with the resurrection itself a shock wave has gone through the entire cosmos: the new creation has been born, and must now be implemented.[2]

IN WHAT FOLLOWS, I will examine the Christological implications of the substitutionary perspective on atonement in relation to three major exemplars of that tradition. Anselm, Calvin, and Barth all agree that the crucifixion reveals that Christ, as true God and true human, is the Mediator who gives himself, the eternal sacrifice of atonement, in order to accomplish reconciliation between God and humankind. This discussion will

---

1. Augustine, *Concerning the City of God Against the Pagans*, 380.
2. Wright, *Christian Origins and the Question of God*, 239.

serve as the basis for showing how the substitutionary tradition can take the major concerns of the nonviolent atonement theorists into account.

I will begin with Anselm. In his scholastic reasoning about the incarnation, Anselm underscores Christ's voluntary obedience and his self-giving sacrifice from the eternal perspective of the Triune God. Yet Anselm's understanding of sacrifice is inadequate. It cannot easily be harmonized with the *Christus victor* motif, and it misses the full depth of the divine self-giving. Secondly, despite his primarily forensic understanding of atonement, Calvin is able to integrate biblical priestly-sacrificial imagery with Christ's conquest over the hostile powers. He is able to do this because he has a strong grasp of the unity of Christ's person and work. Thirdly, Barth offers a powerful forensic account of Christ's substituting work and its implications for a socio-political implications of the atonement as liberation. Yet I will suggest that for both Calvin and Barth, their forensic views of substitutionary atonement would be strengthened by greater attention to the cultic motif. Lastly, I will conclude that Christ's cultic-sacrificial death at the cross is the common ground between nonviolent and substitutionary perspectives on atonement, helping to overcome the ahistorical and overly transcendent tendencies of substitutionary atonement theories.

4.1 Anselm's Cultic-Feudal Perspective on Christ's Atoning Death

The Incarnate Son of God for Humankind's Sin as Debt to God

Anselm argues for the absolute necessity of the compensation of God's honor by the Mediator, who must be God-man. Anselm insists that because atonement is something "which none but God can make and none but human ought to make, it is necessary for the God-human to make it."[3] According to Anselm, the necessity of atonement consists in two logical factors. One is the personal obligation of human beings to satisfy God's honor, and the other is the divine power of God to fulfill the duty of sinners. From these two indispensable presumptions about the purpose of Christ's saving work, Anselm rightfully reasons that Christ must be a God-human who is able to accomplish the divine responsibility to restore God's honor. Moreover, Anselm draws attention to the truth

---

3. Anselm, "*Cur Deus Homo*," *Basic Writings*, 259.

that the person of Christ as the Mediator is not just constituted by God's absolute necessity in a passive way. Rather, from the incarnation to the atonement, Christ voluntarily and actively obeys the eternal will of God the Father. Anselm highlights that the Son of God himself spontaneously decides to become the human Jesus by his immutable will.[4] Thus Anselm believes in the infinite value of Christ's self-giving death by his own voluntary will, because Christ gives "himself up to death for the honor of God. For God will not require this from him as a debt, because there will be no sin in him he will not be bound to die."[5] Anselm further explains the Christological qualification of the person of Christ as God-human. As the incarnate, eternal Son of God himself, he is able to give whatever he wills with his own divine sovereignty. There cannot be any human inevitability in the person and work of Christ.

> As he is both God and man, in connection with his human nature, which made him a man, he must also have received from the divine nature that controls over himself which freed him from all obligation, except to do as he does. In like manner, as one person of the Trinity, he must have had whatever he possessed of his own right, so as to be complete in himself, and could not have been under obligations to another, nor have need of giving anything in order to be repaid himself.[6]

Correspondingly, Anselm' mediatorial Christology emphasizes the paradoxical truth of Christ's incarnation, in which Christ assumes "a sinful substance" as the descendant of Adam and Eve, without committing a single sin.[7] It is the vicarious humanity of Christ *pro nobis*. The hypostatic unity of the true humanity and eternal deity in the person of Christ is the ground for the restoration of creation.

> Since it is fitting for that man to be God, and also the restorer of sinners, we doubt not that he is wholly without sin; yet will this avail nothing, unless he be taken without sin and yet of a sinful substance. But if we cannot comprehend in what manner the wisdom of God effects this, we should be surprised, but with reverence should allow of a thing of so great magnitude to remain hidden from us.[8]

4. Anselm, "Cur Deus Homo," *Basic Writings*, 285.
5. Anselm, "Cur Deus Homo," *Basic Writings*, 160.
6. Anselm, "Cur Deus Homo," *Basic Writings*, 296.
7. Anselm, "Cur Deus Homo," *Basic Writings*, 279.
8. Anselm, "Cur Deus Homo," *Basic Writings*, 279.

Yet although Anselm believes in Christ's assumption of our fallen human nature in a literal sense, at the hermeneutical level Anselm indeed supports his unfallen humanity by insisting that the humanity of Christ does not have "mortality."[9] Thus Anselm fails to substantially apply the patristic principle that what was not assumed was not redeemed.[10] For Anselm, while the primary problem of sin is dishonor to God in a transcendental and relational dimension, the immanent corruption of the world is only a derivative issue. Rather than biblically describing the incarnate Son of God's assumption of our sinful humanity—Christ sovereignly achieves salvation of the fallen creation in his own person—Anselm hastily turns to speculate on Christ's sinlessness itself, in order to emphasize the functional implication of the commercial restitution of God's honor in the atonement. The impeccability of Christ's human nature is the divine medium through which the infinite value of Christ's self-sacrificial deity to atone for the entire debt of sinful humankind is communicated to restore God's honor. Anselm's soteriology indeed indicates that the sinlessness of the incarnate Son of God is more directly "related to the atonement event, than to the incarnation."[11] For Anselm, there is no doctrinal concept of Christ's salvific suffering at the cross, because humankind's redemption depends on the "innocence" of his humanity.[12] It necessarily follows that apart from Christ's person as the Mediator, the perfect human being, death itself is the decisive point of Christ's atonement. It is regrettable that Anselm's Christological ambiguity blurs the organic relationship between Christ's person in the incarnation and his work of atonement. Thus, according to Balthasar, Anselmian satisfaction theory never allows the essential "contact" between the reality of human sin and the atoning work of Christ, on the ground that "Christ's death is placed on one side of the scales and the sins of the world on the other; his death overbalances the world's sin because of the free will nature and divine value of the former."[13] Due to the meritorious perspective on the death of Christ in Anselm's *Cur Deus Homo*, there is discontinuity between the atonement event and his incarnation, without considering the vicarious humanity of Christ *pro nobis*. In this regard, Anselm's

9. Anselm, "*Cur Deus Homo*," *Basic Writings*, 269.

10. For an excellent reflection on the fathers' ideas on the incarnation, see Torrance, "The Mind of Christ in Worship," *Theology in Reconciliation*, 139–214.

11. McIntyre, *St. Anselm and His Critics*, 152.

12. Hart, "A Gift Exceeding Every Debt," 348.

13. Balthasar, *Theo-Drama IV*, 260.

objectively satisfactory type of atonement overemphasizes the saving work of Christ, rather than his person as the eternal Mediator between God and sinners. Since the human life of Jesus only plays a temporary role in preparing his death, there is no room for a vicarious and sovereign role in the humanity of Christ. Thus Anselm places the historical and human event of Christ's self-giving sacrifice in the eternal-immanent dimension within the Triune God.

> In fact, that honor belongs to the whole Trinity. Therefore, since he himself is God, the Son of God, he offered himself for his own honor to himself, as he did to the Father and the Holy Spirit. That is, he offered his humanity to his divinity, which is itself one of the three persons . . . The Son freely offered himself to the Father. For it is in this way that we most aptly express it, both because the whole Godhead, to whom as man he offered himself, is understood in the reference to the one person, and because when we hear the names of Father and of Son we feel a certain boundless gratitude in our hearts, when it is said that the Son entreats the Father in this way for us.[14]

This is the theologically aesthetic dimension of the eternal Son's act of self-offering to the Father's divine honor. Christ's self-giving can be subjectively realized in a Christian life of endless thanksgiving. Christ's spontaneous offering of himself to God can "remit all debt since he has earned a reward greater than all debt, if given with the love which he deserves."[15]

In order to avoid any overly literal understanding of Christ's sacrifice as a "payment," we need to positively assess Anselm's own theological methodology of "contemplative reason," which "moves unceasingly from meditation to prayer."[16] David Bentley Hart argues that Christ's cultic-sacrificial death for God's honor is his eternal "gift" of unsurpassable love:

> Christ's sacrifice belongs not to an economy of credit and exchange, but to the Trinitarian motion of love, it is given entirely as gift, and must be seen as such: a gift given when it should not have needed to be given again, by God, and at a price that we, in our sin, imposed upon him. As an entirely divine action, Christ's sacrifice merely draws creation back into the eternal motion of divine love for which it was fashioned. The violence that befalls

---

14. Anselm, "*Cur Deus Homo*," *Basic Writings*, 269–97.

15. Anselm, "*Cur Deus Homo*," *Basic Writings*, 300.

16. Olsen, "Hans Urs Von Balthasar and the Rehabilitation of St. Anselm's Doctrine of the Atonement," 53–54.

Christ belongs to our order of justice, an order overcome by his sacrifice, which is one of peace.[17]

For Anselm, there is no division or contradiction between God and Christ in the crucifixion, because the Son of God voluntarily dedicates the eternal sacrifice of himself through "his humanity" to the Father, in order to make atonement for human sin. There can be neither God's divine judgment against sin nor Christ's triumphant conquest over evil in Anselm's contemplation of the celestial offering in front of the throne of God's eternal glory. However, rather than holistically explaining the simultaneity of Christ's atoning death for God and humankind, Anselm exclusively concentrates on describing the upward movement of Christ's eternal sacrifice to God. What is lacking is the saving work of the incarnated Son of God with, for, and in us. It is no accident that with regard to the cultic perspective, Anselm never mentions Christ's priestly-sacrificial atonement *pro nobis*, which the New Testament evidently testifies, because he only exegetes a small sample of biblical passages regarding Christ's will to obey God.[18] Besides, according to Anselm, the voluntary will of Christ is definitively from his deity, not from his vicarious humanity.[19] While Anselm firmly believes in the mediatorship of Christ as God and human, for Anselm Christ's humanity is no more and no less than his atoning death itself, which must be dedicated to reinstate God's honor.

More seriously, Anselm's objective atonement model draws attention to the eternal glorification of Christ's death as something separated from his historical life and ministry on the earth. It is regrettable that for Anselm, Christ's earthly life and ministry have no soteriological value. Anselm wrongly separates Christ's person from his self-sacrificial death for God's honor, because Christ's voluntary death is indeed the sole factor in atonement. Anselm contends that "nothing can be more severe or difficult for man to do for God's honor, than to suffer death voluntarily when not bound by obligation; and man cannot give himself to God in any way more truly than by surrendering himself to death for God's honor."[20] This is Anselm's scholastic glorification of Christ's salvific death, which can be legitimately criticized by the modern non-violent atonement theologians. If Christ's human death itself brings about humankind's reconciliation

---

17. Hart, "A Gift Exceeding Every Debt," 348.
18. Anselm, "*Cur Deus Homo*," *Basic Writings*, 210, 211, 300.
19. Anselm, "*Cur Deus Homo*," *Basic Writings*, 210.
20. Anselm, "*Cur Deus Homo*," *Basic Writings*, 2712.

with God, Anselm's view of atonement falls to the level of a commercial transaction between God and sinners. David Brown explains Anselm's commercial interpretation of the death of Christ as an excessive surplus to pay back all the debts of sinners:

> That is why for Anselm even the God-man Christ is in no sense compensating for human misconduct in the perfect life he leads. He is merely fulfilling the destiny of human nature which God made possible in creating it that way. Compensation or recompense must therefore, Anselm contends, lie elsewhere, and this he believes he has found in Christ's death. According to traditional Christian teaching, human nature is intended for eternal life and human beings die only because of the fall. Therefore a life voluntarily surrendered to death has nothing to do with the teleology of human nature. It is something returned to God that is not owed, a purely gratuitous act, and, because it is the life of a human being who is also God, an offering of infinite worth.[21]

Brown strives to make an apology for Anselm's separation of Christ's death from his own person. Nevertheless, Anselm fails to comprehend the continuity between Christ's life, crucifixion, and resurrection for our salvation. Since the human life of Jesus only plays a temporary role in making his death possible, there is no room for a vicarious and sovereign role in the humanity of Christ. While it is true that Christ's crucifixion is the central event of the atonement, it cannot be the be-all and end-all. Rather, Christ's atoning work initiates from God's eternal election in Christ and actualizes through the incarnation and his earthly life and ministry and finally culminates in the self-sacrificial event of crucifixion in our sinful place. In the Anselmian commercial formulation of Christ's atoning death, the hermeneutical principle of the unity and distinction of Christ's person in his work and the work in his person is impaired by Anselm's over-emphasis on Christ's saving death apart from Christ himself. In this sense, Anselm's speculations on Christ's death itself as meriting eternal reward deserve to be fairly criticized by nonviolent atonement scholars. God's perfect being in Anselm's atonement model confirms that Christ's death to God's honor is an ahistorical and eternal event in the Triune God's being and act beyond human time and space. Along with the divine and eternal dimension of the crucifixion, Anselm would have done better to explore the historical and biblical actuality of Christ's atoning death for the sake of the salvation of humankind.

21. David Brown, "Anselm on Atonement," 293.

The Ontological Unnecessity of Christ's Victory over Evil

The reason why Anselm never substantially deals with the problem of evil is that Anselm follows the Augustinian understanding in which "evil is nothing, an absence of good."[22] From the divine perspective of God's sovereignty, it is plausible that for Anselm there can be neither a dualistic conflict nor equal relationship between Satan and God. Anselm claims that "neither the devil nor man belong to any but God, and neither can exist without the exertion of divine power."[23] Since both the devil and humankind are the fallen creation of God, the hostile powers cannot have their own independent right of possession over sinners beyond God's sovereign reign. Even if humans misunderstand Satan to have a just power of punishment over them, there is still the fact that "God's inconceivable wisdom, which happily controls even wickedness, permitted it."[24] The underlying idea of Anselm's rejection of the *Christus victor* motif is that there is neither a necessity for Christ to redeem humans enslaved under Satan, nor a military conquest over Satan. Those issues seriously impair God's sovereignty over the entire creation. Provided that in the case of *Christus victor* there is a dualistic conflict between God and the evil powers, there would be an inevitable justification of the fatalistic phenomenon of humankind's victimization. Rather, it is through Anselm's elimination of the devil from the salvation drama that humans have responsibility for their own sins.[25] The devil is nothing but the evil executor of God's righteous verdict over sinful humankind.

> The devil is said to torment men justly, because God in justice permits this, and man in justice suffers it. But when man is said to suffer justly, it is not meant that his just suffering is inflicted by the hand of justice itself, but that he is punished by the just judgment of God.[26]

However, Anselm rightly puts a double qualification on the role of Satan. Even if the evil powers indirectly carry out God's judgment, they

---

22. Evans, *Anselm*, 67.
23. Anselm, "Cur Deus Homo," *Basic Writings*, 201.
24. Anselm, "Cur Deus Homo," *Basic Writings*, 202.
25. See Southern, *St. Anselm and His Biographer*, 85–96, and Hopkins, *A Companion to the Study of St. Anselm*, 189–90.
26. Anselm, "Cur Deus Homo," *Basic Writings*, 203.

Christ the Mediator's Self-Sacrificial Atonement Pro Nobis

invariably remain evil themselves.[27] Moreover, Anselm acknowledges that God must be engaged in humankind's "liberation" from the devil.[28] There seems to be a glimpse of the *Christus victor* motif. Anselm mentions that "Christ is said to be exalted on this account, because he endured death."[29] The crucified Christ's exaltation, including his resurrection and ascension, not only positively means "a reward of his obedience" but also paradoxically reveals his divine "omnipotence" in the crucifixion itself.[30]

Nonetheless, Christ's atoning work at the cross does not have a direct effect on the liberation of humans enslaved under evil. Although Anselm intends to deny Satan's jurisdiction over sinful humankind in *Christus victor*, he seems to inevitably justify human victimization by evil, insofar as it is caused by God's sovereignty. Anselm's scholastic contemplation of God's power and responsibility to restore his fallen creation is "too limited to deal with oppression," including oppression caused by structural evils beyond human reason in a yet-suffering world.[31] Anselm's theological deletion of Satan's destructive and enslaving power over fallen humanity makes it likely that God's honor-centered atonement is radically inclined to deny the destructiveness of evil at a socio-political and spiritual level. Anselm's commercial understanding of God's satisfaction fails to have the holistic perspective that embraces the problem of human victimization and suffering in society.

The decisive reason why there is no room for the *Christus victor* motif in Anselm's feudalistic atonement theology is that Anselm rejects a violent concept of God's punishment against sin and evil. The scholastic perspective on the restoration of God's honor disregards God's righteous judgment that annihilates the power of sin, death, and evil. It is regrettable that Anselm fails to contemplate the most dramatic point of Christ's substitution or "damnation" for our sins, because Christ under God's condemnation paradoxically consumes the evil powers of sin, death, and even hell.[32] This is the divine simultaneity of Christ's substitutionary death for our sins and his apocalyptic conquest over the hostile powers. Anselm fails to see that Christ's human humiliation and voluntary obedience to

27. Anselm, "*Cur Deus Homo*," Basic Writings, 203.
28. Anselm, "*Cur Deus Homo*," Basic Writings, 203.
29. Anselm, "*Cur Deus Homo*," Basic Writings, 209.
30. Anselm, "*Cur Deus Homo*," Basic Writings, 209.
31. Flora A. Keshgegian, "The Scandal of the Cross," 489.
32. Balthasar, *Theo-Drama IV*, 287.

the crucifixion is inseparable from his divine exaltation and apocalyptic victory in his resurrection. Without the saving power and righteousness revealed in the crucifixion of Christ, there is no way to guarantee the reality of the enslaved humans' liberation from the hostile powers.

4.2 Calvin's Biblical Reflection on Christ's Sacrifice and Victory For Us

Christ's Mediatory, Priestly-Sacrificial Atonement

According to Calvin, Christ himself is the sole mediator who can overcome the problem of sin, fallen humans' alienation from the holy God himself. Thus Christ as the Mediator is the unique savior to "bridge the gulf" between humankind and God.[33] We need to note that Calvin's doctrine of sin directly relates the personal iniquities of sinners to the universal effect of their sins as guilt, which brings about their eternal destruction under the evil powers.

> So great was the disagreement between our uncleanness and God's perfect purity! Even if man had remained free from all stain, his condition would have been too lowly for him to reach God without a Mediator. What, then, of man: plunged by his mortal ruin into death and hell, defiled with so many spots, befouled with his own corruption, and overwhelmed with every curse?[34]

Since the wages of sin is death (Rom 6:23), sinners have to take personal responsibility for their own sins. Although Calvin's concept of sin has a strong theological affinity with Anselm's, as the personal and direct problem of guilt in front of God, Calvin's idea of sin never remains at the dimension of the broken relationship between God and sinners. Hence, for Calvin, Christ's eternal mediatorship as fully God and fully human is the objective basis for the atonement. Calvin believes that the purpose of Christ's incarnation is "to restore us to God's grace as to make of the children of men, children of God; of the heirs of Gehenna, heirs of the heavenly kingdom."[35] In this way, Calvin overcomes Anselm's scholastic reasoning about the restoration of God's honor by focusing on his

---

33. Calvin, *Institutes* II.12.1.
34. Calvin, *Institutes* II.12.1.
35. Calvin, *Institutes* II.12.2.

Christ the Mediator's Self-Sacrificial Atonement Pro Nobis

sovereign grace to save his children from sin and death, as well as the evil powers of hell.

The principle of vicarious substitution *pro nobis* permeates Calvin's biblical understanding of the person and work of Christ. Firstly, Calvin considers it imperative that Christ be fully God and fully human.[36] Without ceasing to be the Son of God, the incarnate Christ shares the same human nature as we. This is precisely the way in which the God-human Jesus can not only give us "the inheritance of the heavenly kingdom" but also fulfill "his task to swallow up death" and "to conquer sin."[37] Regarding the person of Christ as the Savior, Calvin understands the two different functions of Christ's deity and humanity in the atonement. Because of the divine nature, Christ prevails over the power of death; simultaneously, through Jesus' human nature he is able to die for our sins. Calvin asserts,

> Since neither as God alone could he feel death, nor as human alone could he overcome it, he coupled human nature with divine that to atone for sin he might submit the weakness of the one to death; and that, wrestling with death by the power of the other nature, he might win victory for us.[38]

Next, Calvin goes on to argue that the atoning work of Christ is to take the forensic punishment of God upon his vicarious humanity, in order to satisfy the requirement of "God's righteous judgment."[39] Calvin insists,

> The second requirement of our reconciliation with God was this: that man, who by his disobedience had become lost, should by way of remedy counter it with obedience, satisfy God's judgment, and pay the penalties for sin. Accordingly, our Lord came forth as true human and took the person and the name of Adam in order to take Adam's place in obeying the Father, to present our flesh as the price of satisfaction to God's judgment, and, in the same flesh, to pay the penalty that we had deserved.[40]

As the theological heir of Anselmian objective theory, Calvin attempts to re-vindicate the idea of satisfaction in the biblical revelation. Yet we should attend to Calvin's understanding of penal substitution through the lens of the uniqueness of Christ's person and work. Christ's

---

36. Calvin, *Institutes* II.12.2.
37. Calvin, *Institutes* II.12.2.
38. Calvin, *Institutes* II.12.3.
39. Calvin, *Institutes* II.12.3.
40. Calvin, *Institutes* II.12.3.

death is not the victimization of a human Jesus by evil, but God the Son's self-sacrificial death for sinners under God's judgment. While Calvin firmly believes the forensic metaphor of God's satisfaction to be the divine reality of salvation, in his view of atonement there are two different ideas of vicarious punishment and sacrifice "side-by-side."[41]

At this point, I would raise a theological question as to how the two different concepts of punishment and sacrifice can be harmonized in Calvin's doctrine of atonement. In my judgment, the priesthood of Christ as the Mediator plays a central role in incorporating both the penal view of the crucifixion and the sacrificial perspective. Although the two themes of penal substitution and sacrificial death are interrelated in Calvin's doctrine of atonement,[42] I claim that for Calvin, the high priesthood of Christ plays an essential role in unifying the different atonement models, in order to describe the mystery of Christ's death for us according to the biblical testimony. Calvin manifestly maintains that Christ as "our High Priest" solely performs the ministry of reconciliation between God and sinners.[43] Calvin says:

> As a pure and stainless Mediator he is by holiness to reconcile us to God. But God's righteous curse bars our access to him, and God in his capacity as judge is angry toward us. Hence, an expiation must intervene in order that Christ as Priest may obtain God's favor for us and appease his wrath. Thus Christ to perform this office had to come forward with a sacrifice.[44]

According to Ronald S. Wallace, although Calvin mentions Jesus as completing forensic substitution in the context of God's judgment and the satisfaction of the law, Calvin never relies on the penal idea that one must fulfill the law so that others may be set free.[45] Rather, the death of Christ on the cross is nothing other than a sacrifice in the primary sense.[46] As a result, we come to realize that the foundation for Calvin's penal substitutionary doctrine is Christ's priesthood and the precious blood that he shed upon the cross. In order to grasp the core of Calvin's biblical understanding of Christ's priestly office, we must scrutinize

---

41. Paul, *The Atonement and the Sacraments*, 103.
42. Calvin, *Institutes* II.16.6.
43. Calvin, *Institutes* II.15.6.
44. Calvin, *Institutes* II.15.6.
45. Wallace, *Calvin's Doctrine of the Christian Life*, 5.
46. Wallace, *Calvin's Doctrine of the Christian Life*, 5.

Calvin's theological exegesis on Christ's priesthood and his eternal sacrifice once and for all in the Epistle to the Hebrews.[47]

First of all, Calvin points out that the incarnation is the starting point for reconciliation between God and sinners, in that Christ assumed our human nature for the sake of atonement. Calvin insists that "having purposed to make atonement for sins, he put on our nature that we might have in our own flesh the price of our redemption; in a word, that by the right of a common nature he might introduce us, together with himself, into the sanctuary of God."[48] Calvin believes in the continuity between the incarnation and crucifixion, because there is one indivisible reality existing between the two events, as seen through the lens of the vicarious humanity in Christ's priesthood. Like Calvin, Torrance maintains that "the priest-hood of the incarnate Son" is equal to "the vicarious humanity of Jesus," for the Son of God took the same flesh and blood as we, so that he would be an eternal priest before God, in order to offer himself as a sacrifice for sins.[49] In this sense, I argue that for Calvin, the body of Christ as a high priest is the vicariously human guarantee of reconciliation that "initiated from the incarnation of fallen nature, so that it culminated in the cross of Christ."[50]

Next, we need to examine Calvin's theological answer to these questions: Why did Christ as the high priest become a sacrifice? How was it possible? Peterson insists that for Calvin, the priesthood of Christ is "unique," because "he is the only one to be both priest and sacrifice for sin."[51] Van Buren emphasizes that in order to complete the work of the high priesthood in the Old Testament, "Christ fulfilled the whole of the sacrificial system, by becoming that substitute for us which was prefigured by the sacrificial victim."[52] Calvin claims: "Although God under the law commanded animal sacrifice to be offered to himself, in Christ there was a new and different order, in which the same one was to be both priest and sacrifice. This was because no other satisfaction adequate for our sins, and no man worthy to offer to God the only-begotten Son, could be

---

47. All the quotations are from *Calvin's New Testament Commentaries*.
48 Calvin, *Commentary on Heb 2:17*.
49. Torrance, *Theology in Reconciliation*, 110.
50. Ahn, 'The Humanity of Christ," 150.
51. Peterson, *Calvin and the Atonement*, 56.
52. Van Buren, *Christ in Our Place*, 70.

found."[53] It is much more striking to realize that according to John Frederick Jansen, insofar as Christ is our priest and sacrifice, "Christ is not the expression of a principle of atonement, but is himself the atonement."[54] In this sense, Christ's priestly office confirms the dynamic unity of Christ's person and work in distinction, because Christ is our priest; simultaneously, he is our sacrifice. Calvin explains the reason why Christ as a priest should become a sacrifice for the sake of reconciliation.

> The priest without a sacrifice is no peacemaker between God and man, for without a sacrifice sins are not atoned for, nor is the wrath of God pacified. Hence, whenever reconciliation between God and man takes place, this pledge must ever necessarily precede. Thus we see that angels are by no means capable of obtaining for us God's favor, because they have no sacrifice. The same must be thought of prophets and apostles. Christ alone then is he, who, having taken away sins by his own sacrifice, can reconcile God to us.[55]

According to the Chalcedonian Definition, for Calvin, Christ is true God; simultaneously, he is a true human being in the person of the Mediator.[56] In the same way, for Calvin, Christ is an eternal priest; simultaneously, he is an eternal sacrifice. Calvin proclaims that we cannot think of Christ's atoning work apart from his person, because we are saved by the sacrificial death of the person of Christ himself. Calvin asserts that "without Christ there is no purity nor salvation, so nothing without blood can be either pure or saving; for Christ is never to be separated from the sacrifice of his death."[57] Here we find a dynamic principle of unity for Christ's person in the work and the work in the person. For the purpose of demonstrating Christ' self-sacrificial work in the person of his high priesthood, Calvin claims that the vicarious act of Christ's sanctification and consecration in his own body accomplished our salvation.

> He should appear before God as a Mediator for us. In the first place, the word "sanctuary" is fitly and suitably applied to the body of Christ, for it is the temple in which the whole majesty of

53. Calvin, *Institutes* II.15.6.

54. John Frederick Jansen, *Calvin's Doctrine of the Work of Christ*, 93–94. Jansen mentions that for Calvin, Christ's priesthood cannot be separated from kingship, in that "redemption" consists of "the reconciliation of God" and "the dominion of God."

55. Calvin, *Commentary on Heb* 5:1.

56. Calvin, *Institutes* II.12.2.

57. Calvin, *Commentary on Heb* 9:22.

> God dwells. He is further said to have made a way for us by his body to ascend into heaven, because in that body he consecrated himself to God, he became in it sanctified to be our true righteousness, he prepared himself in it to offer a sacrifice . . . He then entered into heaven through his own body, because on this account it is that he now sits at the Father's right hand; he for this reason intercedes for us in heaven, because he had put on our flesh, and consecrated it as a temple to God the Father, and in it sanctified himself to obtain for us an eternal righteousness, having made an expiation for our sins.[58]

Wallace explains that Calvin, reasoning from "the analogies of consecration by the sprinkling of blood," grasps "in Christ's death, the perfecting of his own self-sanctification to his eternal priesthood on our behalf."[59] Christ's self-sanctification in his own body and consecration of the body as sacrifice to God are the manifestation of Christ's vicarious humanity *pro nobis*, through which Christ not only sanctifies our fallen nature but also saves all of us.[60] Moreover, it is remarkable that according to Calvin, since the sanctified humanity of Christ as a priest goes together with his act of offering himself to God, Christ is both a priest and sacrifice. Torrance insists that "the inherent oneness of the Offer and the Offering" in the priestly office of Christ unites "the Patristic emphasis upon the Being of God in his acts" and "the Reformed emphasis upon the Acts of God in his being."[61] Calvin also joins the two emphases into the high priesthood of Christ. At the heart of the mystery of atonement in Calvin's exegesis of Hebrews lies the simultaneity of Christ's work and person. In terms of "Christ as priest," Edmondson accurately describes Calvin's view on the person of Christ in his atoning work by contending that "Reconciliation is not something that happens to Christ, but something that he does, that he offers, that he accomplishes."[62] Here we can see how Calvin harmonizes the being of Christ in his act and the act in his being from the perspective of Christ's priestly office. Calvin simultaneously emphasizes both who Christ as the Mediator is in his self-offering to God and what Christ did in his vicarious humanity, so that Calvin can demonstrate the dynamic unity of Christ's person and work in atonement. Therefore, the

58. Calvin, *Commentary on Heb 9:11*.
59. Wallace, *Calvin's Doctrine of the Christian Life*, 6.
60. Ahn, "The Humanity of Christ," 156.
61. Torrance, *Theology in Reconciliation*, 133–35.
62. Edmondson, *Calvin's Christology*, 112.

work of Christ's self-offering is inseparable from his person as vicarious humanity, the high priesthood.

Yet, commenting on the desperate prayer of Christ, Calvin describes Christ's atonement in the forensic setting of God's condemnation and the consequence of death through the motif of *Christus Victor*. Following the biblical testimony, Calvin continuously integrates all the aspects of Christ's atoning work into his person.

> He [Christ] saw in it the curse of God, and that he had to wrestle with the guilt of all iniquities, and also with hell itself? Hence was his trepidation and anxiety; for extremely terrible is God's judgment. He then obtained what he prayed for, when he came forth a conqueror from the pains of death, when he was sustained by the saving hand of the Father, when after a short conflict he gained a glorious victory over Satan, sin, and hell.[63]

Finally, Calvin underlines the eternal efficacy of Christ's priestly sacrifice to God, because Christ perfectly accomplished the work of atonement in the person of the Mediator himself. Since Christ, the Mediator as the high priest, stands forever between God and fallen humanity, Christ's self-offering in his own body is eternally effective.

> The virtue of the one sacrifice is eternal and extends to all ages. And he says since the foundation of the world, or from the beginning of the world for in all ages from the beginning there were sins which needed expiation. Except then the sacrifice of Christ was efficacious, no one of the fathers would have obtained salvation; for as they were exposed to God's wrath, a remedy for deliverance would have failed them, had not Christ by suffering once suffered so much as was necessary to reconcile men to God from the beginning of the world even to the end.[64]

Calvin confirms that Christ's death is perfectly and eternally sufficient for the sake of reconciliation between God and sinners. What Christ had done once and for all goes together with who Christ is. The work of Christ is in his person; simultaneously, the person is in the work. Therefore, Jesus Christ himself was, is, and will be the living sacrifice from eternity to eternity. Calvin can properly proclaim Christ as the Mediator between God and sinful humankind by reflecting the biblical truth on Christ's priestly-sacrificial atonement *pro nobis*.

63. Calvin, *Commentary on Heb* 5:17.
64. Calvin, *Commentary on Heb* 9:26.

However, it is somewhat regrettable that Calvin's Christology tends to focus on Christ's atoning work rather than his own person. The great Reformer's principal concern is how believers can receive the benefit of Christ's salvation, because, according to Charles Partee, "the primary focus of the Protestant Reformation was soteriological rather than Christological."[65] Due to the over-accentuation of Christ's substitutionary atonement "for us," Calvin fails to offer a substantial exposition on the relationship between Christ's deity and his humanity in the hypostatic person. Calvin distinguishes Christ's Sonship and eternal deity from the incarnated Christ's earthly life and true humanity.[66] However, regarding the communication of Christ's natures in his own person as the Mediator, Calvin seems to hesitate about the direct contact between the deity and humanity of Christ. Calvin believes that "since Christ, who was true God and also true man, was crucified and shed his blood for us, the things that he carried out in his human nature are transferred improperly, although not without reason, to his divinity."[67] Calvin's Christological interpretation of the "improper transferal" indirectly shows that God's satisfaction by Christ's atoning death exclusively depends on his vicarious humanity,[68] whereas the deity of Christ as the beloved Son of God must not endure God's wrathful judgment and cannot experience the human Jesus' death. Calvin's Christological concern over the distinction between the deity and humanity of Christ paradoxically blurs his objective confirmation of the actual unity of the two natures in Christ's saving work.[69] Provided that Christ is the eternal Mediator, Calvin needs to fully preserve the

---

65. Partee, *The Theology of John Calvin*, 144.

66. Calvin, *Institutes* II.14.2.

67. Calvin, *Institutes* II.14.2.

68. Calvin, *Institutes* II.16.10. According to Calvin, "Christ's body was given as the price of our redemption, but that he paid a greater and more excellent prince in suffering in his soul the terrible torments of a condemned and forsaken man."

69. Allen, "Calvin's Christ," 393–94. R. Michael Allen points out the hermeneutical limitations, as follows: "This discussion of Calvin's careful manner of discussing the relation of the two natures of Christ is not to suggest that he had no doctrine of the *communicatio idiomatum*, rather it must be noted that his discussion of the *communicatio* does not operate on the ontological level. Calvin discusses the *communicatio* within his hermeneutical discussion of New Testament texts regarding the person and nature(s) of Christ. Calvin refers to the *communicatio* as a 'figure of speech' . . . The *communicatio* refers specifically to the instances whereby what is proper to one [human] nature (i.e., shedding of blood) is predicated of the other nature (i.e., divinity). Note that, in these instances, the particular attribute is not being attributed to the person of Christ (the 'hypostatic union') but to the other nature."

unity of the two natures, without weakening the hermeneutical distinction throughout his substitutionary atonement theology.

Furthermore, although Calvin takes a Christological interpretation of Christ's priestly-sacrificial atonement, he seems simply satisfied with his overarching emphasis on God's divine satisfaction by Christ' propitiatory death. Rather than underscoring the revelation of Christ's self-sacrificial love for sinners, Calvin often seems to place the hermeneutical emphasis on Christ's appeasement of God's wrath.

> Propitiation is added, because no one is fit to be a high priest without a sacrifice. Hence, under the Law, no priest entered the sanctuary without blood; and a sacrifice, as a usual seal, was wont, according to God's appointment, to accompany prayers. By this symbol it was God's design to shew, that whosoever obtains favor for us, must be furnished with a sacrifice; for when God is offended, in order to pacify him a satisfaction is required.[70]

In this regard, as his critics claim, given that propitiation of God's vindicatory justice takes priority over the expiation of sin by Christ's self-sacrificial blood, it inevitably appears to nonviolent atonement theologians that Calvin pushes himself toward a justification of God's violence against the human victim Jesus. Yet the nonviolent atonement scholars should keep in mind that for Calvin there is no propitiation of God's wrath without the expiation of our sins in the objective sense. More decisively, Calvin does not provide us with his own account of how the cultic, forensic, and military metaphors of atonement are dynamically related to each other in the person and work of Christ. However, in spite of these limitations, we can compassionately conclude that Calvin's theological reflection on Christ's cultic-substitutionary death is not so much based on the socio-cultural influence of Calvin's own historical period as on the solid Christological interpretation of biblical revelation.[71]

---

70. Calvin, *Commentary on 1 John* 2:2.

71. Fiddes, *Past Event and Present Salvation*, 100. By underling the subjective and personal application of salvation as "healing," Paul S. Fiddes misconstrues the whole of Calvin's doctrine of atonement as an objective type of penal substitutionary atonement that is solely based on Christ's "passive obedience." Fiddes fails to realize Christ's "active obedience" in his own self-giving, which Calvin biblically describes.

Continuity Between God's Judgment and Christ's Conquest Over Evil

Calvin dynamically engages penal substitutionary doctrines of atonement with a classical type of *Christus Victor*. Calvin argues for Christ's victory over evil powers against the background of Christ's vicarious punishment by God. Calvin affirms that "it was expedient at the same time for him to undergo the severity of God's vengeance, to appease his wrath and satisfy his just judgment. For this reason, he must grapple hand to hand with the armies of hell and the dread of everlasting death."[72] At the moment when Christ was judged in our sinful place, he was "victorious and triumphed over" the hostile powers.[73] Here we see that the penal aspect of Christ's atoning death is simultaneously related to the military image of Christ, the eternal conqueror over the evil powers of sin and death. It is through Christ's death that sin as guilt must be punished by God the eternal judge. At the same time, evil as power is overcome by Christ, the eternal Son of God. For Calvin, God's judgment in Christ's crucifixion never contradicts God's victory in Christ's resurrection. Rather, God's judgment against sin and evil already confirms his victory over the evil powers in the crucifixion. In contrast to Aulén's theological deletion of God's justice against sin from his power to liberate humans from the evil powers, Calvin proceeds in the biblical way to integrate God's forensic judgment and Christ's satisfaction of the divine law into Christ's conquest over the diabolic principalities. As Henri A. G. Blocher rightly puts it, Satan is described as "the *Accuser*" in the juridical setting of the heavenly court (Rev 12:10; Job 1:6–12; Zech 3:1).[74] More essentially, the biblical theme of *Christus victor*, unlike Aulén's overemphasis on Christ's deity over his humanity in the mythological language of cosmic war, is concretely embodied in the incarnate Christ's human obedience to the Father, including his earthly life and ministry to the point of the cross.[75] Christ's penal substitutionary death for our sins is related to his conquest over the evil powers, because by the saving power of Christ's blood—that is, his satisfaction of God's divine law—not only are the devil's accusations cancelled, but the hostile powers are "disarmed" (Col 2:14, 15).[76] It

---

72. Calvin, *Institutes* II.16.10.
73. Calvin, *Institutes* II.16.11.
74. Henri A. G. Blocher, "Agnus Victor," 82.
75. Blocher, "Agnus Victor," 85.
76. Blocher, "Agnus Victor," 82–83.

is no accident that for Calvin, God's judgment of sin brings about Christ's conquest over sin, death, devils, and hell, because Christ's penal substitution sets sinners free from the enslavement of the hostile powers. Citing Hilary of Poitiers's arguments, Calvin confirms that Christ's substitutionary death is the objective ground of his victory over death and hell.

> He bore the weight of divine severity, since he was "stricken and afflicted" (cf. Isa 53:5) by God's hand, and experienced all the signs of a wrathful and avenging God. Therefore, Hilary reasons: by his descent into hell we have obtained this, that death has been overcome. In other passages he does not differ from our view, as when he says: "The cross, death, hell—These are our life." In another place: "The Son of God is in hell, but man is borne up to heaven." And why do I quote the testimony of a private individual when the apostle, recalling this fruit of victory, asserts the same thing, that they were "delivered who through fear of death were subject to lifelong bondage"? [Heb 2:15]. He had, therefore, to conquer that fear which by nature continually torments and oppresses all mortals. This he could do only by fighting it. Now it will soon be more apparent that his was no common sorrow or one gendered by a light cause. Therefore, by his wrestling hand to hand with the devil's power, with the dread of death, with the pains of hell, he was victorious and triumphed over them, that in death we may not now fear those things which our Prince has swallowed up [cf. 1 Pet 3:22].[77]

We can note the crux of Calvin's Christological interpretation of atonement. By vicariously bearing God's judgment against sin, death, and hell, the crucified Christ annihilates the power of sin and death. In this way, Christ's substitutionary death accomplishes the conquest of the hostile powers in his own person. Moreover, God's judgment and the Satanic powers of death and hell overlap in Calvin's understanding of Christ's death. Calvin states that "the Son of God had been laid hold of by the pangs of death that arose from God's curse and wrath—the source of death."[78] The two contradicting motifs of God's righteous judgment and Christ's divine victory over Satan exemplify Calvin's principle of unity in distinction. Without relying on the theological background of dualistic conflict between God and evil, Calvin can argue for Christ's fierce combat and glorious conquest over the powers of sin and death. Rather, because

77. Calvin, *Institutes* II.16.11.
78. Calvin, *Institutes* II.16.10.

Christ the Mediator's Self-Sacrificial Atonement Pro Nobis

of God's sovereign permission granted to the evil powers, the incarnated Son of God defeats them, without underestimating the dramatic effect of Jesus' salvific suffering at the cross. Thus God's judgment of evil is the manifestation of God's righteous sovereignty over the entire creation in Christ himself.

Likewise, as Peterson rightly puts it, Christ's vicarious humanity under God's judgment plays a decisive role in accomplishing the salvation of sinful humankind, because it reveals the substitutionary dimension in Calvin's doctrine of *Christus Victor*.[79]

> We must look to the point of his fear. Why did he dread death except that he saw in it the curse of God, and that he had to wrestle with the sum total of human guilt, and with the very powers of darkness themselves. Hence the fear and anxiety, because the judgment of God is more than terrifying. He got what he wanted inasmuch as he emerged from the pains of death as Conqueror, was upheld by the saving hand of the Father, and after a brief encounter gained a glorious victory over Satan, sin, and the powers of hell.[80]

Christ's substitutionary death plays an instrumental role in actualizing the divine conquest of evil, because it puts an end to the power of death in the paradoxical se. In this way, Christ's conquest over the hostile powers not only takes place in a divine-transcendental dimension, but also becomes a historical-immanent event for humankind.

More importantly, we can see Calvin's incipient idea of God's apocalyptic judgment in Christ's atoning death for us, because the crucifixion is the beginning of the new life in Christ. By relating the substitutionary motif to that of *Christus Victor*, Calvin Christologically confirms the continuity between atonement and resurrection in the person of Christ himself.

> For the lively assurance of our reconciliation with God arises from Christ having come from hell as the conqueror of death, in order to show that he had the power of a new life at his disposal. Justly, therefore, does Paul say that there will be no gospel, and that the hope of salvation will be vain and fruitless, unless we believe that Christ is risen from the dead (1 Cor 15:14). For then did Christ obtain righteousness for us, and open up our entrance into heaven; and, in short, then was our adoption ratified,

---

79 Peterson, *Calvin and the Atonement*, 72–74.

80. Calvin, *Commentary on Heb 5:7*. Cited from Peterson, *Calvin and the Atonement*, 72.

when Christ, by rising from the dead, exerted the power of his Spirit, and proved himself to be the Son of God.[81]

4.3 Barth's Penal-Cultic Substitutionary Doctrine of Atonement and the Socio-Political Implications of Christ's Apocalyptic Victory

Barth's Mediatorial Christology of God in Christ

Just as Barth discusses God's being (II/1) with his reconciling act in Christ (IV/1), he deals with the person of Christ as God-human (§59.1, "The Way of the Son of God into the Far Country") before addressing his atoning work *pro nobis* through the lens of both a forensic and cultic formulation (§59.2, "The Judge Judged in Our Place").[82] Above all, the alpha and omega of Barth's Christological understanding of atonement is the divine and voluntary "obedience" of the Son of God in "his self-humiliation, his way into the far country."[83] In radical contrast to the prodigal son who disobeys his human father in Jesus' famous parable (Luke 15:11–32), the Son of God himself fully obeys God's will for the salvation of fallen humankind and the evil world, which are alienated from God's covenant of love and justice. Barth strives to justify how God's deity can be maintained throughout the incarnation, because atonement is "a matter of the mystery of his deity in his work *ad extra*, in his presence in the world."[84] Barth highlights that throughout God's divine humiliation of becoming the human Jesus, Christ himself never ceases to be the eternal of Son of God himself.

> Even in the form of a servant, which is the form of his presence and action in Jesus Christ, we have to do with God himself in his true deity. The humility in which he dwells and acts in Jesus Christ is not alien to him, but proper to him . . . It is his sovereign grace that he wills to be and is amongst us in humility, our God, God for us. But he shows us this grace, he is amongst us in humility, our God, God for us, as that which he is in himself, in the most inward depth of his Godhead. He does not become

---

81. Calvin, *Commentary on Matt 28:1*.
82. Hieb, *Christ Crucified in a Suffering World*, 106.
83. Barth, *Church Dogmatics* IV/1, 177.
84. Barth, *Church Dogmatics* IV/1, 177.

another God. In the condescension in which he gives himself to us in Jesus Christ he exists and speaks and acts as the One he was from all eternity and will be to all eternity.[85]

It is through the incarnation that the Son of God becomes Jesus, a humble man. However, at the heart of the *novum mysterium* of God's own self-humiliation in Christ lies his saving righteousness and power in the person of the Mediator.[86] God himself in Christ determines and accomplishes the entire atonement for the fallen creation. Barth confirms, "the truth and actuality of our atonement depends on" God in Christ himself.[87] Furthermore, against the nonviolent atonement theologians who completely deny Christ's deity in the incarnation and crucifixion, Barth prophetically warns that "a God who found himself in this contradiction can obviously only be the image of our own unreconciled humanity projected into deity."[88] The caricature of Barth as a "neo-orthodox" theologian unconcerned with the humanity and immanence of God is falsified by passages like this:[89]

> We may believe that God can and must only be absolute in contrast to all that is relative, exalted in contrast to all that is lowly, active in contrast to all suffering, inviolable in contrast to all temptation, transcendent in contrast to all immanence, and therefore divine in contrast to everything human, in short that he can and must be only the "Wholly Other." But such beliefs are shown to be quite untenable, and corrupt and pagan, by the fact that God does in fact be and do this in Jesus Christ.[90]

In his mature work, Barth rejects a one-sided concept of God as "Wholly Other," because there is no such timeless transcendence of God's being and work as fundamentally severed from the historical and immanent dimension of our world. Rather, the living God revealed in Christ embraces all the human contradictions of sin, evil, and death as

---

85. Barth, *Church Dogmatics* IV/1, 193.
86. Barth, *Church Dogmatics* IV/1, 193.
87. Barth, *Church Dogmatics* IV/1, 193.
88. Barth, *Church Dogmatics* IV/1, 186. Italics mine.
89. For the theological issues, see Mangina, "Mediating Theologies." According to Mangina, "Barth's Christology demands a stronger account of church and sacraments than he himself supplied," Mangina, "Mediating Theologies," 427.
90. Barth, *Church Dogmatics* IV/1, 185–86.

"his own" things in Christ himself, in order to reconcile the entire fallen creation to himself.[91]

Yet, according to Barth, since God in Christ takes fallen humankind and the evil world upon his own person, the crucifixion means God's self-sacrificial judgment in Christ himself. More seriously, God's self-humiliation in Christ to the point of crucifixion would mean his self-annihilation. In this regard, it seems unreasonable that the crucified Son of God under his own judgment can save those who are under the divine accusation. Thus Barth is obliged to clarify the Christological implications of his views about God in Christ at the crucifixion. Barth contends that the crucifixion has nothing to do with the death of God or his self-annihilation.

> God gives himself, but he does not give himself away. He does not give up being God in becoming a creature, in becoming man. He does not cease to be God. He does not come into conflict with himself. He does not sin when in unity with the man Jesus. He mingles with sinners and takes their place. And when he dies in his unity with this man, death does not gain any power over him. He exists as God in the righteousness and the life, the obedience and the resurrection of this man.[92]

The biblical truth that Jesus is the Son of God means that Christ himself has God's own eternal sovereignty even at the moment of the crucifixion. For Barth, God in Christ was, is, will be God, without collapsing into the merely human god of the nonviolent atonement theologians. Regarding the eternal deity of Christ, there is no vulnerability to sin and death, nor inevitability dominated by hostile powers. From the incarnation onwards, through the entire life and ministry and even violent death of Christ, the living and almighty God in Christ sovereignly acts for the salvation of sinners.

Along with the ontological supposition of Christ's deity, Barth simultaneously sets forth a salvific role for his true humanity. Barth underlines that as a true human being like one of us, Christ had to be exposed to human temptation and suffering.

> In himself he was still the omnipresent, almighty, eternal and glorious One, the All-Holy and All-Righteous who could not be tempted. But at the same time among us and for us he was quite

---

91. Barth, *Church Dogmatics* IV/1, 185.
92. Barth, *Church Dogmatics* IV/1, 185.

different, not omnipresent and eternal but limited in time and space, not almighty but impotent, not glorious but lowly, and open to radical and total attack in respect of his righteousness and holiness.[93]

It must be noted that without any theological ambiguity, Barth emphasizes that from the incarnation onward, Christ takes the fallen human nature *pro nobis*.

> The Word assumes our human existence, assumes flesh, i.e., he exists in the state and position, amid the conditions, under the curse of sinful man. He exists in the place where we are, in all the remoteness not merely of the creature from the Creator, but of the sinful creature from the Holy Creator. Otherwise his action would not be a revealing, a reconciling action.[94]

Barth's view of Christ's assumption of human fallenness confirms the crux of Pauline soteriology. Here Barth's genius lies in dynamically engaging the forensic motif of God's judgment with Christ's hypostatic union—a union of the Son's deity and the human Jesus' fallen humanity in his own person.

> In that he takes our place it is decided what our place is. In that he allows himself to be sentenced as man, sentence is pronounced on us. The wrath of God against all ungodliness and unrighteousness of men, who hold the truth in unrighteousness, is revealed, and revealed concretely and finally from heaven (Rom 1:18), in the fact that God gives himself not only to encounter the man against whom he must and does turn his wrath but to *take his place*. In Jesus Christ we see who we are by being seen as those we are—being seen as God in him acknowledges what we are, accepting solidarity with our state and being, making himself responsible for our sin.[95]

In this way, Barth not only believes in continuity between the incarnation and atonement, but also declares God's paradoxical power of salvation in the movement of self-humiliation. God in Christ "frees the creature in becoming a creature" and "overcomes the flesh in becoming flesh."[96] The ultimate intention of Barth's Christological reflection is to

---

93. Barth, *Church Dogmatics* IV/1, 184.
94. Barth, *Church Dogmatics* I/2, 155.
95. Barth, *Church Dogmatics* IV/1, 240. Italics mine.
96. Barth, *Church Dogmatics* IV/1, 185.

maintain the eternal deity of the incarnated and crucified Christ as the God of unrighteous humans, as well as to declare the Son of God's true humanity as solidarity with them.

The Judged Judge in Our Sinful Place as the Priest Sacrificing Himself Pro Nobis

Barth's interpretation of reconciliation has both ontic and noetic implications, because God's eternal covenant and will in Christ are actually fulfilled by Christ's atoning death in our human history and space. God's revelation in Christ corresponds to God's act, the reconciliation event in Christ himself. According to Barth, God's revelation of our sin is simultaneously his act of abolishing our guilt by his forgiveness.[97] Barth states that God's ultimate communion with all humanity is culminated in "revelation," and it is "identical with" the "reconciliation" in the person and work of Jesus Christ.[98] God's self-revelation in Christ is one with his reconciliation. Here, the crux of Barth's Christ-centered theology of revelation and reconciliation is the fact that God's noetic revelation is the same as his ontic reconciliation in Jesus Christ himself.[99] With the unity of revelation and reconciliation in Christ, Barth sets forth a doctrine of Christ's substitutionary atonement that is juridically formulated from the outset. In §59.2, "The Judge Judged in Our Place," Barth comprehensively explains the four substitutionary characteristics of Christ's atoning death in the juridical framework, as follows. First, "Jesus Christ was and is 'for us' in that he took our place as our Judge."[100] This fact means that the humbly incarnated Son of God can be the true judge of good and evil, instead of arrogant sinners who arbitrarily judge each other. Second, "Jesus Christ was and is for us in that he took the place of us sinners."[101] This means that although Christ knows no sin, he takes the condemnation of our sins upon himself. Third, "Jesus Christ was and is for us in that he suffered and was crucified and died."[102] From the eternal kingdom of God,

97. Watson, "A Study in St. Anselm's Soteriology and Karl Barth's Theological Method," 494.
98. Barth, *Church Dogmatics* II/1, 274.
99. Barth, *Church Dogmatics* IV/1, 637.
100. Barth, *Church Dogmatics* IV/1, 232.
101. Barth, *Church Dogmatics* IV/1, 236.
102. Barth, *Church Dogmatics* IV/1, 245.

Christ the Mediator's Self-Sacrificial Atonement Pro Nobis

Christ descends in obedience to God's will to the point of crucifixion in the human world of sin and death.[103] Fourth, "Jesus Christ was and is for us in that he has done this before God and has therefore done right."[104] In spite of the negative dimension of God's judgment in Christ, penal substitution is the positive content of God's saving righteousness and his sovereign love *pro nobis*. Barth highlights that God himself is with us in Christ, in order to fulfill the covenant by means of Christ's work of substitution in our sinful place. In Barth's penal substitutionary understanding, Christ is not just the passive "measure" of God's judgment, but the active "Subject" of the forensic event, in that Christ himself "judges and punishes" our sins in his own "righteousness."[105]

Thus, rather than focusing on the punishment that Christ bears in the traditional penal substitution theory, Barth creatively illuminates his own theological concept of "displacement," in which fallen humankind has been displaced by Christ himself, the judged judge in their sinful place.[106] The displacement of our sinful being through Christ's substitutionary death is the key point at which God's own restorative judgment is perfectly accomplished in the person of Christ, not us. The over-accentuation of punishment or satisfaction distorts the integrity of Christ's substitutionary work, which the Holy Scripture witnesses by a variety of images.[107] Thus Barth is concerned with fact that the forensic aspect of Christ's atoning work cannot be overemphasized apart from his own person. According to Barth, even "The Judge Judged in Our Place" is only one of many biblical accounts of the event, although it is perfect by itself.[108] A specific theory of atonement cannot perfectly grasp "the thing itself, the *Sache* of reconciliation," but it just functions as a finger pointing to the full realization of reconciliation.[109] Although Barth is inclined to concentrate on a forensic understanding of the atonement, he properly interprets the quintessence of penal substitution as its substitutionary character, not the forensic judgment or Christ's salvific suffering itself. Since penal substitution itself is only a means to the final goal of

---

103. Barth, *Church Dogmatics* IV/1, 245.
104. Barth, *Church Dogmatics* IV/1, 258.
105. Barth, *Church Dogmatics* II/1, 402.
106. Rutledge, *The Crucifixion*, 518.
107. Johnson, *God's Being in Reconciliation*, 124.
108. Johnson, *God's Being in Reconciliation*, 118.
109. Johnson, *God's Being in Reconciliation*, 118. Quoted from Barth, *Dogmatics in Outline*, 116.

reconciliation in Christ, the biblical motif cannot be overemphasized. Christologically speaking, since the person of Christ must precede his atoning work, even penal substitution should remain as only one of the hermeneutical ways to grasp Christ's atonement, not the sole and absolute perspective. As Adam J. Johnson rightly puts it, according to Barth the theory of substitution cannot be the sole standard by which God's saving work in Christ is judged.

> The doctrine of substitution is a consequence of and not the basis for the unity of the work of Christ. Barth's argument, in other words, is not that the work is unified because it is substitutionary, but rather that it is unified because God is the one present in Christ making this substitutionary work effective.[110]

What I will demonstrate is that, along with the fourfold forensic formulation of Christ's substitution, Barth himself simultaneously believes in the Christological dimension of the cultic metaphor of atonement revealed in the New Testament. Barth strives to avoid the hermeneutical absolutization of penal substitution theory itself, apart from the person of Christ. It is remarkable to see that in his commentary on Romans, Barth strongly argues for the vicarious meaning of Christ's death by demonstrating the substitutionary perspective of the cultic atonement.

> Whom (Christ) God set forth to be a covering of propitiation, through his faithfulness, by his blood. In the Old Testament cultus *the covering of propitiation* (EV. mercy seat; Hebr. *Kapporeth*; LXX *Hilasterion*) . . . it is the place above which God himself dwells . . . the place where, on the great day of atonement, the people were reconciled to God by the sprinkling of blood (Lev 16:14, 15) . . . By the express counsel of God, Jesus has been appointed from eternity as the place of propitiation above which God dwells from which he speaks; now, however, he occupies a position in time, in history, and in the presence of men. The life of Jesus is the place in history fitted by God for propitiation and fraught with eternity—God was in Christ reconciling the world unto himself (2 Cor 5:19).[111]

The atoning death of Christ on the cross means that God's eternity breaks through our history. God's eternal determination to reconcile the world has been completed in time and space. It is through the

---

110. Johnson, *God's Being in Reconciliation*, 124.
111. Barth, *The Epistle to the Romans*, 105.

vicarious sacrifice of Christ himself that God reveals reconciliation in Christ. Barth affirms,

> The propitiation occurs at the place of propitiation—only by blood: only, that is to say, in the inferno of his complete solidarity with all the sin and weakenss and misery of the flesh; in the secret of an occurrence which seems to us wholly negative . . . By his death he declares the impossible possibility of our redemption.[112]

More theologically, in *Church Dogmatics* IV/1, Barth presents a hermeneutical innovation: he argues that the forensic metaphor of the "judge judged in our place" can be equally well represented in cultic terms.[113]

Barth holistically opens a way to engage his forensic formulation of Christ's substitutionary death with his priestly-sacrificial death for us. Barth asserts, "in fact we can equally well describe the work of Jesus Christ as his high-priestly work as his judicial work, and we shall mean and say exactly the same thing."[114] According to Barth, Christ as the eternal priest is the sole "Mediator" between God and sinners in an exclusive sense. Simultaneously, he is the holy "representative" of sinful humankind in the inclusive perspective.

> 1. Jesus Christ took our place as Judge. We can say the same thing in this way. He is the Priest who represented us. He represented a people oppressed by its sins, threatened because of them, and in need of propitiation, a people from which the will of Yahweh is concealed, which will not be instructed properly concerning his rights and law, which cannot really sacrifice or pray for itself. The priest is the mediator and representative who

---

112. Barth, *The Epistle to the Romans*, 105.

113. Barth, *Church Dogmatics* IV/1, 275–76. For excellent research on this topic, see Johnson, "A Temple Theory of the Atonement," in *God's Being in Reconciliation*, 164–96. Johnson paraphrases Barth's proposal using the image of the biblical temple, and he makes three crucial claims: "1. Jesus Christ came as the true temple, 2. Jesus Christ is the one who was abandoned and forsaken in the place of the old temple, 3. In the place of the old, Jesus was the true temple." According to Johnson, instead of the "dialectics" of God's "presence" and his "destroying presence" among the Israelites and the old temple in the Old Testament, it is through Christ's atonement event that "God took himself the nature and fate of the old temple, bearing his own destructive presence in himself, so as to save those upon whom it would otherwise fall."

114. Barth, *Church Dogmatics* IV/1, 277.

by virtue of his office (originally, perhaps, understood in charismatic terms) actually makes possible the access of the people to its god.[115]

Likewise, at the heart of the priestly-sacrificial atonement lies the Christological simultaneity of Christ's deity and his vicarious humanity. As Christ's eternal priestly office reveals his own person as Mediator, his atoning work confirms his self-offering as God-human to God. Barth insists, "Jesus Christ is the One who was accused, condemned, and judged in the place of us sinners. But we can say the same thing in this way: he gave himself to be offered up as a sacrifice to take away our sins."[116] Since "in our place he [Christ] has made a perfect sacrifice," Barth integrates the universal efficacy of Christ's priestly-sacrificial atonement once and for all into the juridical exposition in which "Jesus Christ was just in our place," as he previously notes.[117]

Accordingly, the cultic substitution is the hermeneutical component that connects both the exclusivity and inclusivity of Christ's atoning death *pro nobis*. Because the Son of God's substitutionary death is self-sacrificial and embraces the death of our old sinful nature, believers can participate, by mystical union with Christ, in the salvific efficacy of his crucifixion.

> It is the power of this inclusion that draws the sinner (in his self-exclusion) into a fellowship of life with Jesus. Insofar as Jesus does what we cannot do, his action is primarily exclusive; but insofar as, on the cross, he vouches for us in God's presence—and vouches for us effectively—his action becomes inclusive.[118]

In the exclusive dimension of Christ's atoning work for us, when Christ himself is apocalyptically judged by God's condemnation of evil, we cannot be with him because it would mean the annihilation of our sinful human existence. In Christ's triumph over evil, we cannot be with him because, due to our spiritual weakness, we would be defeated by the hostile powers. By contrast, the cultic atonement has an inclusive spiritual dimension in which we can be crucified with Christ and resurrected with him, in order to become holy and kingly priests for God's kingdom. The most distinctive characteristic of a cultic understanding of atonement

---

115. Barth, *Church Dogmatics* IV/1, 275.

116. Barth, *Church Dogmatics* IV/1, 277.

117. Drury, "The Priest Sacrificed in our Place." Cited from Barth, *Church Dogmatics* IV/1, 224, 281.

118. Balthasar, *Theo-Drama IV*, 351.

is humankind's participation in Christ's atoning work. Matthias Grebe rightly observes that there is a unique dimension of "participatory substitution" in the cultic atonement.[119] Likewise, according to Ephraim Radner, Leviticus reveals that to lay hands on the head of a sacrificial offering is "an effective act of solidarity and participation" that typifies the organic relationship between Christ and sinful humankind.[120] Humans' identification with a sacrificial offering enables the imputation of their sin to the dying animal. Sinners can receive God's grace of forgiveness to remove their sins through the vicarious death of the sacrifice. Witnessing the blood of the sacrifice instead of their own sinful being is inclusively related to their human participation in the entire process of God's atonement.

However, models of penal substitution and *Christus victor* are grounded upon the exclusiveness of Christ's saving work *pro nobis*. Christ must displace our sinful being throughout the atonement, because no one can be vicariously judged by God's judgment and can conquer the hostile powers. Without existential and personal participation in the atoning work of Christ himself, saved sinners can merely receive the divine outcome of Christ's penal redemption and military victory in an absolute or passive way. In the penal and military model of atonement, it is God himself in Christ, or the deity of the Son of God, that is the key point of God's reconciliation with sinful humankind. The humanity of Jesus only plays a functional role in revealing and communicating God's saving power to saved sinners. By contrast, the cultic substitution confirms that the vicarious humanity of Christ *pro nobis* as the eternal Priest and the lamb of God is the contact point through which sinful humans meet the holy God. Under the blood of the Son of God, saved sinners can enter the "holy of holies." Accordingly, it is through, with, and in Christ as the eternal priest *pro nobis* that believers are called to not only dedicate their earthly life as a spiritual sacrifice to God himself but also to sacrifice themselves in service to their neighbors.[121] In this regard, the priestly-sacrificial atonement of Christ has both the indicative and imperative dimension of salvation. The indicative dimension of Christ's

---

119. Grebe, *Election, Atonement, and the Holy Spirit*, 190–92.

120. Radner, *Leviticus*, 54.

121. "Therefore, I urge you, brothers and sisters, in view of God's mercy, to offer your bodies as a living sacrifice, holy and pleasing to God—this is your true and proper worship" (Rom 12:1); "But you are a chosen people, a royal priesthood, a holy nation, God's special possession, that you may declare the praises of him who called you out of darkness into his wonderful light" (1 Pet 2:9).

self-sacrificial death presents us with the ever new and transforming imperative to give ourselves in worship to God and service for the world through the priesthood of all believers in Christ.

Next, more directly and substantially, Barth asserts that concerning the cultic perspective on atonement, God's own self-giving in the Son of God himself is the crux of Christ's priestly-sacrificial atonement.

> It is God himself who not only demands but makes the offering. He makes it in that he the Lord willed to become a servant, in that his Son willed to go into the far country, to become one with us and to take our place as sinners, to die for us the death of the old man which was necessary for the doing of the will of God, to shed our wicked blood in his own precious blood, to kill our sin in his own death.[122]

Barth underlines that Christ's self-giving sacrifice through the crucifixion is the historical reality of God's reconciliation with sinful humankind in himself. It is through the cultic atonement that God not only abolishes the sins that caused our alienation, but also reveals our new identity in Christ himself. He is the personal actualization of God's perfect self-sacrificial love *pro nobis*.[123]

More importantly, Barth goes on to argue that without Christ's substitutionary atonement, even "an imputation of the alien righteousness" of the Son of God would be unavailable for the justification of sinners.[124] According to Barth, the salvific efficacy of Christ's death begins in the cultic sense, because the objective ground of God's justification of sinners is Christ's self-sacrifice. The perfect and historical self-giving of Christ is God's saving righteousness by which sinners are justified by faith in Christ. In this sense, Barth's atonement theology not only indicates the priority of cultic over juridical understanding, but also demonstrates the hermeneutical compatibility of the cultic and penal motifs. As Hunsinger rightly puts it, the cultic metaphor of Christ's blood lies at the heart of the Apostle Paul's forensic declaration of sinners' justification:

> Seen as a juridical event, Christ's cross is the place of judgment where God has "condemned sin in the flesh," satisfying "the just requirement of the law" (Rom 8:3, 4), yet in a way that brings unexpected acquittal to the guilty since "we [have been] justified

---

122. Barth, *Church Dogmatics* IV/1, 280.
123. Barth, *Church Dogmatics* IV/1, 282.
124. Barth, *Church Dogmatics* IV/1, 283.

by his blood" (Rom 5:9). Here the motif of Christ's blood again pertains primarily to the *extra nos* and the *pro nobis* aspects of the cross. "Justified by his blood" stands in dramatic counterpart to the more familiar phrase "justified by faith," underscoring the provenience of divine grace.[125]

Barth accurately points out that while it was appropriate for the Reformed orthodox theologians to set forth Christ's substitutionary atonement under the name of Christ's priestly office, "the only trouble was that their expositions under this title did at their heart slip into forensic notions."[126] As Barth mentioned above, a violent interpretation of God's punishment against sinners is alien to a biblical notion of atonement.[127] However, it is odd that without self-critical reflection on the forensic tendency in the Reformed tradition, Barth justifies the hermeneutical priority of penal over cultic substitution, because he believes the atonement to be culturally accessible and theologically comprehensible.

> If we ourselves have refrained from presenting the whole in this [cultic] framework it is for two reasons. First, and quite simply, material which is already difficult would have been made even more difficult by trying to understand it in a form which is now rather remote from us. Second, and above all, we are able to see the matter better and more distinctly and more comprehensively under the four selected concepts taken from the forensic area of biblical thinking than would have been possible even at the very best if we had committed ourselves radically to a cultic view.[128]

Eberhard Jüngel rightly observes that Barth places the divine humiliation of the Son of God in the priestly office of Christ.[129] Following Calvin's biblical understanding, in which the reconciling work of Christ belongs to his eternal priesthood,[130] Barth assumes that Christ as the Judge judged in our sinful place implies the Priest who sacrifices himself *pro nobis*. Yet although both Calvin and Barth acknowledge the biblical priority of the cultic metaphor over forensic, commercial, and military metaphors, both of them overaccentuate the forensic aspect of Christ's

---

125. Hunsinger, *Disruptive Grace*, 362–63.
126. Barth, *Church Dogmatics* IV/1, 275.
127. Barth, *Church Dogmatics* IV/1, 275.
128. Barth, *Church Dogmatics* IV/1, 275.
129. Jüngel, *Karl Barth, a Theological Legacy*, 48.
130. Calvin, *Institutes* II.15.6.

substitutionary death. We should be alert to the absolutization of the forensic (including penal) dimensions of atonement. In order to holistically integrate multiple other motifs into their soteriologies, Calvin and Barth would have done better to start from the cultic understanding, which they themselves admit is more faithful in biblical terms.

However, my critical argument with Barth is not about the doctrinal content of Christ as the judge judged in our place, but about the hermeneutical priority assigned to the forensic perspective over the cultic one. My own holistic interpretation of Christ's priestly-sacrificial atonement event never rejects the forensically ontological dimension of substitutionary atonement—Christ must bear the penalty of God's judgment against fallen humanity and sin itself *pro nobis*—the penal substitution theory in the Reformed tradition and the ontologically modified one of Barth. The cultic perspective hermeneutically reinforces how the radical substitution of Christ for sinners and ontological sacrifice for their iniquities and fallen nature simultaneously takes place in his own person—the eternal priest and the lamb of God. Thus I argue that the cultic perspective on Barth's doctrine of atonement does not necessarily mean the ontological replacement of the forensic dimension of God's judgment through Christ's substitutionary death *pro nobis*. It is, nevertheless, odd to see that, according to Grebe, in order to logically engage with the doctrine of election in Christ, Barth's atonement theology should be solely interpreted from the cultic perspective of Christ's self-offering sacrifice for sinners, not the juridical standpoint of punishment against sin itself.[131] By biblically employing

---

131. Grebe, *Election, Atonement, and the Holy Spirit*, 3. Grebe argues that Barth's theological exegesis is incorrect, because "Christ did not bear sins in the way the Azazel-goat did (by bearing them upon itself and thus taking divine punishment)." Rather, the cultic atonement of Christ only means "a sin offering," and Christ did not, therefore, bear sin on the cross in a penal sense. We may critically observe the absolutizing tendency of a sacrificial motif in the doctrine of atonement in D. M. Baillie and Gunton. Baillie believes that the biblical core of the atonement event is "the eternal love of God dealing *sacrificially* with the sins of the world," because, as C. H. Dodd argues, there is no room for a violent concept of the "propitiation" of the righteous God's "wrath." See Baillie, *God Was in Christ*, 189. More seriously, following the Anselmian motif of restoration, Gunton argues that Christ's sacrifice has nothing to do with "a punitive substitution" that is a sort of external "transaction" between God and humankind. Rather, the sacrifice is "a divine action from within the heart of the human condition" that changes "the human relationship to God"; Gunton, *The Actuality of Atonement*, 124–27. But, as Barth rightly argues, for God's restorative judgment in Christ's priestly-sacrificial death, the cultic and forensic perspectives on atonement are not mutually exclusive in the ontological sense.

Existenzstellvertretung, Grebe solidly re-illuminates Barth's cultic understanding of atonement in his theological exegesis on Leviticus 16.

> *Existenzstellvertretung* is understood to be an atoning death, a vicarious offering of one's life as an equivalent for the forfeited life of another. *Existenzstellvertretung* should be seen as a concept making sense of the theology of cultic atonement and events in the Old Testaments, in particular in Leviticus. To contend that atonement is *Existenzstellvertretung* is to argue that the ungodly are redeemed from their sinful nature by participating in the death of the sacrifice through which they come into contact with the transcendent and holy God. The slaying of the sacrificial animal should not be seen as a punishment of the animal, nor should the priestly offering of the blood be seen as a human work to appease an angry deity. Instead the sin offering and the sprinkling of the blood should be seen as a salvific act (restoring the covenantal fellowship previously breached by sin) enabled by God himself.[132]

Accordingly, I basically agree with Grebe's critique of the hermeneutical weaknesses in Barth's forensically oriented doctrine of atonement. Barth himself modifies a penal substitution theory by neutralizing a violent motif of God's retributive punishment against sinners. Yet he is still inclined to explain the entire atonement processing through the lens of the forensic logics and formulation, without fully harmonizing the cultic perspective into his atonement theology. However, the decisive point with which I cannot but disagree is that for Grebe, while there is Christ's cultic substitution for sinful human beings, the ontological event has nothing to do with Jesus' vicarious bearing of their sins in the penal sense. Grebe's division between the ontological event and Christ's bearing of sins is unjustified, because the being of sinners and their sins cannot be separated from each other. Rather, Balthasar asserts that according to the Apostolic soteriology and Luther's Protestant restatement of the dynamic view, the crux of Christ's radical substitution for sinful humankind is the direct and ontological contact with their sins under God's righteous judgment.[133] The incarnated Son of God not only assumes fallen human

---

132. Grebe, *Election, Atonement, and the Holy Spirit*, 68–69.

133. Balthasar, *Theo-Drama IV*, 244–54, 286. "Christ himself is the archetype of the *simul Justus et peccator*. This, for Luther, is the logical consequence of the Chalcedonian formula, for the adopted human nature is essentially sinful and subject to God's judgment," Balthasar, *Theo-Drama IV*, 286. See also Luther, *On the Freedom of a Christian*, 49.

nature itself, but the crucified Christ also takes the curse that human sin causes upon himself. Christ's self-sacrificial substitution event is not merely to embrace the being of sinners, in order to externally justify the new status of their sinful being, but Christ himself, crucified by God's condemnation, wipes out their iniquities by his own blood, in order to declare them righteous in front of the holy God.[134] Grebe's indiscriminate criticism against Barth's Reformed position of atonement goes too far to the extent that it is appropriate for us to believe that cultic restoration of sinful nature can be fulfilled, without the forensic annihilation of sin itself.[135] In this way, Grebe fails to fully consider Barth's integrative thinking on atonement as God's own restorative judgment in Christ himself.

In contrast to Grebe's nonviolent reinterpretation of atonement, God's forensic procedure and declaration of atonement and Christ's cultic-sacrificial death *pro nobis* as the content of the event are in a mutually constitutive relationship with each other in the ontological sense.[136] Grebe attempts to nullify a violent motif and dimension of atonement by accepting the cultic-nonviolent perspective on Christ's substitution for sinners. Yet it seems evident that Grebe cannot get out of the hermeneutical dilemma between God's violent punishment of sin and evil and his nonviolent restoration of sinful human nature and the fallen world. More seriously, like Anselm and nonviolent atonement theologians, Grebe exclusively focuses on the epistemological and ontological positivity of God's restorative work of salvation in Christ, overlooking the negative dimension of God's judgment against sin and evil.

> According to Barth's view, Christ's death on the cross was God's "negative act" that, in light of Easter, was undertaken with a "positive intention." The notion of an act that was both "negative" and "positive" suggests the primary aim of the cross was to deal with sin. But the true emphasis of the New Testament understanding of the cross is to reconcile humanity to God—not merely deal with the barrier of sin—"in Christ God was reconciling the world to himself" (2 Cor 5:19). Although Barth's conclusion about the new status of humanity is in line with our

---

134. "God did this by sending his own Son in the likeness of sinful flesh to be a sin offering. And so he condemned sin in the flesh" (Rom 8:3). "Since we have now been justified by his blood, how much more shall we be saved from God's wrath through him!" (Rom 5:9).

135. Grebe, *Election, Atonement, and the Holy Spirit*, 183.

136. For the holistic view on atonement, see Cass, "Christ Condemned Sin in the Flesh."

interpretation of the cross-event (the "turning of man" and "his positing afresh" [*seine neue Setzung*] into a new and positive relationship with God) we have seen that the whole Christ-event should not be seen as an act that was both negative and positive but rather was a wholly positive act by Jesus that brought humanity into fellowship with God.[137]

Typically, this is the hermeneutical dualistic perspective in which a number of modern theologians are unconsciously inclined to underline a positive corollary of Christ's atoning death for us, avoiding the negative process of how the crucified Christ overcomes the burden of sin and evil in his own person.[138] Rather than pushing a dichotomous question of whether Christ's atoning death is penal or cultic not, we need to have a more balanced and holistic view of the cultic-penal substitutionary atonement of Christ. The juridical dimension of God's judgment against sin and evil in the atonement event are is to be taken into Christ's self-giving sacrifice for sinful humankind, with a hermeneutical distinction in the ontological unity.

Moreover, due to an Alexandrian Christological bent, there is a monophysite dualistic understanding of deity and humanity in Barth's doctrine of reconciliation.[139] Barth essentially places Christ's atoning work *pro nobis* in the juridical context of God's universal judgment against all humankind. In spite of the annihilation of fallen humanity in the divine judgment against Christ, God as the sovereign subject of the event is the eternally living God himself, for his own restorative salvation of all the sinners in the world.

> God is supremely God, that in this death he is supremely alive, that he has maintained and revealed his deity in the passion of this man as his eternal Son. Moreover, this human passion does not have just a significance and effect in its historical situation

---

137. Grebe, *Election, Atonement, and the Holy Spirit*, 193. Italics mine.

138. Paradoxically speaking, Grebe's exclusive understanding of the sacrificial-restorative death of Christ, which I criticize, enables me to have my own constructive critique of the forensic absolutization in the penal substitution theory of atonement, because according to the biblical revelation on reconciliation, a cultic metaphor accompanies the forensic one side by side.

139. Waldrop, "Karl Barth's Concept of the Divinity of Jesus Christ," 263. Charles T. Waldrop makes the criticism that according to Barth, "everything has already happened in God, and therefore God's act *ad extra* seems to have no inherent value. If Jesus' real life is lived eternally with God prior to this becoming a man in time, how could his life in time be very important?"

within humanity and the world. On the contrary, there is fulfilled in it the mission, the task, and the work of the Son of God: the reconciliation of the world with God. There takes place here the redemptive judgment of God on all men. To fulfil this judgment, he took the place of all men, he took their place as sinners. In this passion there is legally reestablished the covenant between God and man, broken by man but kept by God. On that one day of suffering of that One there took place the comprehensive turning in the history of all creation—with all that this involves.[140]

As John Thompson rightly puts it, according to Barth, God in the divinely humbled Christ is the sovereign subject of self-judgment in our sinful place.[141] Hence, the deity of Christ plays a decisive role in accomplishing God's reconciliation with sinful humankind in Christ himself. It cannot be exaggerated that the person and work of Christ is attributable to his eternal deity. By contrast, in Jesus' true humanity *pro nobis*, according to Barth, since Jesus Christ is the judge judged in our place, "in his vicarious humanity He bears the just judgment of God on our sin being made sin for us."[142] Therefore, it is regrettable Barth's Chalcedonian understanding of Christ's deity and humanity is limited. The deity has the positive effect of salvation, whereas the humanity has the negative dimension of judgment.[143] If Barth exclusively focuses on maximizing the penal and military motif, the dualistic problem unavoidably emerges in a way similar to the case of nonviolent atonement theories.

Correspondingly, Barth's restorative concept of God's judgment in Christ has its own tendency toward universalism.[144] As Barth insists,

140. Barth, *Church Dogmatics* IV/1, 247.

141. Thompson, "Christology and Reconciliation in the Theology of Karl Barth," 209.

142. Thompson, "Christology and Reconciliation in the Theology of Karl Barth," 211.

143. Yet Barth confirms the positive role of Jesus' vicarious humanity in the doctrine of sanctification as a constitutive dimension of reconciliation. Barth, *Church Dogmactics* IV/2, §64.3 "The Royal Man"

144. Even though Barth insists that universalism should not be an object of Christian faith, he believes that with a humble prayer of eschatological hope, we may have "openness to the possibility," because "the unexpected work of grace" would be "received only as a free gift" (IV/3, 477–78). According to Hunsinger, Barth's own theological perspective on universalism is "reverent agnosticism" on the eschatological corollary of Christ's atoning death, because he not only argues against Origen's rationalism of universal restoration, but also moves beyond the Augustinian tradition's

if Christ is the electing God and the elected human, then the whole of humanity is already elected in the humanity of Jesus and he is the only one reprobate in God's righteous judgment.[145] But then there is the theological probability that everyone will be ultimately saved in Christ, on the ground that the Son of God himself can never be eternally abandoned by the Father. From the forensic formulation of atonement, Barth's Christologically reoriented doctrine of election and reprobation demonstrates that Jesus' sinful humanity is the passive object of God's election and judgment from eternity, whereas the deity of the Son of God is the active subject in electing and reconciling all humankind in himself. God's "No" in the crucifixion is God's wrathful judgment against fallen humankind and their sins, and it is negated by "the Yes of the reconciling will of God," which is the eternal and final decision of the Father.[146] God's election and reconciliation in Christ's deity negates the reprobation—fallen humankind's negation of God's faithfulness and love—through his humanity, which is judged by God himself. By faithfully following the divine paradox of sin and grace (Rom 5:20:21), Barth focuses on illuminating the asymmetrical understanding of God's grace in Christ—his "Yes" to human sin, which is their rebelling "No." In Christ's person, provided that God's eternal deity in Christ infinitely overwhelms Jesus' historical humanity, God's reconciliation must be the positive and restorative consequence of his negative and forensic judgment against Jesus' vicarious human nature, which embraces the whole of humankind and their sins. Even if Barth attempts a Christological representation of the penal

---

biblicalism on an eternal hell as God's punishment. Hunsinger, "Hellfire and Damnation," 427. More constructively, in order to deny the theological possibility of universal salvation in Barth's theology, David W. Congdon argues that God's reconciling work in Christ has "a double contingency," because an objective contingency of divine reconciliation in Christ always accompanies saved humankind's subjective contingency of participation in "the apostolic mission of Jesus." Congdon, "Apokatastasis and Apostolicity." For the human subjectivity of Barth's theology, see Mangina, *Karl Barth on the Christian Life*. Nonetheless, G. C. Berkouwer rightly objects that Barth's Christologically modified approach to Calvin's double predestination logically leads up "*apocatastasis*," the doctrine of universal salvation, though Barth struggles to deny the unavoidable conclusion. G. C. Berkouwer, *The Triumph of Grace in the Theology of Karl Barth* (Grand Rapids, Mich.: W. B. Eerdmans, 1956), 112. For an evangelical critical evaluation on the universal implication on Barth's atonement theology, See, Garry, "Karl Barth and the Doctrine of the Atonement," *Engaging with Barth: Contemporary Evangelical Critiques*, 232–72.

145. Barth, *Church Dogmatics* II/2, 95. IV/1, 309.
146. Barth, *Church Dogmatics* II/1, 397; IV/1, 309.

process of atonement in the cultic perspective, Christ's deity seems to be directly related to the universal efficacy of the divine reconciliation, without fully substantiating the biblical implication of the eternal priest's atoning work by his vicarious humanity.

However, we may critically accept that for Barth, neither a theological principle nor the consequence of universalism supersedes the sovereignty of God's divine freedom in the living Son.[147] Rather, Barth's universalizing tendency needs to reflect his own "inclusive Christology," according to the typology between Adam and Christ that the Apostle Paul describes in Romans 5.[148] Barth himself believes in a dynamic representation of the living Christ's personal and historical encounter with those who are elect in himself from eternity. Yet since Barth argues for God's universal sovereignty over all humanity in Christ, he definitely neglects the ontological distinction between Christians and non-Christians from the human side.[149] At this point, Barth himself should have reconsidered Calvin's biblical insight into how the universality of God's grace can be harmonized with the particularity of the faith of the elect in Christ. Although Christ died for all, the salvific efficacy of the atonement event is not to be applied by both "the godly and the ungodly" in an "indiscriminate" way.[150]

The Apocalyptic and Socio-Political Dimension of Christ's Atoning Death

Similar to Weaver's narrative *Christus Victor*, Barth also places a heavy emphasis on the fact that "Jesus is Victor."[151] There is no doubt that Barth's doctrine of atonement is essentially in line with *Christus Victor*, because Barth glorifies the triumph of Christ over the evil power of darkness.[152] According to Barth, Jesus is our "Redeemer from sin and death and the

---

147. Greggs, "'Jesus is Victor.'"

148. Mangina, *Karl Barth: Theologian of Christian Witness*, 127.

149. Mangina, *Karl Barth: Theologian of Christian Witness*, 77. "Judas is not the same as Paul; the unbeliever is not the same as the believer."

150. Calvin, *Institutes* II.16.6. For Calvin's biblical interpretation on Christ's atoning death for all, see Boersma, "Calvin and the Extent of the Atonement," and Kevin D. Kennedy, "Hermeneutical Discontinuity between Calvin and Later Calvinism."

151. Barth, *Church Dogmatics* IV/3.1, 165–274.

152. Bloesch, *Jesus is Victor!*, 43.

Christ the Mediator's Self-Sacrificial Atonement Pro Nobis

devil."[153] Yet there is an essential difference between the classic type of *Christus Victor* and Barth's view on Christ's victory. Above all, there is no dualism between God and evil in Barth's doctrine of atonement. God in Christ has already conquered the power of darkness. As the eternal light of God, Christ himself reveals his definitive victory over sin, death, and the devil. As a result, Barth rejects the idea of "ransom theory," in which devils have rights over human beings, because they do not have "a divine potentiality" but only "exist as non-being."[154] In the nonviolent atonement theory, Jesus cannot save himself without God's proclamation of resurrection, in which God nonviolently overcomes evil by forgiving the sinners who killed his Son. In this case, the nonviolent Jesus is not the active savior of sinners, but a passive victim who needs the salvation of God. However, according to Barth, Jesus Christ is "the key point and consummation" of God's work of "creation, reconciliation, and redemption."[155] By dynamically incorporating the two motifs of God's forensic judgment and *Christus Victor* into the person of Christ himself, Barth declares that Christ accomplishes reconciliation with God and conquest over the evil powers in his own person. The biblical metaphor that Barth employs is Christ as the eternal light of God, as the Gospel of John witnesses: "The light shines in the darkness, and the darkness has not overcome it" (John 1:5). The motif of light is used to reveal the universality of Christ's atoning work for the entire fallen creation.

> As reconciliation is reconciliation of the world, of all men, it applies to the whole world, to all men . . . That it applies to all in this twofold sense means that as the light of life shines in the darkness, the world and all men come within the reach of its beams, but as it shines in the darkness, the world and all men are still in the sphere of darkness.[156]

Barth places a heavy emphasis on the "overwhelming" power of the light over the darkness. While it seems to be a dualistic conflict between light and darkness from a literal perspective, there cannot be in fact an equal confrontation between the evil power of darkness and Christ himself as the eternal light.

---

153. Barth, *Church Dogmatics* IV/1, 766. Regarding the Christian faith, Barth follows Luther's confession.
154. Barth, *Church Dogmatics* II/1, 563.
155. Barth, *Church Dogmatics* II/2, 149.
156. Barth, *Church Dogmatics* IV/3.1, 191.

> Hence we cannot in any sense understand in static terms the relationship between him and the surrounding world of darkness. It is certainly not *dualistic*. We do not have the equilibrium of opposing forces, as though darkness had the claim and power finally to maintain itself against light, as though its antithesis, opposition and challenge to light, its restricting of it, rested on an eternal and lasting order.[157]

However, Barth does not overlook the seriousness of the evil that persistently resists the eternal reign of Christ.

> On the other hand, it is not monistic. The power of light is not so overwhelming in relation to that of darkness that darkness has lost its power altogether, as though its antithesis were already removed, its opposition brushed aside, its challenging and restricting of light of no account. The only alternative is to think of it in terms of dynamic teleology, namely, in relation to the power of light, Word, and revelation as this is active in great superiority yet has not so far attained its goal but is still wrestling toward it, being opposed by the power of darkness, which even though it yields in its clear inferiority, is still present and even active in its own negative and restrictive way. A history is here taking place; a drama is being enacted; a war waged to a successful conclusion.[158]

Here Barth totally rejects any theological dualism in which God and evil are equally matched, as if a king had to desperately suppress his rebellious enemies in a human situation. At the same time, Barth denies the naively positive belief that evil has already been annihilated by God in Christ. Rather, Barth proposes a third way between God's eternal sovereignty in Christ and the historical persistence of evil. Barth's theology of atonement cannot be simply defined as a divine and objective achievement of God's reconciliation in Christ, as if the historical and subjective application to humankind and the world were unnecessary. Rather, as Barth himself underlines, because of the "dynamic teleology" in his theology, God's reconciling work continuously accompanies the apostolic and evangelical participation of Christians as the faithful witnesses of Christ's saving truth. They are sent into God's kingdom to minister to the yet-suffering world in the darkness of untruth.

---

157. Barth, *Church Dogmatics* IV/3.1, 168. Emphasis mine.
158. Barth, *Church Dogmatics* IV/3.1, 168. Emphasis mine.

It is of great importance that Barth boldly declares an apocalyptic dimension in the substitutionary death of Christ by interrelating the two motifs of God's judgment against sin and his victory over evil. Barth proclaims that "the activity of the second Adam who took the place of the first, who reversed and overthrew the activity of the first in this place, and in so doing brought in a new man, founded a new world and inaugurated a new æon—and all this in his passion."[159] Christ's self-sacrificial death not only declares the death of the fallen creation—God's judgment against sin and evil in the world—but also reveals his own eternal life-giving death—the foundation for the renewed creation in himself. Like Calvin, Barth thinks the penal dimension of the atonement demonstrates both God's objective reconciliation with the fallen creation and the divine triumph over the evil powers of sin, death, and even hell.

> As the Judge, as the judged, as the One who in his own person has accomplished the judgment, he is the end of the old æon and the beginning of the new. He is the righteousness which dwells in the new heaven and the new earth (2 Pet 3:13). We wait for him when, placed in him and with him at this turning-point of the times, we wait for this new heaven and new earth. He sits on the throne and says: "Behold, I make all things new," and more than that: "It is done. I am Alpha and Omega, the beginning and the end" (Rev 21:5)—He, this righteous man.[160]

In his realized eschatology, Barth underlines that Christ's death is already the objective guarantee of the new creation in Christ himself. More significantly, as Mangina rightly points out, God's judgment against fallen humanity through Christ's atonement has the "apocalyptic" dimension of divine recreation.

> When Barth speaks of judgment, he means an apocalyptic event, God's action of restoring and renewing the whole creation. At the cross, God does not bring about any possibility immanent in the first creation—although as ordered to the covenant, creation itself remains "very good." Human sin is by definition the rejection of grace; how then could it manifest a capacity for receiving grace? Rather, God saves the world at the cross by remaking it. The death of Jesus Christ is God's negation of the world, the end of the world as a sphere shaped by human agency and striving. At the cross, nothing less took place than the end of history:

---

159. Barth, *Church Dogmatics* IV/1, 254.
160. Barth, *Church Dogmatics* IV/1, 257.

"Human history was actually terminated at this point" (IV/1, 734). In the terms set by apocalyptic, the new creation can only appear by a radical act of divine remaking: "everything old has passed away; see, everything has become new!"[161]

The dynamic and all-inclusive dimension of reconciliation in Christ confirms that the whole fallen world under God's apocalyptic judgment is already apocalyptically transformed into the new creation through the crucified Christ himself. What is at stake is the eternal light of Christ's reconciliation, which starts to shine forth in the life of Christians in order to open their eyes to the eternal truth of *Christus Victor*. They can then sacrifice themselves in liberating those who are oppressed by the darkness of structural evils in the yet-suffering world.

> According to the Gospel of Luke and the Epistle of James, as also according to the message of the prophets, there follows from this character of faith a political attitude, decisively determined by the fact that man is made responsible to all those who are poor and wretched in his eyes, that he is summoned on his part to espouse the cause of those who suffer wrong. Why? Because in them it is manifested to him what he himself is in the sight of God; because the living, gracious, merciful action of God towards him consists in the fact that God himself in his own righteousness procures right for him, the poor and wretched; because he and all men stand in the presence of God as those for whom right can be procured only by God himself. The man who lives by the faith that this is true stands under a political responsibility. He knows that the right, that every real claim which one man has against another or others, enjoys the special protection of the God of grace. As surely as he himself lives by the grace of God he cannot evade this claim. He cannot avoid the question of human rights. He can only will and affirm a state which is based on justice. By any other political attitude he rejects the divine justification.[162]

Here Barth underscores the Christian calling to witness God's reconciling and liberating truth in Christ. Just as God himself achieves reconciliation with sinful humankind in Christ, so Christians must take the socio-political responsibility for the liberation of suffering humans for the sake of Christ's kingdom. Mangina identifies a core idea of Barth's

---

161. Mangina, *Karl Barth: Theologian of Christian Witness*, 127. Emphasis mine.
162. Barth, *Church Dogmatics* II/1, 387.

political ethics that is based on the doctrine of God. Since "the God confessed by Christians is a God who is for the human being," "a genuinely evangelical church must take the risk of" dealing with the socio-political problems in our world.[163] Likewise, according to Helmut Gollwitzer, Barth's doctrine of evil clearly shows that "on the human plane, this disempowerment of nothingness, which has already occurred, does not mean quietism, however, but fearlessness and irreverence toward evil."[164] For Barth, a horizontal liberation of sinful victims from evil powers is inseparable from the vertical reconciliation between them and God, because "it is only within humanity's true horizon, which is the reconciling work of God through Jesus Christ, that true liberation can be experienced and pursued."[165] Thus, beyond the limited scope of "a spiritual reconciliation," which Anselm and Calvin emphasize, Barth's hamartiology not only emphasizes "a spiritual reality" of personal sin in front of God, but also embraces "the social aspects" of structural evil in the world.[166] Divine reconciliation is inseparable from human liberation, just as the eternal deity of Christ and his vicarious humanity *pro nobis* are hypostatically united in the person of Christ. In contrast to liberation theologians, who focus on the suffering humanity of Jesus apart from his divine aseity as the Son of God, Barth pursues a holistic *telos* for Christian liberation, distinguished from a political ideology of liberation itself.[167] Liberation is always essentially linked with God's own reconciliation with sinners and the authentic freedom of the sinful victims in Christ.

Thus Barth himself not only embraced a theological position of "uncompromising resistance against National Socialism" during the Second World War, but also after the war he took a politically critical stance against both "an ideological anti-Communism" and "a Christian glorification of Communism."[168] Barth's Christian and political perspectives boldly testify that there is no Lord except Jesus Christ, because all the human ideologies of socio-political prosperity and peace, no matter whether conservative or liberal, are nothing but the sins of hubris and illusion. Only the crucified and resurrected Christ himself reigns in his

163. Mangina, *Karl Barth: Theologian of Christian Witness*, 192.
164. Gollwitzer, "Kingdom of God and Socialism," 96.
165. Barter, "A Theology of Liberation in Barth's *Church Dogmatics* IV/3," 155.
166. Johnson, *God's Being in Reconciliation*, 156.
167. See Sobrino, *Jesus the Liberator*. For an evangelical critique, see Hieb, *Christ Crucified in a Suffering World*.
168. Barth, *Against the Stream*, 102–3.

created and saved world. The salvific efficacy of Christ's atoning death *pro nobis* embraces the entire dimension of sinful humankind and the fallen world. Thus, the universality of God's reconciliation with humanity is substantially related to their liberation from evil at both spiritual and socio-political levels. Nathan D. Hieb rightly observes that for Barth there is a Christological simultaneity of reconciliation that is already accomplished in Christ, and his liberation is now ongoing through his faithful followers.[169] The former is the eternal grounding for the latter in the historical sense.

The Barthian doctrine of atonement also illuminates the juridicalizing dimension of *Christus Victor*. The deity of God himself in the human Jesus takes the initiative to exercise divine power, love, and justice. Barth's theological description of Jesus' revelation of his reconciliation here and now tends to blur the distinction between his eternal deity and vicarious humanity. Even Torrance, a sympathetic commentator, concedes that for Barth, Christ's vicarious humanity does not play a decisive role in fulfilling God's reconciliation, because the eternal light that symbolizes Christ's deity already triumphs over the power of darkness as nothingness.

> Christ seemed to be swallowed up in the transcendent Light and Spirit of God, so that the humanity of the risen Jesus appeared to be displaced by what he called "the humanity of God" in his turning toward us . . . the priestly office of Jesus Christ has been allowed to fall into the background without being fully integrated with the vicarious ministry of Christ as the obedient Son and Servant, which had its affect on his account of the ministry of the ascended Jesus Christ.[170]

According to Barth, if the divine victory of Christ is categorized as a corollary of his prophetic office,[171] it would not be unfair to argue that the human agony and death of Jesus, caused by the structural evils in the world, are already overshadowed by his deity, which conquers the power of darkness. Provided that the Son of God's deity is the active subject of his conquest over the hostile powers, it inevitably follows that the incarnated Christ plays only a functional role in manifesting God's apocalyptic judgment against sin and evil. Here I modestly suggest that Barth needs to place Christ's victory in his kingship rather than his prophetic office, in

---

169. Hieb, *Christ Crucified in a Suffering World*, 241.
170. Torrance, *Karl Barth, Biblical and Evangelical Theologian*, 184.
171. Jüngel, *Karl Barth*, 48.

Christ the Mediator's Self-Sacrificial Atonement Pro Nobis

order to vindicate his original intention to proclaim Christ's mediatorial work to be divine and human.[172]

4.4 Systematic Theological Review

Here I will recapitulate the mediatorial Christologies of Anselm, Calvin, and Barth.

1. All three assume a Christological ontology in which Christ is both fully God and fully human, because he is the sole Mediator between God and humankind. No sinful human being can enter God's kingdom without the mediatorial work of the Son of God, Christ himself revealed in the Holy Scripture.

2. All three affirm the the Christological substance of the Chalcedonian Definition. There is the hypostatic union of eternal deity and vicarious humanity in Christ's unique person *pro nobis*. The mediatorial Christologies essentially concentrate on the Son of God's eternal deity, which is the ontological starting point of the atonement. At the same time, Christ's vicarious humanity plays an important role in communicating God's saving work in Christ to the fallen creation. His incarnation, public ministry, crucifixion, and resurrection have the divine, objective, and ontological *telos* of sinners' salvation from sin and evil. The substitutionary view of atonement is the hermeneutical key by which the person and work of Christ is described and explained.

3. The biblical and ecumenical view of substitutionary atonement can guarantee Christ's *Munus Triplex* in a balanced way.[173] The incarnate Son of God is the eternal light of God that not only *prophetically* reveals the darkness of sin and evil, but also *militarily* overcomes the hostile powers, because he *sacrificially* gives himself for the fallen world. But the crucified Christ does not give himself away at the cross, because he is the eternal Son of God himself.

4. The primary motif of the crucifixion is Christ's voluntary obedience to the eternal will of God, who loves and saves humankind in Christ.

---

172. Terry, *The Justifying Judgment of God*, 147.

173. Even Anselm's satisfaction theory indirectly nuances Christ's victory as his "exaltation," but also prophetically teaches us the infinite value of Christ's sacrifice for God and sinners. Anselm, *"Cur Deus Homo," Basic Writings*, 209.

From the ontological perspective of divine reconciliation, the crucified Son of God reveals God's saving righteousness, in order to set sinners free from the divine condemnation. The spiritual liberation of enslaved humankind from the hostile power is the ontological consequence of Christ's objective reconciliation.

5. All three theologians affirm ontological continuity between the crucifixion and resurrection of Christ in his own person as God-human. The doctrine of substitutionary atonement substantially accords with Pauline soteriology. Paradoxically speaking, the crucified Christ—in his own self-"sacrificial" atonement under "God's judgment"—is the resurrected Son of God himself who can bring about the "ontological renewal" of the fallen world in his own person as God-human.[174] In the substitutionary view of atonement, there cannot be any dualistic conflict between Christ and evil, because evil is already ontologically negated by the crucifixion of Christ himself.

As we have seen, Christ's self-sacrificial death is the common ground between nonviolent and substitutionary atonement theologians. While, according to Brock, the crucifixion is Jesus' prophetically self-giving death that encourages the oppressed to protest against evil, both Schwager and Weaver acknowledge that there is a cultic dimension to Christ's nonviolent atonement for us.[175] Instead of a forensic or ethical approach to atonement, which cause God's direct violence against his Son or his indirect violence through evil, the cultic perspective provides a new hermeneutical breakthrough in the conversation between modern-nonviolent and classical-substitutionary camps. I make the constructive argument, therefore, that the Christologically cultic substitutionary views of Anselm, Calvin, and Barth can satisfy Weaver's theological requirement: a nonviolence that makes possible "the action of others without denying their freedom or harming their person."[176] First, since Christ spontaneously obeys God the Father's plan to save fallen humans, his atoning death *pro nobis* is a sovereign decision by Christ's own

---

174. Beker, *Paul the Apostle*, 209–11. Beker asserts, according to the Apostle Paul, "the event of cross and resurrection cohere in a single meaning. Paul correlates God's act of love in Christ (Rom 3:25) and the obedience of Christ (Rom 5:19; Phil 2:6). Thus, the death of Christ is both God's 'own' love for the world (Rom 5:6–8) and God's judgment over human sin (1 Cor 1:18–23); it is both Christ's obedience, self-surrender, and sacrificial love for us and God's surrender of 'his own Son' (Rom 8:32)."

175. See Chapter 2.

176. Weaver, *The Nonviolent Atonement*, 9.

voluntary will to sacrifice himself for sinful victims and the suffering world. Second, the person of Christ as the Son of God cannot be harmed by the cultic atonement, because as the eternal priest, Jesus Christ nonviolently dedicates himself as the eternal sacrifice to the Father.

4.5 Constructively Critical Reflection

Modern theologians criticize that the evangelical tradition of substitutionary atonement has tended to underestimate the seriousness of structural evils. To illustrate, the twentieth-century evangelical theologian John Stott claims that the overcoming of evil essentially means Christ's conquest over evil principalities and authorities. Christ calls us to participate in a spiritual war, not active resistance to socio-political evils.[177]

> It has been suggested that Paul himself had begun to "demythologize" the concept of angels and demons, and that he sees them rather as structures of earthly existence and power, especially the state, but also tradition, convention, law, economics, and even religion. Although this attempted reconstruction is popular in some evangelical (as well as liberal) groups, it remains unconvincing. The addition of "in the heavenly realms" in the Ephesians passages, and the antithesis to "flesh and blood" in Ephesians 6:10, not to mention the world-wide extent of the powers' influence, seems to me to fit the concept of supernatural beings much more readily, although of course such beings can and do use structures as well as individuals as media of their ministry.[178]

Against the subjective demythologization of biblical texts, such an objectively revelation-centered interpretation focuses on the spiritual and transcendental powers of Satan as a personal being. It does so to such an extent that the evangelical tradition of atonement tends to overlook socio-political evils in the concrete and historical context, as if

---

177. "Finally, be strong in the Lord and in his mighty power. Put on the full armor of God, so that you can take your stand against the devil's schemes. For our struggle is not against flesh and blood, but against the rulers, against the authorities, against the powers of this dark world and against the spiritual forces of evil in the heavenly realms" (Eph 6:10–12).

178. Stott, *The Cross of Christ*, 150. Yet, it must be noted that the founding leader of the Lausanne movement, Stott definitely proclaims Christians' socio-political responsibility, because they must resist against structural evils in the fallen world, with the primary urgency of evangelization of unreached people. See Stott, *The Lausanne Covenant*.

they were already overcome by Christ himself. Yet both Christians and non-Christians witness the obvious persistence of evil and the historical actuality of destroying powers.

While Anselm and Calvin in their own historical context, and even twentieth-century modern evangelicals, tend to concentrate on the vertical dimension of Christ's atoning efficacy between God and sinners, Barth has his own balanced understanding that enables both reconciliation and liberation. However, for Barth, the universal objectivity of Christ's triumph as the eternal light over evil as darkness reveals that he has already and totally annihilated all the hostile powers of sin, death, and demons, in both heaven and earth, through his crucifixion and resurrection two thousand years ago.[179] It is somewhat regrettable that his realized eschatology in Christ seems to lack the urgency of apocalyptic transformation for the suffering world in the future. However, if I sympathetically defend Barth's original intent and that of Anselm and Calvin, the eternal sovereignty of Christ in his atonement is considered the objective ground for humankind's unshakable hope of salvation here and now. Without God in Christ's present victory over the evil powers, all the human efforts to fight against the spiritual and socio-political structural evils in the world would be futile. It must be noted that for Barth Christ's atoning death never dissolves our personal identity and the seriousness of contemporary issues of violence and evil. Since "Jesus Christ is the same yesterday and today and forever" (Heb 3:8), Christians as his faithful witnesses must now participate in Christ's work of liberating suffering humankind from the structural evils that are already defeated by the crucifixion and resurrection, and which will be eschatologically annihilated by his *parousia*.

At this point, in order to correct the perception that Christ's sovereignty in his atonement justifies violence and evil as the instruments of salvation, I modestly suggest to substitutionary atonement theologians that they should focus on the historical understanding of Jesus' death as human victimization by structural evils in the world, before directly addressing the saving aspect. What is at stake is God's divine disclosure of fallen humanity's violence in the social-structural dimension. It is to be

---

179. Barth, *Church Dogmatics* III/3, 367. Barth asserts that evil "is only an echo, a shadow, of what it was but is no longer, of what it could do but can do no longer," because "it is broken, judged, refuted, and destroyed at the central point, in the mighty act of salvation accomplished in Jesus Christ, is valid not merely at that point but by extension throughout the universe and its activity." Thus, for Barth, evil as "nothingness" never has any ontological involvement in God's creation, but only remains as "falsehood" at the epistemological dimension.

noted that in spite of God's sovereignty in atonement, the historical and direct agents of Jesus' death are the Pharisees, chief priests, and Pilate, as the evil representatives of religious and political governing powers. As Jürgen Moltmann rightly observes, Jesus' messianic movement and self-confession as the Son of God in front of the high priest not only brings about the religious accusation of blasphemy in the context of Second Temple Judaism, but also finally provokes the crucifixion as the Roman Empire's public execution.[180] This fact proves that he had to be an innocent victim of the Roman Empire's violent dominion, in order to maintain the *status quo* between the Romans and Jews.[181] Regarding the hermeneutical order of Christ's atonement, Moltmann's theology of the cross rightly starts from a historical perspective on the human suffering of Christ—why Jesus dies at the hands of evil powers in a socio-political sense—and reaches to the divine suffering in the theological perspective—why the Son of God should be abandoned by God the Father in the crucifixion.[182] Although we must be alert to Moltmann's indiscriminate absolutization of God and Christ's suffering, which is the ontological collapse of God's eternal aseity in Christ,[183] I believe that the historical and socio-political perspective on Christ's suffering and victimization by evil can reinforce the hermeneutical weakness of the substitutionary atonement theologies. The deity and sovereignty of Christ as the Mediator should not be overaccentuated to the point of overlooking the anthropological issue of violent victimization, as if the incarnated and crucified Christ were impassible and invincible. If Christ's deity solely played an essential role in atonement, his humanity would only be a functional

180. Moltmann, *The Way of Jesus Christ*, 160–63.

181. Moltmann, *The Way of Jesus Christ*, 160–63.

182. Moltmann, *The Crucified God*. See Chapter 4, "The Historical Trial of Jesus," and Chapter 5, "The Eschatological Trial of Jesus Christ."

183. For an excellent critique of Moltmann's theology of God's suffering, see Balthasar, *Theo-Drama IV*, 321–23. For Bathasar, in Moltmann's theological thinking, "we come across another form of identification, nearer to Hegel. For him, the cross is not the privileged (and ultimately the solely valid) locus of the Trinity's self-revelation. Rather it is the locus of the Trinity's authentic actualization"; Moltmann, *The Crucified God*, 190. Since, according to Moltmann, the Triune God is "an open eschatological process for men on earth, with the Cross as its origin" (Moltman, *The Crucified God*, 192), Balthasar objects that "Moltmann is sucked into the undertow of Whitehead's 'process theology' which 'overcomes the dichotomy between immanent and economic Trinity, as well as that between God's nature and his inner tri-unity.'" For an evangelical understanding of God's suffering at the crucifixion, see Ngien, *The Suffering of God According to Martin Luther's Theologia Crucis*.

instrument of God's salvation. That would be a modern version of Apollinarianism, on which evangelical soteriology is incessantly tempted to rely. Rather, the vicarious humanity *pro nobis* that the Son of God takes upon himself not only reveals existential solidarity with humankind in the violent world, but also demonstrates his saving power to heal the sinful victims who have been alienated from the holy God.[184] Given that Jesus Christ is fully human and fully God, the nonviolent perspective on the death of Jesus cannot but ultimately correspond to the substitutionary understanding of atonement. The holistic perspective on atonement is based on the Christological simultaneity of Jesus' vulnerable humanity and his omnipotent deity. In this way, we can confess with nonviolent atonement scholars that the crucifixion of Christ exposes his courageous concern for the socio-political liberation of suffering humankind, but we can also confess with the substitutionary atonement theologians that it reveals humanity's reconciliation with God as the objective basis for the present and eschatological liberation of sinful victims.

---

184. From the substitutionary view, Torrance creatively engages Christ's reconciliation with a nonviolent metaphor of healing. He rightly observes that "he [Christ] *healed* the ontological split in human beings through the hypostatic and atoning union which he embodied within it, thereby integrating image and reality in and through a human life of perfect sincerity, honesty, and integrity in the undivided oneness of his person as Mediator." Torrance, *The Mediation of Christ*, 69.

Conclusion

Towards a Holistic Perspective on Atonement Theology

It was divine "necessity"—the necessity of God's gracious and non-coercive love—that the love of God be fully expressed in all its vulnerability in Jesus Christ. It was sinful human "necessity" of a world order of our own making—that this one who mediated God's forgiveness and inaugurated the reign of God characterized by justice, freedom, and peace should become the victim of our violence because he threatened the whole world of violence that we inhabit and will to maintain.[1]

WE HAVE OBSERVED THAT nonviolent views of atonement focus on the vulnerable humanity of Jesus and his victimization at the cross, at the expense of his deity. By contrast, the substitutionary view illuminates both the eternal deity and vicarious humanity of Christ, with the priority of Christ's divine nature over the human one. I constructively conclude that from a nonviolent viewpoint, Christ's self-sacrificial death is the common denominator between nonviolent and substitutionary views of atonement. Yet the substitutionary view proves that the Son of God's

---

1. Migliore, *Faith Seeking Understanding*, 189. This is Migliore's balanced view of the simultaneity of Jesus' human victimization and his self-sacrifice under God's sovereignty.

self-sacrifice is the objective foundation of God's reconciliation with sinful humankind and their liberation from evil. In this concluding chapter, I will summarize the strengths and weaknesses of these two contrasting perspectives on Christ's death for us, in order to set forth a holistic understanding of the atonement.

The Nonviolent Perspective on Atonement

According to the nonviolent theories of Brock, Schawager, and Weaver, Christ's crucifixion is an inevitable death—in an objectively *violent* sense—because of dualistic conflict between a God of nonviolence and the evil of violence. The nonviolent perspectives aim to absolve God from the ethical issue of violence in Christ's death at a literal level, because the death of Christ is ultimately caused by the dualistic conflict between a good but powerless God of nonviolence and the evil power of violence. The theological dualism between "negatives" such as violence, crucifixion, death, judgment, and the evil powers and "positives" such as nonviolence, resurrection, life, restoration, and God is deeply embedded in the nonviolent atonement theories in an epistemological sense. The theological discontinuity between God's saving work and human victimization is attributed to the separation of Christ's two natures. The nonviolent atonement by a powerless God is grounded upon the nonviolent Jesus. He is nothing but the victimized representative of suffering humankind. Without accomplishing his atoning work, God inevitably takes advantage of the human Jesus at the crucifixion, in order to reveal the evil powers by his passive death. The theological logic of human inevitability in the nonviolent atonement theories corresponds to their functional Christologies. In the critical sense, the nonviolent atonement theories aggravate urgent issues surrounding victimization and violence by reason of the absence of God's sovereignty and Christ's deity in the cosmic tragedy. It cannot be denied that the ethical-anthropocentric views of the nonviolent atonement models re-illuminate the destructive actuality of structural evils at a phenomenal and immanent level. The ethical realization of God's kingdom, Christ's nonviolent life and ministry, and his prophetic life and cultic death are the theological continuities between both the modern-nonviolent and classical-substitutionary approaches to Christ's death.

The Substitutionary Perspectives

Anselm, Calvin, and Barth declare Christ's sovereign self-giving in atonement—in an ethically *nonviolent* way—for the sake of God's reconciliation with sinful humankind and his deliverance of the victimized sinners from the hostile powers of sin, death, and devils. A hermeneutical ground for the substitutionary doctrines of Anselm, Calvin, and Barth is the Chalcedonian formulation of the person of Christ as God and human: a mediatorial Christology. In order to avoid portraying any dualistic conflict between God and the hostile powers, the substitutionary approaches confirm that the objective reconciliation between God and fallen humankind is accomplished by the atoning efficacy of the Mediator, Christ, *pro nobis* once and for all. The nonviolent atonement scholars believe Christ's penal substitutionary death to be the unethical justification of God's intrinsic violence, which oppresses victimized humankind. Yet their criticism is unconvincing, because God's judgment against human sin is not achieved by the victimized Jesus as *only human*, but in his person as *God and human*, the Meditator. The human victimization belongs to a non-ethical category of evil and violence, because it is an isolated event that separates Christ's death from his own Mediatorship. But, despite the negative phenomenon of Christ's death under God's judgment, penal substitution involves the positive, life-giving dimension of Christ's priestly atoning ministry in his own sacrifice. More importantly, according to Barth, the penal-cultic substitution finally brings about apocalyptic triumph over evil and the restoration of fallen humankind in Christ. At the same time, we need to keep in mind that if the substitutionary perspectives tend to absolutize specific motifs like Anselm's feudalistic-cultic restoration of God's honor or Calvin and Barth's forensic judgment by the divine justice, the over-emphasis might ironically impair the hermeneutical integrity of God's sovereignty in Christ, as if there were an absolute standard judging the whole atonement event. In this regard, the divine and objective dimension of Christ's substitution can be misconstrued as ahistorical and transcendental by its modern critics.

Toward A Holistic Perspective on Atonement

This book has pursued a constructively critical conversation between nonviolent and substitutionary perspectives on atonement for the purpose of reflecting theological motifs and Christological implications. I critically engage Rita Nakashima Brock, Raymund Schwager, and J. Denny Weaver's nonviolent approaches with the substitutionary doctrines of St. Anselm, John Calvin, and Karl Barth. Above all, I have critically analyzed nonviolent perspectives on atonement by employing four hermeneutical frames: negative epistemology, negative ontology, positive epistemology, and positive ontology.[2] We have critically realized that the dualism between the violent negativity of evil and nonviolent positivity of God lie at the heart of the nonviolent perspective on atonement. Nonetheless, there still remains a decisive theological question: how can a purely nonviolent God annihilate all the evils in the suffering world and recreate the negativity into positivity? It seems to be ironic that Brock, Schwager, and Weaver's "nonviolent" concepts of God unconsciously presuppose God's sovereign intervention on the issue of evil and violence. As Weaver proves in his exposition of Christ's apocalyptic resurrection, at the end of Christ's crucifixion, the nonviolent God should be able to be, at least, "violent" in the active sense of overcoming evil and violence and unilaterally completing the ontological transformation of the evil into good. With the divine paradoxical involvement, the negative epistemology of Jesus' human victimization by evil radically jumps into the positive ontology of God's nonviolent restoration. Therefore, the human-ethical nonviolence that nonviolent atonement theologians uncritically absolutize must be theologically modified in the light of God's own sovereign nonviolence against sin and evil for the sake of the ontological restoration of the suffering world into the new creation in Jesus Christ.

We have critically reviewed the claim that the nonviolence-oriented functional Christologies of Brock, Schwager, and Weaver inevitably cause an ontological collapse of Christ's deity and the hermeneutical denial of his divine sovereignty as a Savoir. I demonstrate that in contrast to the Christologies of nonviolent atonement scholars, the mediatorial Christologies of Anselm, Calvin, and Barth have proved their own ontological and hermeneutical integrity. Yet we have constructively observed that Christ's self-sacrificial death on the cross is the common grounding between both nonviolent and substitutionary atonement theology. Thus, I do my own constructive critique of the hermeneutical absolutization of the penal metaphor in the atonement theologies of Calvin and Barth. There is a hermeneutical logic of Christ's penal substitution that is followed by the cultic one in Calvin and Barth's forensically oriented

---

2. See the Introduction, "Research Questions."

atonement theology. Thus, I suggest to switch the order, to properly relocate Christ's eternal priesthood *pro nobis* at the center of the atonement event. Substitutionary atonement theologians need to reconfirm the cultic perspective as the starting point of Christ's atonement event, in order to solve the theological problem of divine violence that nonviolent atonement scholars misconstrue. Here I suggest a cultic perspective on atonement as a holistic model on the ground that the self-giving sacrifice of Christ the eternal priest can be both substitutionary and nonviolent. Without violent coercion, Christ voluntarily dedicates himself as the perfect sacrifice for atonement and for the salvation of sinners. The person of Christ as the eternal priesthood has never been violently destroyed by sin and evil. Christ's self-sacrificial death took away the sins of the entire world once and for all.[3]

However, my cultic sacrifice-oriented perspective on atonement never makes unnecessary the other two biblical motifs of judgment and victory. Unlike the misconstruals of nonviolent atonement theologians, interestingly including Anselm, a cultic metaphor of Christ's death for sinners is ontologically connected with the forensic dimension of God's judgment against sin and evil. It is crucial to reflect that God's apocalyptic judgment—God's own nonviolent resistance against sin and evil, which is yet ontologically restorative for his suffering creation—is voluntarily done by Christ's self-giving sacrifice on the cross. More decisively, "Since we have now been justified by his blood, how much more shall we be saved from God's wrath through him!" (Rom 5:9). In Pauline soteriology, the precious blood of the crucified Jesus—the cultic symbol of Christ's atoning death for us—simultaneously translated into the forensically ontological foundation of salvation.[4] At the heart of Christ's atonement event lies the Son of God's self-sacrificial downward movement from the incarnation to the point of crucifixion.

At the same time, we need to pay attention to the fact that in the substitutionary atonement theologies, the three biblical metaphors of sacrifice, judgment, and victory are "overlapped" with each other in the hermeneutical sense. Even though I argue for a hermeneutical priority of the cultic perspective over judgment and victory in Christ' atonement,

---

3. "He [Christ] has appeared once for all at the culmination of the ages to do away with sin by the sacrifice of himself" (Heb 9:26).

4. My theological interpretation is deeply indebted to Dr. Hunsinger's short but thoughtful article: Hunsinger, "Epilogue: Meditation on the Blood of Christ," in *Disruptive Grace*, 361–63.

there is an ontic and noetic simultaneity of the three events in Christ's atoning death *pro nobis*, with distinction in unity. The incarnate Son's self-sacrificial death in the atonement reveals that the crucified Christ nonviolently forgives our sins, freely offers eternal life and righteousness to sinful humankind, and vicariously bears the curse of sin and death in his person for us. It is through the marvelous exchange in Christ's substitutionary death that the Son of God righteously judges sin and evil and triumphantly conquers the hostile powers. These ontological and epistemological dimensions of the atonement event as Christ's saving work are inseparable from his unique person, the Mediator, understood in Chalcedonian terms as both the eternal Son of God and the human Jesus of Nazareth. What I attempt to underline is the ontological simultaneity of the principal biblical metaphorical events of atonement from the dynamic Christological principle that Christ's person is in his atoning work *pro nobis* and his work is in his person. Atonement theology must be essentially Christological, in order to avoid the hermeneutical absolutization of one specific motif such as nonviolence, victory, or even retributive or restorative justice.

Furthermore, although I criticize nonviolent perspectives on atonement, I never disregard the nonviolent-ethical implication of Jesus' atoning death. Rather, there must be a genuine Christian life as the nonviolent representation of Christ's substitutionary death for the salvation of sinners. As the Apostle Paul declares, "while we wait for the blessed hope—the appearing of the glory of our great God and Savior, Jesus Christ, who *gave himself for us to redeem us* from all wickedness and to purify for himself a people that are his very own, eager to do what is good" (Titus 2:13–14), Christ's substitutionary atonement in his own person as God-human *pro nobis* reveals God's saving power and gracious righteousness in Christ, by which Christian life is practically lived in a self-sacrificial and peaceful way.

I conclude that theological reflection on the atonement is rendered problematic when any specific motif is absolutized, thereby opening the door to ideological projection of human needs. This holds true for theories that emphasize the nonviolent character of atonement as much as for any other model. In this book, I suggest a holistic viewpoint of atonement that critically incorporates elements of both traditional substitutionary theories, with their emphasis on the reconciliation between God and sinful humankind, and contemporary nonviolent theories, with their emphasis on the disclosure of structural evil by Jesus' life and death. These dimensions of atonement are inseparable from the person of Christ, understood in Chalcedonian terms as both the eternal Son of God and the human Jesus of Nazareth. I demonstrate that the nonviolent models' emphasis on Jesus' victimization by structural evils can co-exist with his sacrificial death, insofar as he takes sin, evil, and divine judgment into his own divine-human person. By not bypassing the historical and socio-political view of the crucifixion by evil, the substitutionary perspective can deal with the urgent issue of human victimization that the nonviolent view raises. God's disclosure of his solidarity with victims is inseparable from his act of actually liberating them from the violent powers of this world and reconciling them to himself. With an integrative approach, I argue that the substitutionary perspectives are much more holistic than the nonviolent theories. The mystery of substitutionary atonement will be praised eternally by those who proclaim what Christ has done once and for all, and who live a self-sacrificial life for his kingdom of justice and love.

Bibliography

Ahn, Hojin. "The Humanity of Christ: John Calvin's Understanding of Christ's Vicarious Humanity." *Scottish Journal of Theology* 65.2 (2012) 145–58.
Allen, Michael R. "Calvin's Christ: A Dogmatic Matrix for Discussion of Christ's Human Nature." *International Journal of Systematic Theology* 9 (2007) 393–94.
Anselm. *Basic Writings*. Edited by Thomas Williams. Indianapolis: Hackett, 2007.
Aquinas, Thomas. *Summa Theologica*. New York: Benziger, 1947.
Augustine. *Concerning the City of God against the Pagans*. Edited by Henry Scowcroft Bettenson. Harmondsworth, UK: Penguin, 1972.
Aulén, Gustaf. *Christus Victor: An Historical Study of the Three Main Types of the Idea of the Atonement*. Edited by A. G. Hebert. London: SPCK, 1931.
Baark, Sigurd. "Seeking Out the Enemy on His Own Ground: Problems and Proof in Dialectical Theology." PhD diss., Princeton Theological Seminary, 2013.
Baillie, D. M. *God Was in Christ: An Essay on Incarnation and Atonement*. New York: Scribner, 1955.
Balthasar, Hans Urs von. *Theo-Drama: Theological Dramatic Theory. IV: The Action*. San Francisco: Ignatius, 1998.
Barter, Jane A. "A Theology of Liberation in Barth's *Church Dogmatics* IV/3." *Scottish Journal of Theology* 53.2 (2009) 154–76.
Barth, Karl. *Against the Stream: Shorter Post-War Writings, 1946–52*. Edited by Ronald Gregor Smith. New York: Philosophical Library, 1954.
———. *Church Dogmatics*. Edited by Geoffrey William Bromiley et al. New York: T. & T. Clark, 2009.
———. *Dogmatics in Outline*. Translated by G. T. Thomson. London: SCM Press, 1949.
———. *The Epistle to the Romans*. London: Oxford University Press, 1968.
———. *Learning Jesus Christ through the Heidelberg Catechism*. Translated by Shirley C. Guthrie Jr. Grand Rapids, MI: Eerdmans, 1964.
———. *Protestant Theology in the Nineteenth Century: Its Background & History*. Translated by Brian Cozens and John Bowden. Grand Rapids, MI: Eerdmans, 2002.

Bauckham, Richard. *God Crucified: Monotheism and Christology in the New Testament.* Grand Rapids, MI: Eerdmans, 1999.

Beker, Johan Christiaan. *Paul the Apostle: The Triumph of God in Life and Thought.* Philadelphia: Fortress, 1980.

Belousek, Darrin W. Snyder. *Atonement, Justice, and Peace: The Message of the Cross and the Mission of the Church.* Cambridge, UK: Eerdmans, 2012.

Berkhof, Louis. *Systematic Theology.* Grand Rapids, MI: Eerdmans, 1946.

Berkouwer, G. C. *The Triumph of Grace in the Theology of Karl Barth.* Edited by Harry R. Boer. Grand Rapids, MI: Eerdmans, 1956.

Blocher, Henri A. G. "*Agnus Victor*: The Atonement as Victory and Vicarious Punishment." In *What Does It Mean to Be Saved?: Broadening Evangelical Horizons of Salvation*, edited by John G. Stackhouse, 67–91. Grand Rapids, MI: Baker Academic, 2002.

Bloesch, Donald G. *Jesus Is Victor!: Karl Barth's Doctrine of Salvation.* Nashville: Abingdon, 1976.

Boersma, Hans. "Calvin and the Extent of the Atonement." *Evangelical Quarterly* 64 (1992) 333–55.

———. *Violence, Hospitality, and the Cross: Reappropriating the Atonement Tradition.* Grand Rapids, MI: Baker Academic, 2004.

Bonhoeffer, Dietrich. *Ethics.* London: SCM Press, 1971.

Borg, Marcus. "Executed by Rome, Vindicated by God." In *Stricken by God?: Nonviolent Identification and the Victory of Christ*, edited by Brad Jersak and Michael Hardin, 150–63. Grand Rapids, MI: Eerdmans, 2007.

Bradbury, Rosalene. *Cross Theology: The Classical Theologia Crucis and Karl Barth's Modern Theology of the Cross.* Eugene, OR: Pickwick, 2011.

Brock, Rita Nakashima. *Journeys by Heart: A Christology of Erotic Power.* New York: Crossroad, 1988.

———. *Proverbs of Ashes: Violence, Redemptive Suffering, and the Search for What Saves Us.* Edited by Rebecca Ann Parker. Boston: Beacon, 2001.

Brown, Benjamin J. "The Dramatic Soteriology of Raymund Schwager: Analysis and Evaluation." PhD diss., The Catholic University of America, 2007.

Brown, David. "Anselm on Atonement." In *The Cambridge Companion to Anselm*, edited by Brian Davies and Brian Leftow, 279–302. Cambridge, UK: Cambridge University Press, 2004.

Brown, Joanne Carlson, and Rebecca Parker, "For God So Loved the World?" In *Christianity, Patriarchy, and Abuse: A Feminist Critique*, edited by Joanne Brown Carlson and Carole R. Bohn, 1–30. New York: Pilgrim, 1989.

Calvin, John. *Calvin's New Testament Commentaries.* Edited by David W. Torrance and Thomas F. Torrance. Grand Rapids, MI: Eerdmans, 1959.

———. *Institutes of the Christian Religion.* Edited by John Thomas McNeill and Ford Lewis Battles. Philadelphia: Westminster, 1960.

Cass, Peter I. M. "Christ Condemned Sin in the Flesh: A Study in the Soteriology of T. F. Torrance with Particular Reference to the Relationship between the Incarnation and Atonement and the Ontological and Forensic Metaphors and Their Ecumenical Significance." PhD diss., Princeton Theological Seminary, 2008.

Cha, Jaeseung. "Calvin's Concept of Penal Substitution: Acknowledgement and Challenge." In *Restoration through Redemption: John Calvin Revisited*, edited by H. van den Belt, 113–33. Boston: Brill, 2013.

Coakley, Sarah. "What Does Chalcedon Solve and What Does It Not? Some Reflections on the Status and Meaning of the Chalcedonian 'Definition.'" In *The Incarnation: An Interdisciplinary Symposium on the Incarnation of the Son of God*, edited by Stephen T. Davis, Daniel Kendall, and Gerald O'Collins, 143–63. New York: Oxford University Press, 2002.

Congdon, David W. "Apokatastasis and Apostolicity: A Response to Oliver Crisp on the Question of Barth's Universalism." *Scottish Journal of Theology* 67.4 (2014) 464–80.

Deme, Daniel. *The Christology of Anselm of Canterbury*. Aldershot, UK: Ashgate, 2003.

Dodd, C. H. *The Bible and the Greeks*. London: Hodder & Stoughton, 1935.

Dorner, Isaak August. *History of Protestant Theology: Particularly in Germany, Viewed According to Its Fundamental Movement and in Connection with the Religious, Moral, and Intellectual Life*. New York: AMS Press, 1970.

Downie, Alison. "Discerning Redeeming Communities: Rita Nakashima Brock and Elizabeth A. Johnson in Dialogue." PhD diss., Duquesne University, 2009.

Drury, John L. "The Priest Sacrificed in our Place: Karl Barth's Exegesis of Hebrews in *Church Dogmatics* IV/1 §59.2." Paper presented at First Annual Barth Conference, Center for Barth Studies, Princeton Theological Seminary, May 2006.

Duff, Nancy J. "Atonement and the Christian Life: Reformed Doctrine from a Feminist Perspective." *Interpretation* 53.1 (January 1999) 21–33.

Edmondson, Stephen. *Calvin's Christology*. New York: Cambridge University Press, 2004.

Eichrodt, Walther. *Theology of the Old Testament*. London: SCM Press, 1961.

Evans, G. R. *Anselm*. Wilton, CT: Morehouse-Barlow, 1989.

Feuerbach, Ludwig. *The Essence of Christianity*. New York: Harper & Row, 1957.

Fiddes, Paul S. *Past Event and Present Salvation: The Christian Idea of Atonement*. Louisville: Westminster John Knox, 1989.

Finlan, Stephen. *Problems with Atonement: The Origins of, and Controversy about, the Atonement Doctrine*. Collegeville, MI: Liturgical, 2005.

Fiorenza, Elisabeth Schüssler. *In Memory of Her: A Feminist Theological Reconstruction of Christian Origins*. New York: Crossroad, 1983.

———. *Jesus: Miriam's Child, Sophia's Prophet: Critical Issues in Feminist Christology*. New York: Continuum, 1994.

Galvin, John. "Jesus as Scapegoat? Violence and the Sacred in the Theology of Raymund Schwager." *The Thomist* 46 (1982) 173–94.

Girard, René. *I See Satan Fall Like Lightning*. Maryknoll, NY: Orbis, 2001.

———. *The Scapegoat*. Baltimore: Johns Hopkins University Press, 1986.

———. *Things Hidden Since the Foundation of the World*. Stanford, CA: Stanford University Press, 1987.

———. *Violence and the Sacred*. Edited by Patrick Gregory. New York: Continuum, 2005.

Gollwitzer, Helmut. "Kingdom of God and Socialism in the Theology of Karl Barth." In *Karl Barth and Radical Politics*, edited by George Hunsinger, 77–120. Philadelphia: Westminster, 1976.

Gorringe, Timothy. *God's Just Vengeance: Crime, Violence, and the Rhetoric of Salvation*. Cambridge, UK: Cambridge University Press, 1996.

Gowan, Donald E. *Theology of the Prophetic Books: The Death and Resurrection of Israel*. Louisville: Westminster John Knox, 1998.

Graham, Jeannine M. *Representation and Substitution in the Atonement Theologies of Dorothee Sölle, John Macquarrie, and Karl Barth*. New York: Peter Lang, 2005.

Grebe, Matthias. *Election, Atonement, and the Holy Spirit: Through and Beyond Barth's Theological Interpretation of Scripture*. Edited by David Ford. Eugene, OR: Pickwick, 2014.

Greggs, Tom. "'Jesus is Victor': Passing the Impasse of Barth on Universalism." *Scottish Journal of Theology* 60.2 (2007) 196–212.

Grimsrud, Ted. "Pacifism and Knowing: 'Truth' in the Theological Ethics of John Howard Yoder." *Mennonite Quarterly Review* 77.3 (July 2003) 403–15.

Gunton, Colin E. *The Actuality of Atonement: A Study of Metaphor, Rationality, and the Christian Tradition*. Grand Rapids, MI: Eerdmans, 1989.

Hart, David Bentley. "A Gift Exceeding Every Debt: An Eastern Orthodox Appreciation of Anselm's *Cur Deus Homo*." *Pro Ecclesia* 7.3 (1998) 333–49.

Helm, Paul. *John Calvin's Ideas*. Oxford: Oxford University Press, 2006.

Hengel, Martin. *The Atonement: A Study of the Origins of the Doctrine in the New Testament*. London: SCM Press, 1981.

Hieb, Nathan D. *Christ Crucified in a Suffering World: The Unity of Atonement and Liberation*. Minneapolis: Fortress, 2013.

Holmes, Stephen R. "Can Punishment Bring Peace? Penal Substitution Revisited." *Scottish Journal of Theology* 58 (2005) 104–23.

———. "Penal Substitution." In *T. & T. Clark Companion to Atonement*, edited by Adam J. Johnson, 295–314. London: Bloomsbury T. & T. Clark, 2017.

Hopkins, Jasper. *A Companion to the Study of St. Anselm*. Minneapolis: University of Minneapolis Press, 1972.

Hunsinger, George. *Disruptive Grace: Studies in the Theology of Karl Barth*. Grand Rapids, MI: Eerdmans, 2000.

———. "Election and the Trinity: Twenty-Five Theses on the Theology of Karl Barth." *Modern Theology* 24.2 (April 2008) 179–98.

———. *The Eucharist and Ecumenism: Let Us Keep the Feast*. Cambridge, UK: Cambridge University Press, 2008.

———. "Hellfire and Damnation: Four Ancient and Modern Views." *Scottish Journal of Theology* 51 (1998) 406–34.

Jansen, John Frederick. *Calvin's Doctrine of the Work of Christ*. London: J. Clark, 1956.

Jenson, Robert W. *Systematic Theology I*. New York: Oxford University Press, 1999.

Johns, Loren L. "'A Better than Sacrifice' or 'Better Than Sacrifice'? Michael Hardin's 'Sacrificial Language in Hebrews.'" In *Violence Renounced: René Girard, Biblical Studies, and Peacemaking*, edited by Willard M. Swartley, 120–31. Scottdale, PA: Herald, 2000.

Johnson, Adam J. *God's Being in Reconciliation: The Theological Basis of the Unity and Diversity of the Atonement in the Theology of Karl Barth*. New York: T. & T. Clark, 2012.

Johnson, Elizabeth A. *She Who Is: The Mystery of God in Feminist Theological Discourse*. New York: Crossroad, 2002.

Jones Paul Dafydd. "Barth and Anselm: God, Christ, and the Atonement." *International Journal of Systematic Theology* 12.3 (July 2010) 257–82.

Jones, Serene. *Feminist Theory and Christian Theology: Cartographies of Grace*. Minneapolis: Fortress Press, 2000.

———. "Women's Experience Between a Rock and a Hard Place: Feminist, Womanist, and Mujerista Theologies in North America." In *Horizons in Feminist Theology: Identity, Tradition, and Norms*, edited by Rebecca S. Chopp and Sheila Greeve Davaney, 33–53. Minneapolis: Fortress, 1997.

Jüngel, Eberhard. *Karl Barth, a Theological Legacy*. Translated by Garrett E. Paul. Philadelphia: Westminster, 1986.

Kennedy, Kevin D. "Hermeneutical Discontinuity between Calvin and Later Calvinism." *Scottish Journal of Theology* 64 (2011) 299–312.

Keshgegian, Flora A. "The Scandal of the Cross: Revisiting Anselm and His Feminist Critics." *Anglican Theological Review* 82.3 (2000) 475–92.

Kryst, Thomas E. "Interpreting the Death of Jesus: A Comparison of the Theologies of Hans Urs von Balthasar and Raymund Schwager." PhD diss., The Catholic University of America, 2009.

Love, Gregory Anderson. *Love, Violence, and the Cross: How the Nonviolent God Saves Us Through the Cross of Christ*. Eugene, OR: Cascade, 2010.

Levering, Matthew. *Sacrifice and Community: Jewish Offering and Christian Eucharist*. Malden, MA: Blackwell, 2005.

Luther, Martin. *On the Freedom of a Christian: With Related Texts*. Indianapolis: Hackett, 2013.

Mangina, Joseph. "Hans Boersma's Violence, Hospitality, and the Cross." *Scottish Journal of Theology* 61.4 (2008) 494–502.

———. *Karl Barth on the Christian Life: The Practical Knowledge of God*. New York: Peter Lang, 2001.

———. *Karl Barth: Theologian of Christian Witness*. Aldershot, UK: Ashgate, 2004.

———. "Mediating Theologies: Karl Barth between Radical and Neo-Orthodoxy." *Scottish Journal of Theology* 56 (2003) 427–43.

———. *Revelation*. Grand Rapids, MI: Brazos, 2010.

McCormack, Bruce L. "For Us and Our Salvation: Incarnation and Atonement in the Reformed Tradition." *Greek Orthodox Theological Review* 43.1–4 (1998) 281–316.

———. "Grace and Being: The Role of God's Gracious Election in Karl Barth's Theological Ontology." In *The Cambridge Companion to Karl Barth*, edited by J. B. Webster, 92–110. Cambridge, UK: Cambridge University Press, 2000.

———. "The Ontological Presuppositions of Barth's Doctrine of the Atonement." In *The Glory of the Atonement: Biblical, Historical & Practical Perspectives: Essays in Honor of Roger Nicole*, edited by Roger R. Nicole, Charles E. Hill, and Frank A. James, 346–66. Downers Grove, IL: InterVarsity, 2004.

McGrath, Alister. *The Making of Modern German Christology: From the Enlightenment to Pannenberg*. Oxford: Basil Blackwell, 1986.

McIntyre, John. *St. Anselm and His Critics: A Re-Interpretation of the Cur Deus Homo*. Edinburgh: Oliver and Boyd, 1954.

Meyer, J. R. "Athanasius's Use of Paul in His Doctrine of Salvation." *Vigiliae Christianae* 52.2 (1998) 146–71.

Migliore, Daniel L. *Faith Seeking Understanding: An Introduction to Christian Theology*. 3rd ed. Cambridge, UK: Eerdmans, 2014.

Moltmann, Jürgen. *The Crucified God: The Cross of Christ as the Foundation and Criticism of Christian Theology*. New York: Harper & Row, 1974.

———. *The Way of Jesus Christ: Christology in Messianic Dimensions*. Minneapolis: Fortress, 1993.

Morris, Leon. *The Cross in the New Testament*. Grand Rapids, MI: Eerdmans, 1999.

Muller, Richard A. "Was Calvin a Calvinist?" *Life and Word* 5 (2012) 59.

Ngien, Dennis. *The Suffering of God According to Martin Luther's Theologia Crucis*. New York: P. Lang, 1995.

Niebuhr, H. Richard. *The Kingdom of God in America*. Chicago: Willett, 1937.

Olsen, Glenn W. "Hans Urs von Balthasar and the Rehabilitation of St. Anselm's Doctrine of the Atonement." *Scottish Journal of Theology* 34.1 (1981) 49.

Ollenburger, Ben C., and Amy L. Barker. "The Passion and God's Atonement." *Mennonite Life* 59 (2004). https://mla.bethelks.edu/ml-archive/2004June/ollenburger_barker.php.

Owen, John. *The Death of Death in the Death of Christ*. Edinburgh: Banner of Truth, 1967.

Packer, J. I. *In My Place Condemned He Stood: Celebrating the Glory of the Atonement*. Edited by Mark Dever and J. Ligon Duncan. Wheaton, IL: Crossway, 2007.

Partee, Charles. *The Theology of John Calvin*. Nashville: Westminster John Knox, 2008.

Patterson, Stephen J. *Beyond the Passion: Rethinking the Death and Life of Jesus*. Minneapolis: Fortress, 2004.

Paul, Robert S. *The Atonement and the Sacraments: The Relation of the Atonement to the Sacraments of Baptism and the Lord's Supper*. London: Hodder and Stoughton, 1961.

Peterson, Robert A, Sr. *Calvin and the Atonement*. Geanies House, Ross-shire, UK: Mentor, 1999.

Radford Ruether, Rosemary. *Sexism and God-Talk: Toward a Feminist Theology*. Boston: Beacon Press, 1993.

Radner, Ephraim. *Leviticus*. Grand Rapids, MI: Brazos, 2008.

Reesor-Taylor, Rachel. "Anselm's *Cur Deus Homo* for a Peace Theology: On the Compatibility of Non-Violence and Sacrificial Atonement." PhD diss., McGill University, 2007.

Root, Michael. "Dying He Lives: Biblical Image, Biblical Narrative, and the Redemptive Jesus." *Semeia* 30 (1984) 155–69.

Rutledge, Fleming. *The Crucifixion: Understanding the Death of Jesus Christ*. Cambridge, UK: Eerdmans, 2015.

Schwager, Raymund. *Jesus in the Drama of Salvation: Toward a Biblical Doctrine of Redemption*. New York: Crossroad, 1999.

Sherman, Robert. *King, Priest, and Prophet: A Trinitarian Theology of Atonement*. New York: T. & T. Clark International, 2004.

Smythe, Shannon Nicole. *Forensic Apocalyptic Theology: Karl Barth and the Doctrine of Justification*. Minneapolis: Fortress, 2016.

Sobrino, Jon. *Jesus the Liberator: A Historical-Theological Reading of Jesus of Nazareth*. Maryknoll, NY: Orbis, 1993.

Sölle, Dorothee. *Christ the Representative: An Essay in Theology After the Death of God*. London: SCM Press, 1967.

Sonderegger, Katherine. "Anselmian Atonement." In *T. & T. Clark Companion to Atonement*, edited by Adam J. Johnson, 175–94. London: Bloomsbury T. & T. Clark, 2017.

Southern, R. W. *St. Anselm and His Biographer*. Cambridge, UK: Cambridge University Press, 1963.

Stalcup, Sondra. "What about Jesus? Christology and the Challenges of Women." In *Setting the Table: Women in Theological Conversation*, edited by Rita Nakashima Brock, Claudia V. Camp, and Serene Jones, 107–32. St. Louis, MO: Chalice, 1995.

Stork, Peter. "The Drama of Jesus and the Non-Violent Image of God: Raymund Schwager's Approach to the Problem of Divine Violence." *Pacifica: Journal of the Melbourne College of Divinity* 20.2 (2007) 185–203.

Stott, John R. W. *The Cross of Christ*. Downers Grove, IL: InterVarsity, 1986.

———. *The Lausanne Covenant: Complete Text with Study Guide*. Peabody, MA: Hendrickson Publishers, 2012.

Strassen, Glen H., and Michael L. Westmoreland-White. "Defining Violence and Nonviolence." In *Teaching Peace: Nonviolence and the Liberal Arts*, edited by J. Denny Weaver and Gerald Biesecker-Mast. Lanham, MD: Rowman and Littlefield, 2003.

Tanner, Kathryn. "Incarnation, Cross, and Sacrifice: A Feminist-Inspired Reappraisal." *Anglican Theological Review* 86.1 (Winter 2004) 35–56.

Terry, Justyn. *The Justifying Judgment of God: A Reassessment of the Place of Judgment in the Saving Work of Christ*. Bletchley, Milton Keynes, UK: Paternoster, 2007.

Thompson, John. "Christology and Reconciliation in the Theology of Karl Barth." In *Christ in Our Place: The Humanity of God in Christ for the Reconciliation of the World: Essays Presented to Professor James Torrance*, edited by Trevor A. Hart, 207–23. Eugene, OR: Pickwick, 1989.

Torrance, Thomas F. *Atonement: The Person and Work of Christ*. Edited by Robert T. Walker and Thomas F. Torrance. Downers Grove, IL: IVP Academic, 2009.

———. *Karl Barth, Biblical and Evangelical Theologian*. Edinburgh: T & T Clark, 1990.

———. *The Mediation of Christ*. Colorado Springs: Helmers & Howard, 1992.

———. *Theology in Reconciliation*. The Torrance Collection. Eugene, OR: Wipf & Stock, 1996.

Van Buren, Paul Matthews. *Christ in Our Place: The Substitutionary Character of Calvin's Doctrine of Reconciliation*. Edinburgh: Oliver and Boyd, 1957.

Voelz, James W. *Mark 1:1–8:26*. St. Louis, MO: Concordia Publishing House, 2013.

Waldrop, Charles T. "Karl Barth's Concept of the Divinity of Jesus Christ." *The Harvard Theological Review* 74 (1981) 241–63.

Wallace, Ronald S. *Calvin's Doctrine of the Christian Life*. Grand Rapids, MI: Eerdmans, 1959.

Watson, G. "A Study in St. Anselm's Soteriology and Karl Barth's Theological Method." *Scottish Journal of Theology* 42.4 (1989) 493.

Weaver, J. Denny. *The Nonviolent Atonement*. Grand Rapids, MI: Eerdmans, 2001.

———. *The Nonviolent God*. Grand Rapids, MI: Eerdmans, 2013.

Webster, John. *Barth's Ethics of Reconciliation*. New York: Cambridge University Press, 1995.

Weingart, Richard E. *The Logic of Divine Love: A Critical Analysis of the Soteriology of Peter Abailard*. London: Clarendon, 1970.

Wendel, François. *Calvin: The Origins and Development of His Religious Thought*. London: Collins, 1963.

Williams, Garry J. "Karl Barth and the Doctrine of the Atonement." In *Atonement Engaging with Barth: Contemporary Evangelical Critiques*, edited by David Gibson and Daniel Strange, 232–72. Nottingham, UK: Apollos, 2008.

———. "Penal Substitution: A Response to Recent Criticism." In *The Atonement Debate: Papers from the London Symposium on the Theology of Atonement*, edited by Derek Tidball, 172–91. Grand Rapids, MI: Zondervan, 2008.

Work, Telford. "Review of *The Nonviolent Atonement*." *Theology Today* 59.3 (2002) 510–13.

Wright, N. T. *Christian Origins and the Question of God, Vol. 3: The Resurrection of the Son of God*. Minneapolis: Fortress, 1992.

Yoder, John Howard. *A Pacifist Way of Knowing: John Howard Yoder's Nonviolent Epistemology*. Edited by Christian E. Early and Ted Grimsrud. Eugene, OR: Cascade, 2010.

———. *The Politics of Jesus: Vicit Agnus Noster*. Grand Rapids, MI: Eerdmans, 1994.

www.ingramcontent.com/pod-product-compliance
Lightning Source LLC
Chambersburg PA
CBHW070253230426
43664CB00014B/2516